CLEAN
MY
SPACE

CLEAN MY SPACE

the secret to CLEANING BETTER, FASTER—and loving your home every day

MELISSA MAKER

AVERY
AN IMPRINT OF PENGUIN RANDOM HOUSE
NEW YORK

FOR CHAD

A
AVERY

an imprint of Penguin Random House LLC
375 Hudson Street
New York, New York 10014

Most Avery books are available at special quantity discounts for bulk purchase for sales promotions, premiums, fund-raising, and educational needs. Special books or book excerpts also can be created to fit specific needs. For details, write SpecialMarkets@penguinrandomhouse.com.

Library of Congress Cataloging-in-Publication Data

Names: Maker, Melissa, author.
Title: Clean my space : the secret to cleaning better, faster—and loving
  your home every day / Melissa Maker.
Description: New York : Avery, an imprint of Penguin Random House, [2017] |
  Includes bibliographical references and index.
Identifiers: LCCN 2016057175 | ISBN 9780735214668 (print)
Subjects: LCSH: House cleaning. | Orderliness. | Storage in the home.
Classification: LCC TX324 .M355 2017 | DDC 648/.5—dc23
LC record available at https://lccn.loc.gov/2016057175
p.   cm.

Printed in the United States of America
10 9 8 7 6 5 4 3 2 1

Book design by Ashley Tucker

CONTENTS

CHAPTER 1

welcome to this book

I'm glad you've picked it up. This is going to be the start of something great for us. Maybe you know me from my YouTube channel or TV appearances. Maybe you are just motivated to try—or are curious about—leading a cleaner, more put-together life. It's a bold move simply to open this book. I know, a book about cleaning the house isn't exactly beach reading. But since we don't get taught cleaning in school anymore (adios, home ec), and it is legitimately a life skill that affects us and our families each day (just think back to your last cleaning-related argument), it is absolutely worth learning about and mastering. I've designed this book to be an easy-to-read reference that offers clear and simple instructions, product recommendations and recipes, basic routines, and self-discovery tools (don't worry, not woo-woo—more like woo-hoo!). I call my approach the **Maker Method**—and I designed it specifically to keep your space cleaner longer, for people like you (and me!), and it works.

I thought about **you** when I wrote *Clean My Space*. I know you. You don't have time to learn how your grandmothers cleaned and you're not down for any Cinderella-style scrubbing; you're a busy person with important things to do. So when I designed this cleaning handbook, I included only the most important things. You won't find any waxing the linoleum or polishing the brass here. I will set you up to get the very best results in the least amount of time without having to read something as technical and complex as *Going Off on a Tangent: A Journey to Mathematic Discoveries* (okay, I made up that book, but I can only imagine how hard that *would* be to read). This book's more like a cookbook, with recipes and easy step-by-step instructions for getting your home the way you want it, along with a dose of friendly encouragement and some fun anecdotes from when I was learning the ropes to get you rolling. I want to show you that maintaining a clean home isn't some secret or a gift that only 4 percent of the human population possesses. It's a teachable skill, and once you get it, transforming a room—no, your entire home!—from college-dorm-type pigsty to design-magazine gorgeous will feel like something you can do with ease and confidence. No matter if you're a busy parent, a young professional, a student, or just about anyone else, this book is designed to teach you exactly how to clean in a quick, fun(ish), and memorable way. Your life will be better for reading this book, I promise!

Why Should You Trust Me to Teach You How to Clean? Because I Hate Cleaning.

I was never even good at it. It made me frustrated, overwhelmed, and certainly caused trouble for me growing up. But since starting my own cleaning service in 2006, I've cracked the code. I've reengineered cleaning. I've trained my staff in this new way and built two successful businesses on this method: in addition to my cleaning service, I now educate hundreds of thousands of people every day on my website and my YouTube channel.

MY STORY

The reason I know I can transform hopeless cases into spic-and-span home dwellers is that I underwent this transformation myself. I was not born the cleaning maven that I am now. In fact, quite the opposite. My mother used to say that crossing my bedroom floor was an Olympic event. My seventh-grade teacher chose to make an example out of my disorganized self one day and dumped the entire contents of my desk onto the floor. I had to clean it up while my classmates watched (hello, therapy). I hated cleaning, and I didn't experience the joy or rewards of a clean personal space. I just felt like it took away from valuable sticker-trading or Nintendo-playing time.

What I did dream about was being an entrepreneur, from a very young age. So when I graduated from business school, no one was surprised when I decided to start my own business. I didn't know yet what *kind* of business, so I kept my eyes and ears open and left it up to the universe to tell me. Imagine my horror, then, when the thing I kept on hearing about was the stress of cleaning house and how hard it was to do it, and for those who wanted to hire it out, how hard it was to find a reliable, trustworthy cleaning person who actually knew what they were doing. I couldn't avoid this constant barrage of the same message even though it was so contrary to who I was. Me? Start a cleaning company? Do you *know* who I am?

Nonetheless, I followed the noise and wrote a business plan and took it to my uncle Larry, my trusted mentor. He told me that in order to be a success, *I'd* have to start cleaning and learning my business from the ground up. When I got over my initial shock, I decided I'd go into it fully, sleeves rolled up and boots to the ground. After eighteen months of research, practice, and hard-core business building—waiting tables at night and cleaning for clients during the day—I was able to quit my serving job and focus on the business full time.

By this point, I had figured out that I could get more done in less time if I reengineered the way I worked. I went through all the general cleaning tasks that needed to be done at each visit in a home (using my creation, the 59-Point Checklist) and tested many techniques, various products (both homemade and store-bought) and, of course, timed and critiqued myself while doing so. I put a lot of hours, money, and energy into it, and what I came out with were vast improvements on how to get the job done well in the least amount of time. I started to write down these ideas and teach new hires how to clean this way (I even managed to convert seasoned employees who'd occasionally throw me a raised eyebrow—*who does she think she is?*). It was awkward at times. I was only twenty-four. But they listened!

Our reputation was incredible and my staff performed their jobs impeccably: I had come up with a better way to clean. In 2008, when the economy took a nose-dive, I worried that my business, just eighteen months old at the time, would have to close down. To my surprise, the business grew fivefold that year! People wanted to come home to a clean space, regardless of how the economy was doing. They'd sooner give up dining out or new handbags before they'd say good-bye to a clean, serene home. I knew I was onto something.

In 2011, my then-fiancé, Chad, and I started making YouTube videos about cleaning. We thought it would help grow the service business in Toronto. What we didn't really consider was how global and prolific YouTube would become, and next thing we knew, we were getting clicks from all over the world. We have since created hundreds of videos that have garnered millions of views. I'm often asked for a whole cleaning routine, or a more holistic approach, that encapsulates all my teachings and simplifications in one place. And that's why I put together this book. I want to teach you all my secrets and show you how to reform your cleaning habits, no matter if you're just starting out or are a veteran home-keeper.

How to Use This Book

You'll want to carefully read this chapter, to help get a lay of the land, and then Chapter 2, "The Basics," to really learn the nuts and bolts of *how* to actually clean and *what* to clean with. Then, read the rest of the book once through, glean what you will from it, and then reference it, like a cookbook, as needed. (Then someday, you can pass this down to your grandchildren as a treasured heirloom, proclaiming how life-changing it was—of course, no pressure.) Sure, it may feel like it takes a long time to clean at first, since you'll be scrubbing with one hand and holding down a page with the other. But remember, you're learning. And if you follow the instructions, after the first few times of trying out a new cleaning technique, tackling an entire space, or whipping up a homemade cleaning product, you'll find you spend less time flipping pages and more time slaying your cleaning task. When you've started to digest it all, turn to Chapter 13, "Routines and Schedules," to make a plan for implementing everything.

GETTING STARTED: THE MAKER METHOD

To have a clean home without quitting your job and devoting yourself to it full-time, you need to know where to focus your energy.

Enter the Maker Method! This is the system I've designed to help you figure out what needs to be cleaned, precisely how to clean it, and when to clean it.

It's just three simple steps:

1. Determine your MIAs

Your whole house does not need to be cleaned all the time. We don't have the time for it, and we're better off trading in what little spare time we do have to do the things that make us happy. So, in step one, you find the **Most Important Areas**, or MIAs, in your home and make those your most regular cleaning focus. We'll deal with those less important areas later, when we have more time or when we do a deeper clean. See, it feels easier already: you have permission to skip things!

When I was researching cleaning, most of the books I read stressed me out. Look up one single task and next thing I knew I needed to commit an hour of my time. No thanks. I decided that the things I was going to clean were only those that mattered *to me*. Baseboards have never bothered me. Foggy windows? Meh, I really don't care. But I can't even think about cooking in a messy kitchen and I feel gross when my kitchen is dirty, so the kitchen is an MIA for me.

On the next page, you will find my MIA quiz. Spend a few minutes looking at the list of spaces in your home and thinking about whether you stress out—or even notice—when this particular space is dirty or disorganized. It will help you understand your MIAs and where you need to focus your cleaning energy.

Now, it's not to say that you won't ever need to clean the areas that aren't important to you. My advice later in the book will help you plan for that (you can even hire someone to do it for you). But getting in touch with your personal priorities will help focus your journey. Count up your *Xs*. In an ideal world, you'll have just, say, ten to fifteen MIAs. As you read though the how-tos for each room, you'll know to prioritize your cleaning to hit your MIAs often and postpone everything else for when you have a bit more time. (In Chapter 13, I'll go more in-depth about how to incorporate your MIAs into your routines and schedules.)

But what happens if most of these categories register as MIAs for you? Then I want you to review your MIA list again, only this time write a number next to each, ranking them by giving a *1* to the absolute *most* important spot and working your way through to less important spots from there. It might feel like a betrayal of your needs—I know! Those messy areas make you crazy!—but we need *some* system for deciding how to prioritize. Trust me on this.

2. Use my cleaning best practices (PTT)

So what happens when you've figured out which areas you want to focus on when you're ready to roll up your sleeves and begin? You'll move on to Chapter 2, where I synthesize the correct **products** for the job (the *P*), the best **tools** (*T*), and, finally, the **techniques** (the other *T*). I teach my staff any time they enter a room to think: PTT. Do I have the Products I need? Do I have the Tools? After that, it's all about Technique. Like a chef preparing a *mise en place*, going through this mental checklist will already make your work more efficient and set you up for a more successful clean. You'll get the basic cleaning technique primer in Chapter 2, then more details of how to accomplish each cleaning task in the room-by-room chapters that make up the bulk of the book.

QUIZ: WHAT ARE YOUR MIAS?

Here's a list of all the major spaces in the house. Note whether each causes a visceral reaction; you simply can't abide for it to be cluttered or dirty (there's a column for each, so you can distinguish). Or, use the shaded row, and you can give the whole darn room an *X*.

When this space is cluttered, I can't stand it (I need this space to be neat).

When this space is dirty, I can't stand it (I need this space to be clean).

FRONT ENTRYWAY		
Furniture and surfaces		
Walls (scuffs and fingerprints)		
Mirrors and windows		
Floor		
Closet		
LIVING ROOM		
Furniture		
Floors		
Walls (scuffs and fingerprints)		
DINING ROOM		
Furniture		
Floors		
Walls (scuffs and fingerprints)		
KITCHEN		
Cupboards and drawers (exterior)		
Counter		
Backsplash		
Appliances (exterior)		
Appliances (interior)		
Furniture		
Walls (scuffs and splatters)		
Trash can		
DEN		
Furniture		
Walls (scuffs and fingerprints)		
TV and electronics		
Media and books		
Floors		
BATHROOM		
Shower and tub		
Toilet		

When this space is cluttered, I can't stand it (I need this space to be neat).

When this space is dirty, I can't stand it (I need this space to be clean).

BATHROOM (continued)		
Walls (marks and splatters)		
Mirrors, medicine cabinet (exterior and windows)		
Vanity top and sink		
Soap dish and toothbrush holder		
Floor		
BEDROOM		
Bed		
Mirrors, artwork, and windows		
Walls (scuffs and fingerprints)		
Closet		
Furniture		
Floors		
HOME OFFICE		
Bookshelf		
Furniture		
Walls (scuffs and fingerprints)		
Computer and components		
Telephone		
Floors		
HALLWAYS AND STAIRCASES		
Staircase		
Walls (scuffs and fingerprints)		
Furniture		
Floors (not including stairs)		
MISCELLANEOUS SPACES		
Windows		
Walls (scuffs and fingerprints)		
Furniture		
Floors		
Washer and dryer		
Closet		

3. Develop cleaning routines and schedules

What this means is building automatic maintenance tasks and little cleaning jobs into your daily and weekly routines, and otherwise taking into account how much time you have to dedicate to cleaning, then making specific appointments and putting them on your calendar. Those daily, weekly, monthly, and annual appointments are important, to be sure, but I find that the little everyday lifestyle tweaks are what will give you serious bang for your buck—removing chores from your big list without adding extra time.

By the time you're through the bulk of this book, you will have very likely already tweaked some of your existing routines. But when you need guidance or an idea of how to form routines—or if you just want to spy on how *I* get things done—that's when you'll turn to Chapter 13.

This might all seem like a lot now, before you've really dived in. But I promise it will start to make sense. The three-step Maker Method keeps your home just the way you want it, and by the time you finish this book, you'll have mastered all three. I find that if you put them into practice, your home will be cleaner, happier, and easier to maintain.

A NOTE ON AN EXPRESS CLEAN VERSUS A TOP-TO-BOTTOM CLEAN

Each room-by-room chapter offers up two routines: the Express Clean routine and the Top-to-Bottom routine. The Express routines are designed to give you the key points to hit when you don't have much time but you want to lightly clean for maximum impact. They can help build your confidence in cleaning if you don't have much experience; they're the *gateway drug* of cleaning. But let me be clear: an Express Clean is a surface clean at best. These cleans are perfect for pre-guest arrivals and quick midweek tidy-ups but *do not replace full cleanings*. Express Cleans focus on tidying and fixing any cleaning faux pas. But a tidy space is not necessarily a truly clean space, and that's where the Top-to-Bottom Cleans come in.

The Top-to-Bottom routines are designed to keep your space cleaner longer, because you're going to be doing things *the right way*. They walk you through each and every task required to properly clean a particular space in your home, start to finish. Rather than move your dirt around (which is what happens if you go about it in not quite the right way), only to have it resettle and look dirty again two days later, I'll teach you how to remove it completely. There may be certain tasks or areas that are not part of your MIAs or don't apply to your space, so you skip those (fist pump!). But the idea here is that you're going to learn how to properly and thoroughly clean any area that *is* important to you. (Don't worry, these jobs won't take all day.)

Once you're ready to attack, set the timer and get moving! I love timing myself because it keeps me accountable and puts the fire under my feet. I don't want to be spending all day cleaning, so if I know how long I've got, I tend to layer on the hustle. You can write your record in the margin, and then watch as you effortlessly shave down that time on subsequent cleanings, just because you know what you're doing. It really happens; I dare you to try!

CHAPTER 2

the basics

The second step of the Maker Method is learning my best practices: the best Products, Tools, and Techniques for every job—or as I call them, the PTT. There was a time when I would reach for old cut-up rags and whatever cleaning products I had in the house to try to clean properly. No wonder I would get frustrated—sometimes the messes would look worse than before I began. I hear about similar frustrations from many of you. Well, once you arm yourself properly, I promise your spaces will not only look clean but *be* clean.

One principle with PTT, though, is that too strong a product, too heavy a tool, or too rigorous a touch can damage an item, so it is wise to always start with the most gentle, basic product, tool, or technique— sometimes a swipe with a clean cloth sprayed with all-purpose cleaner is all you need. You can always level up as necessary depending on the situation. Oftentimes, the most everyday items and methods will clean the majority of the house. You'll work smarter, not harder!

This chapter is packed with everything you need to know about those essential PTTs, but first, two important notes!

A Note on the Topic of "Disinfecting"

Although I am all about clean, you will notice that I don't recommend antibacterial products that claim to obliterate germs on contact. In my research, I have consulted epidemiologists at the CDC, chemists, doctors, and other cleaning professionals, and I have discovered that none recommend the goal of trying to kill germs on every surface all the time. Living in a completely sterile environment is not beneficial to our immune systems, and in fact appears to be harmful. What's more, the incorrect application of these products—that is, relying on them to "disinfect" messes rather than cleaning them up properly—renders them ineffective at best and can often result in spreading germs around at worst. Disinfectants are typically designed solely to disinfect—they don't really clean. Experts agree: physically removing dirt (that is, by scrubbing it away using soap and water) is *the most* important thing you can do for the health of your home; don't worry about disinfecting surfaces unless there is someone in your house with a specific serious health problem (in which case, please talk to your doctor about how to properly clean) or if there's a specific reason to disinfect (Chicken juice! Pet stain! Toddler accident!). At that time, remember, remove the dirt physically first, and *then* disinfect the surface right after with the appropriate product.

A More Fun Note! About Essential Oils

If you watch my videos or read my website, you'll know that I am obsessed with scents. I love essential oils and that powerful aromatic "zing" that they bring to my day. They leave your home smelling much nicer than commercial cleaners (spa-like, even), although the scent won't linger for hours on end like some of those products can (which I also think is a plus). I love them because they allow cleaning to be a little more creative and fun; I am always experimenting with new scent combinations. (Hey, if that helps me look forward to cleaning, I'll take it.)

But I don't just love essential oils for their beautiful smell. Aromatherapists and other alternative healers swear that you can use essential oils to bring about health benefits—such as using them to cheer you up or calm you down and even fight off fungus and bacteria. Though there isn't a ton of hard science to back up the claims, I like to believe they are true, and I find that using the oils is so enjoyable that if hard science one day validates the claims, bonus! Until then, enjoy the placebo effect.

If you do choose to use them, I encourage you to look for 100 percent pure essential oils only—if we want the maximum benefit, we've got to use the purest stuff. Essential oils are readily available at health food stores and many reputable online stores, too.

Here's my starter list of essential oils. It is by no means comprehensive, but there are lots of great websites and organizations dedicated to aromatherapy that you can check out to learn more about essential oils' properties, uses, and blending suggestions.

CITRUS OILS

Citrus oils such as lemon *(Citrus limon)*, grapefruit *(Citrus paradisi)*, lime *(Citrus aurantifolia)*, and sweet orange *(Citrus sinensis)* smell divine and are touted to be antiseptic, disinfectant, antibacterial, antimicrobial, and antifungal. Plus, citrus oils, which come from the rind of the fruit, are highly concentrated in limonene, which is known to help with degreasing and lifting soil off a surface easily. I love mixing citrus with peppermint.

HERBAL OILS

Peppermint oil *(Mentha piperita)*: Antibacterial, antifungal, antimicrobial, and antiseptic and smells like you ripped open a fresh pack of gum. This is great to use on its own or in combination with other herbs or citrus scents. Spearmint *(Mentha spicata)* is a milder alternative and smells equally divine.

Eucalyptus oil *(Eucalyptus globulus)*: If you've ever walked into a steam room at a spa and smelled that fresh, gently sinus-clearing aroma, it's likely eucalyptus that you're encountering. Its medicinal, bracing scent is calming and clearing. Eucalyptus is one of the oldest natural medicine ingredients known to fight viruses and bacteria. It's claimed to be antibacterial, antifungal, antiseptic, antiviral, and disinfectant.

Lavender oil (*Lavandula angustifolia*): Talk about calming, this is the go-to scent! It helps relieve jitters, gives way to a relaxing sleep, and I love using it to prevent mustiness in my washing machine, too. Lavender oil is said to be antibacterial, antifungal, antimicrobial, and antiseptic.

Tea tree oil (*Melaleuca alternifolia*): This was my first essential oil, and it got me hooked! The smell did take some getting used to, but now I associate it with cleanliness. It's extremely versatile and offers up many powerful properties, including antibacterial, antifungal, anti-inflammatory, antimicrobial, antiseptic, antiviral, and disinfectant. I typically use this on its own instead of mixing.

Thyme oil (*Thymus vulgaris*): Thyme is powerful! It's a go-to in natural medicine for disinfectant use. I tend to use this in the all-purpose spray kept in my kitchen. Plus, being an herb, it blends nicely with citrus and other herbs. It is said to be antibacterial, antifungal, antimicrobial, antiviral, and disinfectant.

To maximize the claimed benefits of the essential oils, I like to use a combination of 20 to 30 drops total per 16 fluid ounces (or 500 milliliters). If you just want to diffuse the scent in a product, 5 to 10 drops will be sufficient for the same volume of liquid.

There are several warnings to heed: Don't apply straight essential oils directly to skin, and don't ingest them. Keep them away from children and pets, and speak to your veterinarian to determine which essential oils are safe to use around your pet and in what concentration. If you are pregnant or breastfeeding, speak to your doctor about essential oils; it is widely advised to keep away from them during this time. If you have allergies to the plant, flower, or herb of the oil (say, you're allergic to lavender), refrain from using that essential oil.

Cleaning Products (the *P*)

I believe in keeping cleaning as simple, inexpensive, and nontoxic as possible—and I learned how the hard way.

When I first started my cleaning service in 2006, I went to my local big-box store to stock up my cleaning kit. I filled a hockey duffel bag with cleaning products and tools. But within one week, I started to get red, raw skin, as well as an irritated nose and throat. So I started researching and tinkering with recipes to see if I could whip up more natural versions using common pantry items and get equally as impressive—or even better—results than what I'd get with store-bought items. My business is now at about a 70/30 split—we train our staff to use 70 percent "homemade" solutions by including dish soap, baking soda, and vinegar, and 30 percent store-bought products, for those times when what's available in the store is the simpler or more effective option.

The must-have products and cleaning solutions I recommend are listed alphabetically below. You will find my recipes where homemade is my preference, but I will also include some trusted store-bought alternatives for when you are short on time. I provide the options I would use myself—chosen because they use gentler ingredients, or because in some cases, they simply do the job the best.

NEED-TO-HAVE PRODUCTS

All-purpose cleaner: All-purpose cleaner is my "hero" product. It's good for cleaning almost anything and the starting point for almost any job. I make my own; it's inexpensive and quick to whip up. Plus, my version is safe to use on fancier finishes like natural stone and stainless steel, too. The majority of your home can and should be cleaned with no more and no less than basic soap and water, which is essentially what this cleaner is. This all-purpose cleaner contains alcohol, so it will kill some pathogens. But it will not kill every germ in your house—and that is by design.

ALL-PURPOSE CLEANER

I like to include rubbing alcohol in my all-purpose cleaner because it helps the solution dry faster and leaves fewer streaks. Use an essential oil of your choice, such as lavender, peppermint, or tea tree, if you want fragrance. Always remember to mix up any product in a clean spray bottle and to label that bottle so you know what's in it. Keep cleaning solutions out of reach from pets and children.

1½ cups water

½ cup rubbing alcohol

1 teaspoon gentle dish soap
(Note: If you prefer, you can swap out dish soap for castile soap, but beware that castile soap should never come into contact with vinegar.)

10 drops essential oil (optional)

Combine all the ingredients in an empty spray bottle and shake well.

Store-bought alternatives: *Mrs. Meyer's Clean Day Multi-Surface Everyday Cleaner; Method All-Purpose Cleaner; Biokleen Spray & Wipe All Purpose Cleaner*

Ammonia-free crystal-cleaning spray, such as Brillianté.

Automatic dishwashing detergent: I find tablet formulations more convenient than powders or liquids. They fit easily under the sink and work really well at powering through grease, buildup, and film. Look for concentrated formulations, such as Cascade Complete ActionPacs or Method Smarty Dish dishwasher detergent tablets.

Degreaser: Used to attack stubborn kitchen grease, which looks darker or yellow and feels sticky, this solution helps lift it away from the surface. If your all-purpose cleaner can't do the trick, step it up and use a degreaser. My version uses sweet orange essential oil, which contains d-limonene—a known degreaser. If you don't have that on hand, you can use another citrus fruit's essential oil instead.

DEGREASER

½ cup baking soda
¼ cup dish soap
20 drops sweet orange essential oil

TOOLS
a nonscratching sponge
a microfiber cloth

Mix together the ingredients in a container and apply with a damp sponge. Allow the degreaser to sit on the greasy area for 10 minutes. Scrub the area with the damp sponge, rinse surface well, and buff dry with a microfiber cloth.

Store-bought alternatives: *When it comes to fighting grease, I look for formulations with either citrus oils or enzymes, which can practically melt grease with some dwell time. Products like Citrus Magic Natural Orange Heavy Duty Cleaner/Degreaser and Biokleen All Purpose Cleaner Concentrate fit the bill.*

Dish soap: I find this to be the most versatile and useful cleaning product in the tool kit, both gentle enough on surfaces and tough on grease and dirt; you'll see it over and over as the base of many of my recipes. Remember to keep a stash in the kitchen, too, for its original purpose—washing dishes!

I like dish soaps that are not antibacterial, are gentle, and have no extras like lotion in them. I usually reach for basic formulations, such as Dawn Ultra Dishwashing Liquid, Method Dish Soap, or Ultra Palmolive Original. Castile soap, like Dr. Bronner's Pure-Castile Liquid Soap, is often used in place of dish soap for people who wish to use the most gentle option (you can even use it for body wash). But, castile users, be aware that it cannot be mixed with vinegar.

Disinfectant: Sometimes you want a little more germ-killing power, like when you dribble chicken juices on your countertop or on the floor. But remember, you still need to clean first—spraying just about any disinfectant on top of a puddle full of bacteria will do nothing at all. Take a paper towel and blot up as much as you can (then throw it away!), clean the spot with all-purpose cleaner (and throw that second paper towel away, too). Finally, treat with a disinfectant registered with the EPA (it will have an EPA registration number on the label) according to the label instructions.

Recommendation: Seventh Generation Disinfecting Multi-Surface Cleaner

Floor cleaners: One of the hallmarks of a clean home is a shiny, streak-free floor. Depending on the hard-floor surface you have, you'll need to clean it with the right product.

Tile and vinyl floor cleaners: I try to use vinegar where possible since it cuts grease and leaves no residue (and no odor); however, if you choose to use a detergent-based product, use a tiny amount.

TILE AND VINYL FLOOR CLEANER

1 cup white vinegar or
½ teaspoon dish or castile soap

5 to 10 drops essential oil (optional; pet owners, please discuss safe use of essential oils for your pet(s) with your veterinarian before proceeding)

1 gallon hot water

Add the vinegar (or soap) and essential oil to a bucket, then fill with hot water.

Hardwood and engineered-hardwood floors: These floors are an investment, and using the right product is essential—the wrong one can strip the varnish. Mopping properly is also of importance (see how on page 52)—too much moisture can warp the porous hardwood. If your floor is unfinished, or if it's an old wood floor and some of the finish has started to wear away, then don't use any moisture or product on the floor at all; just dust-mop it with a flat-head mop.

(FINISHED) HARDWOOD FLOOR CLEANER

2 cups water
½ teaspoon dish soap

Mix together in a spray bottle for use with a flat-head mop.

Laminate floors: Laminate flooring can fall victim to hazing, which is caused by the buildup of too much or inappropriate cleaning products. After much trial and error, I developed this recipe. As with hardwood, reducing moisture on the mop is crucial for reducing streaking and keeping the floors in tip-top shape.

LAMINATE FLOOR CLEANER

½ cup rubbing alcohol
½ cup water
½ cup white vinegar

Mix together in a spray bottle for use with a flat-head mop.

Store-bought alternatives: *Since flooring is a big investment, if you opt for a store-bought product, look for one specifically formulated for your particular finish, such as Armstrong Hardwood & Laminate Floor Cleaner, Bruce Hardwood and Laminate Floor Cleaner, and Bona Hardwood Cleaner.*

Natural stone: Natural stone is a delicate little flower and really needs to be treated gently when it comes to cleaning. Vinegar or anything harsh can mar the surface or cause permanent staining.

NATURAL-STONE FLOOR CLEANER

1 quart water
1 teaspoon dish soap
¼ cup rubbing alcohol

Mix together the water (hot is always good), dish soap, and rubbing alcohol in a bucket and use with a mop. If you notice streaks or stickiness left behind, finish up by repeating your mopping with clean water only to remove any residue.

Glass and stainless-steel cleaner: This product is designed for mirrors and windows, glass knobs, and any other glass décor that would be left streaky from the all-purpose cleaner, because of its soapiness. Its gentleness means it's also perfect for scratch-prone stainless steel. Glass cleaners are designed to lift dirt and oil off surfaces and leave a streak-free shine. When cleaning glass, if you find it is quite dusty, dust it first (with a dry flat-weave microfiber cloth) and clean it second, or else you'll notice dusty streaks left behind.

INDOOR-GLASS CLEANER AND STAINLESS-STEEL CLEANER

My basic water-vinegar solution will do the job on most glass—but if you have really stubborn stains, add the cornstarch for an extra (and extra-gentle) bit of abrasion that will help dislodge the dirt. This also does a great job on stainless steel.

1 cup water
1 cup white vinegar
1 teaspoon cornstarch
(optional—for really dirty surfaces)

Add to a spray bottle and shake gently to combine.

Outdoor glass gets dirty with dirt, not dust or fingerprints. Therefore, it needs a cleaner designed to remove the dirt. Suds are okay in this case! The squeegee will remove extra liquid and reveal a beautiful, streak-free shine that will trick your neighbors into thinking you clean 24/7.

GLASS CLEANER FOR OUTDOOR WINDOWS

1 gallon hot water
1 cup white vinegar
1 tablespoon dish soap

Mix all ingredients together well and use with a double-sided squeegee to clean windows to a crystal-clear shine.

Store-bought alternatives: *I like store-bought glass cleaners that not only clean but also help repel water marks, oil, and grease, such as Bon Ami 1886 Original Formula Powder Cleanser and Clean-X Repel Glass & Surface Cleaner.*

Leather cleaner: Most of the time, leather needs little more than a vacuum or a dusting; but when it starts to appear parched or lackluster, I find that an application such as Leather CPR Cleaner & Conditioner will restore its supple sheen.

Oxygen bleach can work wonders, taking on tough stains (think: wine, grease, blood) without harming the material or surface (but be sure to test it on a hidden area first!) and whitening and brightening fabrics. It's a gentler product than chlorine bleach, as it is made of sodium percarbonate and hydrogen peroxide. Once hot water is added to the powder and dissolved, oxygen bubbles are released and help break down stains and dinginess. Even outside of laundry, oxygen bleach has many cleaning applications. Recommendations: look for products that boast oxygen bleach or hydrogen peroxide as ingredients, such as OxiClean or Biokleen Oxygen Bleach Plus.

Stain remover: For laundry stain pretreatments, check out page 243. But for household stains on carpets and upholstery, remove any excess stain matter, then blot the area clean as best you can with a clean paper towel. Now, apply your pretreater.

HOUSEHOLD STAIN REMOVER (to be mixed up fresh every time, then discarded afterward)

2 parts hydrogen peroxide
1 part dish soap

Mix together in a small bowl and apply with a toothbrush or cloth. Let it sit for a few minutes, then rinse with water and blot up excess. Repeat if necessary.

Toilet bowl cleaner: These cleaners break down bacteria, odors, and mineral deposits, to keep the commode looking and smelling fresh.

TOILET BOWL CLEANER

Toilet bowl cleaners don't sound overly fun to make, but this one does work well. My essential oil recommendation is not optional here—tea tree oil is known for its disinfecting properties.

———

½ cup baking soda
½ cup water
¼ cup castile or dish soap
¼ cup hydrogen peroxide
15 drops tea tree oil

Combine the ingredients in a clean squeeze bottle with a cap. Squirt the solution around the toilet bowl, and after a few moments scrub with your brush as usual. Flush . . . and you're done!

Note: Tough toilet rings may require the use of a pumice stone (see page 34).

———

Store-bought alternatives: *Tough water and odors are your worst enemies in the toilet bowl, so I like to go for aggressive but bleach-free solutions like Biokleen Soy Toilet Scrub, Green Works Toilet Bowl Cleaner, and Lysol Hydrogen Peroxide Toilet Bowl Cleaner.*

Tub-and-tile cleaner: For the bathroom, you'll need something that will remove stubborn soap scum—that sticky residue left behind on tiles and tubs from our dirty shower or bath water, that combines by-products of soap, shampoo, body oils, mineral deposits, and dead skin cells—so gross! Here, too, I find that a homemade version is unbeatable.

TUB-AND-TILE CLEANER

To get even more cleaning power, look for a vinegar with a higher acidity percentage—like 6 to 10 percent—which you can find at hardware and health food stores. Be sure to use protective hand and eye gear if you're using this amped-up version; it's strong (and not to be used for salad!). This is safe to use on most bathroom surfaces, including glass, but excluding natural stone.

———

continues >>

½ cup white vinegar, poured into an empty spray bottle

½ cup dish soap

Baking soda, sprinkled as needed on tough areas

TOOLS

a nonscratching sponge

a squeegee

Spray the tub and tiles liberally all over with the solution and let it sit. After about 5 to 10 minutes, re-spray if necessary and scrub it off with a wet, nonscratching sponge; it should come off very easily. If there are stubborn areas, sprinkle baking soda onto the sponge as you scrub; the added abrasion eliminates that soap scum. Rinse the area well and use a squeegee to remove excess moisture and reveal a streak-free shine.

Store-bought alternatives: *I look for bleach-free and mildly abrasive formulations to get rid of soap scum and hard-water stains, such as Bon Ami Powder Cleanser and Bar Keepers Friend Cleanser & Polish. For dealing with mold and mildew, bleach-free, odorless formulations like Concrobium are a good bet.*

TUB, TILE, AND GROUT CLEANER (To remove staining)

This more intense tub-and-tile scrub can also whiten and brighten grout.

¼ cup dish soap

¼ cup baking soda

10 drops essential oil (optional)

Up to 2 tablespoons hydrogen peroxide

TOOLS

a nonscratching sponge

a bristle brush

a squeegee

Mix together the dish soap, baking soda, and essential oil (if using) in a small container, then add just enough hydrogen peroxide to make a paste. Apply the paste onto a damp, nonscratching sponge and scrub the tub, tiles, or grout. Allow the product to sit for 10 minutes, then wet the sponge and scrub again (scrub grout with the bristle brush). Finish up by rinsing the areas well; use a squeegee to dry the area. Discard any extra—this paste does not store well.

MELISSA'S MVP: BAKING SODA

I could write a whole book all about baking soda and its many, many uses.

Baking soda is a chemical compound known as sodium hydrogen carbonate, or sodium bicarbonate (a product so nice, they named it twice!), and it is safe and effective enough to use in almost any household application—remember, it is edible! (What's not to love about that?) Not only does it provide mild abrasion to remove dirt with a gentle scrub, it is also a whitener (baking soda toothpaste!), a deodorizer, and a laundry booster. Have I impressed you yet? Baking soda can act as a substitute for a cream or powdered kitchen or bathroom cleanser, an eraser-style sponge, and almost any deodorizing product (it even works as underarm deodorant!). Baking soda can leave some residue behind, so remember to rinse or wipe well before moving on.

Here are some simple household applications for baking soda; don't be surprised when I mention it throughout the book!

- **Carpets:** Sprinkle on carpets and let sit for 30 minutes to absorb odors and lift out dirt, then vacuum it up.

- **Trash cans/recycling bins:** Sprinkle some in the can or bin if it smells, leave for 20 minutes, then wipe clean with a wet cloth.

- **Kitchen:** For caked-on food on pots, pans, the oven door, or cooktop, create a paste of equal parts dish soap and baking soda, then add a few sprinkles of water until it's got a nice, pudding-like consistency. Apply with a damp, soft sponge and let sit on the surface for about 20 minutes, then wipe off (easily!) with a wet sponge. Rinse well and buff dry with a cloth.

- **Walls:** Sprinkle a little on a cloth slightly dampened with water, and use it to erase marks on the wall (yep, an eraser-style sponge substitute). Wipe the wall clean with a dry cloth.

- **Sinks:** Works great to remove stains from sinks—sprinkle it in and scrub well with a soapy sponge and hot water. Buff with a dry cloth to achieve that high-polish shine. The results are amazing!

SPECIALTY PRODUCTS

Enzyme-based cleaner: Enzymes help break down soil or heavy stains, get rid of odors, and make cleanup jobs much easier; they work by essentially *digesting* the stain, dirt, or grease (nice!) with a little bit of dwell time. You can use them in both laundry and cleaning applications. General home-cleaning options include Biokleen Bac-Out Stain + Odor Remover and Nature's ERADICATOR Multi-Purpose Enzyme Cleaner. Pet-specific enzyme product options include Nature's Miracle and Bissell Stain & Stink with Enzyme Action.

Gasket cleaner: I know, "What?!" You'll need it for only two things: your fridge and your washing machine. But it's a great, gentle way to discourage mildew from setting into the gaskets and stinking up everything.

GASKET CLEANER

1 cup white vinegar
10 drops essential oil

Stir together, then moisten a cloth with it and apply to the gaskets on your fridge or washing machine.

Natural-stone cleaner: Abrasive and acidic products can eat through a sealant and ruin a natural stone finish, so it's important to use a cleaner that's neutral yet effective at cleaning. My all-purpose cleaner recipe (see page 16) is gentle and effective enough to fit the bill.

If you're looking for a store-bought solution, there are several products available for this, including DuPont Granite & Marble Countertop Cleaner + Protector and Method Daily Granite.

Natural-stone sealer: I recommend sealing all natural-stone surfaces; check with your installer first, of course. This will make spills bead up and not set into the stone as long as they are wiped up. This goes for flooring

PANTRY ITEMS

You'll notice that I use these ingredients again and again in lots of different formulations, so it's a good idea to just keep them in the house.

- **3% hydrogen peroxide (what you get in the brown bottle):** a whitener, stain-remover, and chlorine bleach alternative.

- **Borax:** Borax, or sodium borate, is a naturally occurring mineral. While it is not as gentle as baking soda, it mixes well with lemon, vinegar, and water for cleaning purposes and does clean quite well when used properly. Turn to page 144 (bathroom) for my favorite Borax trick.

- **Cornstarch:** Used in glass cleaner; super soft, provides the most gentle abrasion, and wipes off streak-free.

- **Cream of tartar:** Can remove stains when combined with vinegar or lemon juice.

- **Rubbing alcohol:** A quick-drying agent for some of my recipes and a dissolver of oil and grease. It is also known to disinfect.

- **White vinegar:** Can be used as a deodorizer, degreaser, stainless-steel cleaner, glass cleaner, and it does away with soap scum and limescale. Lemon can do almost anything that vinegar does, but there are practical reasons why I recommend vinegar, not least of all the ridiculousness of having to juice a bunch of lemons before cleaning. You can always sub in lemon juice for vinegar if you want to, but be aware that a product with lemon juice in it will go rancid, where vinegar will not, so any big batch meant to last for a while should contain vinegar. Remember, you can always amp up your vinegar game with 6 percent or 10 percent acidity.

and shower walls, too. Sealing should be done every year or two. Product options include DuPont StoneTech BulletProof Sealer and Miracle Sealants 511.

WD-40: It has many home uses (like getting that stiff lock to turn more easily), but I find it is invaluable for removing paint splatters from sinks. If you don't have that particular problem, you can skip it.

Wood cleaner and polish: You can tell if your wood is finished or unfinished by how it behaves if you drop a bead of water on it. If it beads, it is finished; if it absorbs, it is unfinished. I clean my varnished wood with my all-purpose cleaner, and occasionally I'll treat it with some wood polish when it's looking a little lackluster. If your wood is unfinished, don't use any product. Simply wipe with a clean, dry microfiber cloth. Oftentimes, I find I can remove most fingerprints and dust from wood with a microfiber cloth lightly moistened with water.

WOOD POLISH

3 parts olive oil
1 part white vinegar

Mix the oil and vinegar together in a clean spray bottle. Spray on, then wipe well with a paper towel. It's like any good salad dressing—give it a good shake before using to mix the oil and vinegar together.

Store-bought alternatives: *I like to avoid silicone-based furniture polish and ideally find something that cleans and protects without leaving buildup or ruining a finish. Furniture buffs (no pun intended) can opt for Howard Feed-N-Wax Wood Polish & Conditioner, or if you are looking for a plant-based formulation, check out Method Wood for Good Polish.*

Cleaning Tools (the first *T*)

I've included a lot of tools here, simply because not every one will be necessary for your individual space. You can decide which are the most important for you. Again, they are arranged alphabetically. Please note—don't skimp on buying the right tools, because you'll regret it down the line, wasting your time (and money) with efforts that don't pay off. You can't expect a good haircut if the hairdresser has only a pair of rusty scissors.

Broom: From time to time, a good old-fashioned broom comes in handy. I like an angled-style broom for getting into tight corners. For sweeping outside surfaces like decks and patios, look for a corn-husk (or natural-bristle) broom.

Cleaning caddy: Depending on what you decide to use product- and tool-wise, having a cleaning caddy to carry your items around is a great idea. It saves you from having to keep running back and forth to get more gear. I like a plastic caddy that is easy to clean, has at least 6 inches of depth, and is large, to fit a lot in. The Casabella Rectangular Storage Caddy or the Rubbermaid Deluxe Carry Cleaning Caddy are good examples. They're sturdy and the sides are deep so that products don't flop out in transit. You can also soak it when it gets grotty—which it will.

Cleaning toothbrush: Use this to get into really tight spaces. It is handy for brushing out limescale from water fixtures or to clean the hinges of the toilet bowl seat. Keep separate toothbrushes for kitchen and bathroom to avoid cross-contamination (you can easily color-code: green for bathroom, blue for kitchen, etc.). And don't even think about storing it anywhere that you keep your regular toothbrush—yikes, just don't take the risk of that kind of mix-up. To clean and disinfect these, I rinse out debris, then soak them in a hot oxygen bleach solution for 30 minutes, rinse well, and dry.

Clean spray bottles: Whether you upcycle empty cleaning-product bottles or source your own from dollar stores, garden centers, or beauty supply stores, spray bottles are essential for whipping up your own products. I label them with permanent marker so that I always know what concoction is in each bottle.

To get the best results, always make sure your spray bottle and trigger head are clean and ready to receive the new mixture. To clean the bottle, simply empty the contents and fill halfway with water. Swirl around to get out any remaining product, and dump the contents. You may need to repeat this several times to remove all the residue. You'll know it is clean when you don't see any bubbles remaining after swishing the water. To clean the trigger head, fill the bottle halfway with clean water and thread the trigger head back onto the bottle. Now, just squirt the trigger (into the sink) several times and allow the water to flush the system.

Compressed air: This stuff blows dust out of tight spaces, like between the keys of your keyboard. Don't shake the can; and use it in short bursts, not long blasts.

Cotton cloth: Sometimes, albeit rarely, a microfiber cloth won't cut it. Cotton cloths are better to use in very greasy or gritty applications, since grease and grit can be difficult to remove from microfiber. Cotton can handle hot washes if necessary; microfiber can't.

Cotton swabs: These are great little cleaning tools for applying cleaning product to tight spaces where a cloth won't fit, but some absorbency and pressure is needed. Use one side treated, and the other side dry, to remove any moisture.

Double-sided nonscratching sponge: You're probably familiar with the double-sided sponge that most of us use to clean in the kitchen. But read that packaging closely and you'll see that it also comes in a *nonscratching* version, which has just as much scrubbing power but won't ruin your delicate finishes. Still, you'll want to be careful. Some brief guidelines:

- The scrubbing side is used to clean inside pots, inside non-self-cleaning ovens, tiles and grout, the microwave, tubs, and porcelain sinks.

- The soft side is for acrylic tubs and sinks, glass, stainless-steel sinks, countertops, or anything else that can scratch easily.

- Remember to keep sponges used in the kitchen separate from ones used in the bathroom to avoid cross-contamination.

- To clean sponges, rinse in cool, soapy water to remove debris, then boil a pot of water and add the sponge, allowing it to boil for 5 minutes to reduce bacteria counts. Remove with tongs and allow to cool.

Flat-head dust mop: These mops serve double duty: they're the perfect tool for thoroughly cleaning hardwood and laminate floors, and they can be used for quick in-between cleans, too—lightly dampened to pick up debris, or dry to tackle spills. Instead of the floor-cleaning solutions usually sold with these, I just use the appropriate floor-cleaning recipe or store-bought alternative (see pages 18–19) and mop quickly with the grain of the wood to avoid streaks. I recommend having a few spare mop heads handy if you plan to clean several floor surfaces in one go; they get dirty pretty fast. Launder the mop head the same way you would clean a microfiber cloth.

This tool is also fabulous for cleaning walls when the time comes. Pop on a clean microfiber pad and dust the walls using a W-pattern (see page 47). If you want to save money on disposable dust mop heads, try swapping in a clean microfiber cloth and laundering it when done instead!

Gloves, mask (and any other protective gear you wish): For hot-water dishwashing, I like long, cuffed rims (no dishwater down your arm!), a comfortable fit, good thickness, and ideally relative prettiness. Casabella WaterBlock Gloves do the trick. To clean these, simply wash your hands, gloves on, with dish soap, rinse, and remove right-side-out to dry.

I can't remember the last time I wore a mask or protective eyewear, because I keep away from products with warnings. However, it is always good to have these items handy if you are going to use a product that carries safety hazards.

Handheld broom: This little broom is perfect for brushing debris out of tight areas and bringing the mess forth for a vacuum to gather; it also excels at quick one-off cleanups where a large broom isn't required. It stores easily, too.

High-dusting tool: Guess what? Not only did you make your own cleaning products, but now you're going to make your own cleaning tool! Sure, you can buy a high duster, but why spend the money? Instead, drape a general-purpose microfiber cloth over the end of a mop pole or broom handle, then secure it with an elastic, so that it looks like a little ghost. Voilà! You have a duster for getting cobwebs against the ceiling, dust caught in grooves in your moldings; flip it upside down, and you have a low duster for your baseboards.

Iron-handle scrub brush (bristle brush): No, the handle isn't made of iron; it's called this because the brush looks like an iron! This is used specifically for cleaning grout lines and it makes the job easier.

Lint roller: With my two cats, there's always a piece of fluff on me somewhere that needs to be removed; that cat-lady look isn't cute. I look for one that has a large surface and strong adhesive properties, such as the Evercare T-Handle Lint Roller or the Scotch-Brite Lint Roller: I keep one handy in the car, one in my bathroom, one in the front hall closet, and one in my office. They're also great if you have guests coming over and there's no time to vacuum hairy upholstery.

Microfiber cloths: Gone are the days of cut-up T-shirts and cleaning rags that lack absorbency and leave moisture and streaks behind. Microfiber cloths can hold, on average, eight times their weight in water, and clean lint- and streak-free. When I first tried microfiber cloths, I noticed right away how they cut my cleaning time and made my work significantly easier, and my final results were way better. Why would I ever want to clean with anything else? It's called microfiber because each small loop of yarn is sliced tens of thousands of times—each little microfiber picks up and traps dust, dirt, and liquids. These cloths can also last for up to five hundred washes, and that's bang for your buck, if you ask me. You'll find a lot of variety these days to suit different cleaning purposes; these are what I generally like:

- **General-purpose or terry:** Perfect for general-purpose cleaning, such as dusting, wiping, etc. Get a few, to avoid cross-contamination. I recommend five of these.
- **Plush:** Perfect for buffing surfaces to a streak-free shine. Stash one with you when cleaning for this purpose. Have two on hand.
- **Flat-weave:** Used for glass cleaning and delicate, soft surfaces such as flat-screen TVs and electronics. I use one or two for a home cleaning.
- **Waffle-weave:** Heavy-duty drying towels designed to replace dish towels. A pair of these is perfect in the kitchen.
- **Full disclosure:** I love microfiber cloths so much, I have my own line of them! (Maker's Cleaning Cloths are available at MakersClean.com.)

It is important that they are cleaned and cared for properly to ensure they'll last use after use. To clean them, first rinse the cloth well to remove excess debris. Machine wash them *only with other microfiber cloths* (they will pick up particles from regular laundry), using gentle, bleach-free laundry detergent and cool water on a regular cycle, or hand wash with dish soap in warm water and rinse thoroughly. Don't use fabric softener or dryer sheets with these cloths; they will clog the fibers and render the cloth ineffective. It is best to hang them to dry or place in the dryer on low heat.

Microfiber twist mop: While the sponge mop may be a familiar cleaning friend, it has been usurped by a much more effective cleaning tool: the microfiber twist mop. A sponge mop cannot be easily cleaned (those spongy pockets!), meaning you'll mop with a somewhat dirty tool at all times. Further, a sponge mop doesn't have the absorbency that a microfiber mop does, meaning moisture will be left behind, leaving streaks and potentially damaging a hardwood or laminate floor. The best choice for most hard-floor surfaces, like ceramic or sealed-stone floors, is a string-style mop made with microfiber, not cotton strands. Look for something like the O-Cedar/Vileda Supertwist Mop with a wringer bucket, or if you like a twist mop and don't want the fancy bucket, something like the Joy Mangano Miracle Mop will do. Always make sure the mop is nearly dry; this means wringing it out so that there is hardly any water on the mop. Too much water means streaks and potential floor damage. Clean the mop head every few uses, and launder the same way you would microfiber cloths.

Ostrich-feather duster: Despite its exotic pedigree, a genuine feather duster won't set you back too much cash, but it comes in super handy on things that would be way too time-consuming to dust with a cloth, such as the tops of books and elaborate light fixtures. To rid it of excess dust, tap it several times over a yet-to-be-cleaned surface.

Paper towels: I am not a proponent of using paper towels for cleaning aside from areas with high potential for cross-contamination—namely bathroom and kitchen surfaces. Be considerate of the environment when you use paper towels; when you can, try to use a dish towel or a cleaning cloth instead. When it comes to paper towels, look for something absorbent and textured with the option to select the size so that each sheet goes the distance.

Pumice stones are great little helpers around the house. Clearly, you'll use a different one for your pedicure than you will for your toilet (so gross, I know!), but I have a feeling you'll come to love pumice as a cleaning tool. It's a crumbly, slightly abrasive stone that helps remove stains on porous surfaces (think: toilet bowl rings); people swear by pumice to clean their grills and non-self-cleaning ovens, too. I've even seen pumice stones used to depill sweaters and remove pet hair from furniture. For toilet cleaning purposes, look for one that comes on a stick (it's like a pumice corn dog—vegan, of course!), like the Pumie. Make sure you designate one for the toilet and toilet only; these guys are porous and cannot be entirely disinfected.

Rubber broom: This relies on friction to dredge up dirt, dust, and debris locked into carpet fibers. A vacuum performs better at removing those tiny particles, like dust and dander, so I feel rubber brooms are best kept for cleaning spots that would potentially be hard to vacuum, such as carpeted stairs. Wet the rubber tip just a bit to amp up the friction.

Scraper: Those old-fashioned cleaning manuals will often recommend chipping away at a dried-on stain with a razor blade. These tools, made just for the job, are a safer way to go, both for your own sake (who wants to risk a gash or tetanus—worst cleaning day ever?) and for the sake of what you're cleaning (razor blades can scratch or cause real damage to surfaces). My favorite is the SKrAPr. When used with water at a 45-degree angle it can safely remove buildup from virtually any surface. And lay off on the elbow grease! Even with a gentle touch, it will remove small paint splatters and buildup with ease. This tool has significantly improved the look of my glass-top stove.

Squeegee: I recommend having a double-sided squeegee with a rubber blade on one side and a microfiber sponge pad on the other. This makes quick work of cleaning exterior windows or larger interior windows. Some come with a universal threading extension, which means they can be screwed onto a broomstick or mop handle and used to clean windows that may have otherwise been out of reach. You'll remove the dirt and liquid and reveal a crystal-clean shine.

I also recommend using a small rubber-blade squeegee when cleaning tubs, tiles, and glass—it reduces the time you need to spend drying these surfaces to get a streak-free shine. If you keep it in the shower and squeegee the walls daily after the shower has been taken, you will reduce the amount of actual shower-cleaning you need to do. This makes a big difference!

Superfine steel wool: This is only, I repeat only, to be used inside your oven, and even then, only (only!) if it is not a self-cleaning oven.

Toilet bowl brush: I like the toilet bowl brush–plunger combo with ventilation, which allows for drying. It does a good job of concealing these two rather unappetizing bathroom tools nicely and allows them to dry effectively. The Libman Toilet Brush & Plunger Combo is a safe bet. Clean the brush and plunger, as well as the container, by rinsing off debris, then soaking them in a hot oxygen bleach solution for 30 minutes; rinse well and dry.

Trash bags: I've used several generic bags that are so thin they tear, and some bags with poor seams that split right open. Spend the money and get heavy-duty bags. Hefty and Glad are decent choices.

Vacuum: If you have a wedding or big milestone coming up where gifts are given, do register for a great vacuum. While not romantic or flashy, it's a super-practical gift and you'll use it for years. Considerations: You want a vacuum that doesn't lose suction, is light enough to be comfortable to work with, and has a high-power head. Further, you want to ensure you have a nice selection of attachments to suit your needs—if you are a pet owner, look for a powerful upholstery tool. You'll also have to decide whether you prefer a canister or upright model (I prefer a canister), and consider how much storage space you'll have for a vacuum. My preference is to have a bagless model, because you just need to empty the canister as opposed to the hassle of changing out bags. If you are an allergy or asthma sufferer, or if you have pets, I recommend you look for a vacuum with a HEPA filter, too. I have found that in the past few years, vacuums have gotten really good—manufacturers have really stepped up their sucking game. I have had a Dyson for many years but I wouldn't hesitate to recommend a Bissell, a Black & Decker, a Hoover, a Dirt Devil, or a Shark. And, if you have a bigger budget, look at a Miele or a Kirby.

I also have a cordless stick vacuum that gets charged between uses and comes out to clean stairs as well as quick midweek cleanups.

Remember to clean your vacuum canister out after each use, since a full vacuum is a dysfunctional vacuum; the debris prevents suction and can overwork the motor. Get in the habit of doing this and your vacuum will last for years. If you have a model that uses a bag, remember to empty it when it gets full (do a poke test).

Wringer bucket: I find it helpful to have a bucket with a removable cone wringer, like the Libman Clean and Rinse Bucket with Wringer or the O-Cedar/Vileda Quick-Wring Bucket. When the bucket is not in use, you can use it to store products or tools, or for other cleaning tasks like soaking small items or for whipping up a window-cleaning solution. One quick note about buckets: try to keep them on a tiled surface when in use to avoid any moisture damage to wood or stone floors, or place an old placemat underneath.

VACUUM ATTACHMENTS

Crevice tool: For hard-to-reach cracks: where the baseboard meets the carpet, underneath appliances and furniture, in vents and ceiling corners, and in the corners under upholstered furniture.

Bare-floor brush: For hard-floor surfaces: the soft bristles protect the floor from scratching. Also good for walls if needed—just make sure the bristles are clean (you can comb the dirt out of them with the vacuum turned on, and the dust that comes out will get sucked right up).

Dusting brush: A smaller version of the bare-floor brush. Good for window coverings, upholstery, windowsills, and screens.

Upholstery brush: Great for getting pet hair off upholstery; occasionally flip it over and scrape off debris caught in the lint-removal strips while the vacuum is running.

Extension wand: Allows you to reach super high and get super low with all your attachments.

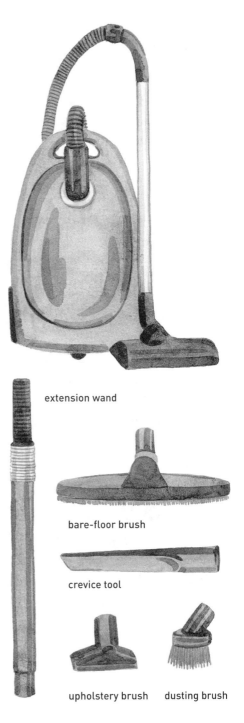

extension wand

bare-floor brush

crevice tool

upholstery brush   dusting brush

SPECIALTY ITEMS

Carpet and upholstery deep-cleaning system: If your home is prone to spills, stains, and accidents (pet or human), this is a good investment. While they don't perform as well as a professional's tools would, they'll do the trick for lifting out stains and odors from soft surfaces. Ours has proven to be invaluable. I've found the Bissell Lift-Off to work well. Remember, you'll need the appropriate solution for the machine, too.

Steam cleaner/garment steamer: Steam cleaning is quite effective but does require you to take the time to learn how to use the tool properly and safely. It can clean surfaces and power through dirt, grease, and ground-in stains. Dirty grout can come clean almost instantly using a steam cleaner; I've watched it liquefy the grime from my overhead exhaust. Further, a quality steam cleaner (as in, one that reaches 212 degrees F at the tip) will also obliterate bacteria. I don't clean with steam on a regular basis, but I can imagine a time when we will all start to.

I look for one that is small and easy to port and store, heats up to at least 212 degrees F at the tip, and has multiple heads for various uses including garment steaming. One product that hits the mark is the Reliable Pronto 100CH Handheld Steamer. Note: I've found that most units require distilled water.

Gear for unfinished spaces: Apartment dwellers, rejoice—you can skip all these items. But if you have an unfinished basement or garage, you'll probably want heavy-duty protective gear (like work gloves with rubber grips, eyewear, and a face mask), a yacht mop, a push broom, a drop cloth, and a shop vacuum. For more on these and how to use them, turn to Chapter 11, "Storage Spaces."

Cleaning Techniques (the second *T*)

After spending ten years deep in the cleaning trenches, I developed these time-saving techniques and best practices to help you get superior results in less time. Even better, they keep your home cleaner longer. So if I may be so bold, forget what you currently know about cleaning and open your mind to this new way. These techniques totally changed the way I cleaned (for the better). I will also explain some basic how-to's here—how to mop, how to vacuum—so that you won't have to read the same instructions over and over throughout the book (unless you want to read about vacuuming again and again!—Can I offer you a job?).

THE 3-WAVE SYSTEM

Have you ever walked into a messy room and felt a strong desire to run the other way? That's because you didn't have a system in place to tackle the cleaning. I get asked *all the time* about **how** and **where** to start cleaning. My formula, the 3-Wave system, is the answer. It has worked for me for years and I teach my staff this method. The idea is that you work around the room three times *with a distinct purpose* with each pass. By the end of the third pass, your space is sparkling and you feel as calm as a cactus in the desert.

You'll work clockwise around the room three times as follows: **wave 1, tidying and organizing**, i.e., putting things that are out of place back where they belong; **wave 2, cleaning**, or dusting, washing, and drying all surfaces except the floors; and **wave 3, floors (plus finishing touches)**. When working clockwise, make the entryway your "12 o'clock" starting point so that you have a consistent start and finish point, and you'll never miss a spot. In rooms with a sink, make the sink your 12 o'clock (you'll use it until the end, so you clean it last!). In each chapter, I'll outline the specifics of each wave for that given space, but here's a primer on what you can expect.

Wave 1: Tidying and Organizing

You can't clean a room that's covered in clutter, and that's why wave 1 is all about tidying. How is a vacuum to be pushed around, or a surface to be dusted, when it's covered with things that don't belong? Remember complaining to your parents about having to clean up before the cleaning person got there? Bingo! That's what we're doing here. (See page 268 for more on hiring a professional.)

The first wave involves picking up trash and recycling, putting things that belong here in order, and removing things that don't belong here. For this wave, you don't need cleaning products; you just need your trash bag/recycling bag and a bin or basket for items that don't belong in that room. I usually place those right in the middle of the room for easy access, so that I don't get off track. Go around the room, scanning from top to bottom, left to right, section by section, for any item that needs to be "dealt with." Any items that don't belong in the room go into the bin; when you're done, you'll leave it outside the door and deal with it after the clean is over.

For the items that you pass that are (sort of) in their right homes (because each item should have a home, as you know), tidy and organize them—nothing too detailed (this isn't the time to reorganize your photo album, see—that's how you get distracted). Position them neatly and attractively.

Wave 2: Cleaning

Now that the room is neat and tidy and free of distraction, you can actually clean it. This means dusting and polishing. To prepare for the second wave, I keep a bottle of all-purpose cleaner in one hand, a clean microfiber cloth in the other, and a dry microfiber cloth thrown over my shoulder so that I can "buff" surfaces and items dry. Spare cloths and glass cleaner are kept close by, too.

High dusting is the first task you're going to tackle (I'll explain how to high-dust later in this chapter). A quick note about high dusting—it's not a job you need to do all the time, but doing it occasionally

wave 1

wave 2

wave 3

will help nab those cobwebs and other dusty collections that gather in corners and horizontal surfaces above eye level (like the tops of cupboards or crown molding). Since dust falls from the top to the bottom,

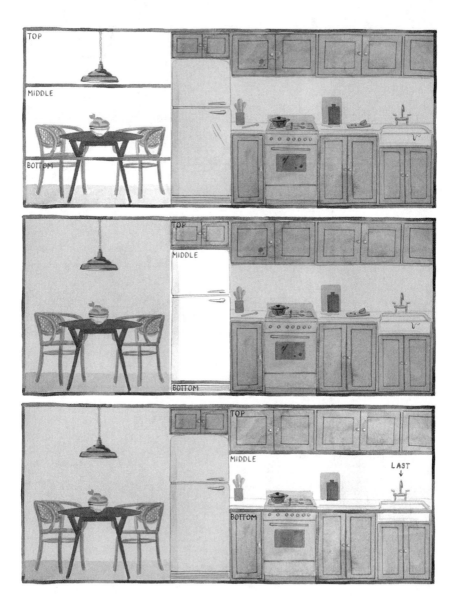

you want to start with high dusting, then move on to lower surfaces. When that's done, put down your high-dusting tool, spray your microfiber cloth so that it's damp, and head back to 12 o'clock. Working section by section, start scanning (top to bottom) and seeking out any fingerprints or marks on the wall, glass surfaces, or horizontal surfaces (like tabletops) that need dusting and polishing, and giving them a swipe with your cloth. You are literally scanning, moving your head up and down as if you were nodding "yes," looking for things that *need* cleaning. Include furniture and room décor in this scan, and clean items as necessary. Finally, points of contact (those things that get touched a million times—knobs and switches) get cleaned, too.

Third and Final Wave: Floors and Finishing Touches

The room is organized and clean, and now it's time to clean the floors, perfect any misses, and remove trash and rogue items.

You start by vacuuming (upholstery first, then floors), then move to mopping if you have hard floors. You gather up the trash bag and bin that you placed outside the door, and deliver the contents to their rightful homes. Finally, look around the room and straighten up anything that missed your attention and replace any temporarily moved items. That's it. You're done!

✓ MORE PRO TIPS!

Pretreat like a boss and let your products do the work for you.

To be fair, many of us learned our ideas about cleaning from TV commercials where a stain magically wipes off after a millisecond of a product being applied. That's not real life. Products need time to loosen dirt, grime, or grease. So if something is particularly stained or greasy in the room that you'll be cleaning, pretreat it before you start your second wave so that it will wipe off easily once you get to it.

Use both hands.

It's almost ridiculous to have to say it, but I've seen people clean with their dominant hand, and the other one just hangs down by their leg like a listless old dog. Using two hands simultaneously means you work twice as fast. Lift with one, clean with the other. Wet cloth in one hand,

ROOM-BY-ROOM OR TASK-BY-TASK?

This is an age-old cleaning debate, and I want to weigh in right now. Many people say, for example, that it's best to do all the vacuuming on one day, instead of dragging that vacuum out for the bedroom on Tuesday, and then have to bring it out again for the den on Wednesday.

Here's my thought: If someone is cleaning their entire house in one shot, then it *does* make more sense to complete one task (actually, I would say, to complete one *wave*) for the entire home, then move on to the next task/wave for the entire home. Most rooms follow a similar 3-wave cleaning pattern, as you will see in each room-by-room chapter. The benefit to doing it this way (aside from a mad calorie burn) is that you really get into a zone—you become laser-focused on the task at hand, and by the last room, you'll be very efficient and speedy.

But, in this book, I focus more on cleaning in smaller, time-restricted chunks depending on what your MIAs are, because I think that's what most people have time for these days. If you choose to clean for 15 minutes per day, I advocate for cleaning by room and *not* by task. When you clean an entire room, everything gets done—you're cleaning from top to bottom, left to right, vacuuming up all the dust on your way out. When you finish that space, that room is entirely cleaned. It will stay cleaner longer and you'll want to keep it that way, since it looks beautiful. When you clean by task over days, your work is never quite done anywhere, and the rooms are always sort-of-clean but also sort-of-not. I don't find that rewarding at all, and for me, the reward is a big part of the positive-feedback loop of keeping my house clean.

dry cloth in the other. You can chop down your cleaning time and look like a natural.

Note your exit route at the beginning when vacuuming and mopping.

Rather than backing yourself into a corner, work from the farthest corner in the room toward the exit. Plug in your vacuum by the exit point; mop your way toward it. That way, you don't have to walk over a beautifully cleaned floor to move on! That's the beauty of making the door or entryway into the room your 12 o'clock starting point. You'll always end at the door.

Check for streaks.

This is a trick that I've taught my staff for years. Mirrors and windows are deceiving; they may look clean head-on, but when you move to another part of the room they can look like a hot mess. In order to make sure they are truly clean, you have to do a dance: Start just a foot away then take one step to the left. Any streaks? Take two steps to the right and look again. See anything new? Finally, center again and crouch down. Look up at the surface, what do you see now? By checking at these four angles, you account for any funny lighting and can see, for real, any streaks or areas left uncleaned. It's like your mirror has drunk truth serum! You can use this trick for any surface (floors, furniture, counters); just find your light source and start grooving.

TWO KEY CLEANING MOVES

Working even one of these techniques into your current cleaning will improve things noticeably; mastering them both will transform the act of cleaning into one that's smooth and efficient—and will enhance the look of your home when you're done.

The **magic letters *S* and *W***: instead of haphazardly circling with your wiping, mixing clean with dirty, use the most efficient motion when

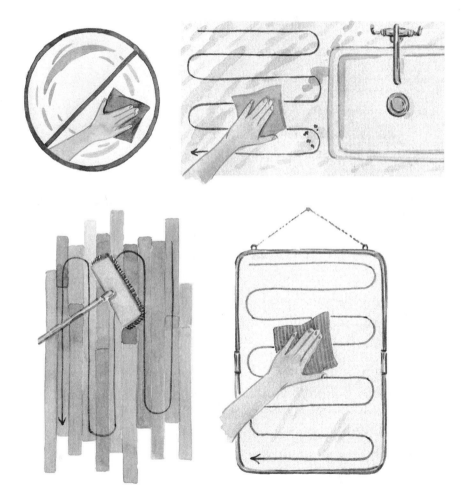

cleaning all horizontal and vertical surfaces, the **S-pattern.** Grab your cloth and begin by starting at the top corner and moving over to the other, then slightly down and back to the opposite side, zigzagging over new areas until you get down to the bottom corner. This is one of the most crucial cleaning moves you need to know! It is more elbow-grease efficient and ensures you cover every inch of a surface without redepositing dirt anywhere.

The vacuuming equivalent is the **W-pattern**, which is most effective and leaves nice cut lines in the carpet. If your room is large, visually divide the space into smaller sections. Begin with the vacuum positioned in the top corner of your section, and line up the vacuum head with the edge of the wall. Pull the vacuum straight down, running parallel to the edge of the wall. Stop and then angle the vacuum head so that it will slightly overlap the straight pass you just made; push up toward the top of the section. Then, pull the vacuum straight down, parallel with the edge of the wall, slightly overlapping the angled pass you just made. Repeat this move, working your way from one side to the other—straight on the downstroke, slightly angled on the upstroke. It's also what you should use when vacuuming upholstery and walls (yes, walls— see page 213!).

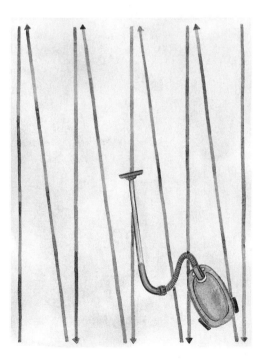

✓ PRO TIP! BECOME YOUR OWN STYLIST

Follow the lead of the great home stagers and always line up items (like magazines or remote controls) **parallel and perpendicular** to the edges of the furniture. Somehow, the mathematical straightness of the lines soothes the eye and suddenly the items left out look curated and deliberate. For example, a tablet, a book, and a cell phone scattered on the night stand will be tidied by stacking them with the largest item on the bottom (tablet), followed by the book, and topped with the phone; line that pile up with the edge of the table.

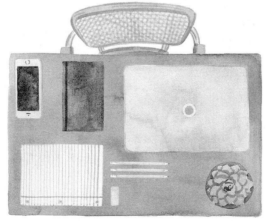

How to Clean

I'll lay out the basics here, but you'll find more tailored specifics in the room-by-room chapters.

HOW TO DUST

For **high dusting**, take your high-dusting tool and head to 12 o'clock. Raise up the tool to the seam where the ceiling meets the wall. Walk it from corner to corner around the room (moving clockwise), dragging it along the corners and edges of the wall and ceiling seams (cobweb central). While you're at it, you can also clean any doorframes, vents, or light fixtures (which—alert!—should be switched off if you are cleaning them, to avoid popping bulbs).

To dust and polish furniture: You want to dust a bare surface; so always begin by carefully removing any items on top (I usually place them to my right on another, uncleaned surface or on the floor beside me). Then, dampen the surface (if the surface can tolerate it) with the appropriate product and start at the top left corner using a general-purpose microfiber cloth folded into quarters, using the most efficient movement, the S-pattern (see page 47), to clean the surface. Flip the cloth over to a dry side and repeat the motion to buff dry. This is done to remove excess moisture and leave a clean, streak-free shine. Then, pick up each item that belongs here and wipe it clean before replacing it neatly. If you need to polish a surface, use the appropriate cleaner *after* dusting. Massage the product in using the S-pattern until you have a nice, even finish. For polishing with an oil-based product, I recommend doing this with a cotton rag or paper towel, since oil doesn't come out of microfiber easily.

Finally, **to dust baseboards**, flip your high duster upside down and go over baseboards in the same manner.

HOW TO CLEAN WINDOWSILLS

You'll see below that I have a technique for when the sill needs a lot of work and when it needs a little. Don't overclean! This is how you do it:

1. Lift any window covering to expose the windowsill.

2. Examine the windowsill and track.

3. If very dirty:
   a. Use a dry cleaning toothbrush to loosen dirt and debris.
   b. Vacuum up dirt using the brush attachment.
   c. Spray with all-purpose cleaner (page 16) and allow the product to sit for a few moments to loosen the remaining dirt.
   d. Use a cleaning toothbrush to agitate the product and lift out the dirt from the sills and tracks.
   e. Use a paper towel to blot up the product and the dirt, being sure not to regrind it into the sill or track.

4. If relatively clean:
   a. Use a cloth dampened with all-purpose cleaner and wipe the track and sill.

HOW TO CLEAN BLINDS

Same story: I don't advise that you tackle the blinds every time—they don't get as dusty as sills do on a regular basis. Just give them a quick inspection, and if they look fine, move on. If they need a clean:

1. Pull blinds to their "closed" position—this will give you the best opportunity to check for dirt and dust.

2. For horizontal slatted blinds (wood, metal, plastic, composite):
   a. Quickly dust the surface with a dry general-purpose microfiber cloth, starting with the top three slats and working your way from left to right, moving down until you reach the bottom.

b. Quickly spot-check for any stains or marks and wipe them away with a damp microfiber cloth.

c. Turn blinds all the way over to the other side and repeat *a* and *b*.

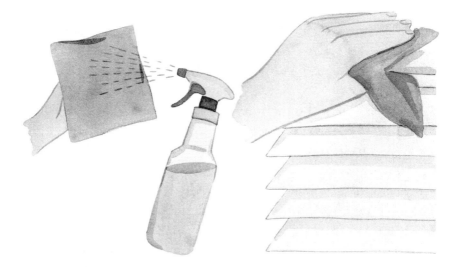

3. For plastic or vinyl vertical slatted blinds:

   a. Spray your general-purpose microfiber cloth with all-purpose cleaner and lift one slat up toward you.

   b. Starting at the top of the slat, wrap your cloth around the slat (just fold it in half over the slat), and gently pull the cloth down toward the tip of the slat. This helps remove dust, dirt, and stains all at once.

   c. Repeat until done.

4. For fabric blinds:

   a. Starting at the top of the blind, use your vacuum with the brush attachment to vacuum up any dust. Depending on the design of the blind, work horizontally from top to bottom, or vertically from left to right, whichever feels more sensible.

HOW TO VACUUM

Begin by removing as many obstructing pieces as possible—that way you don't have to maneuver around the room with a clunky vacuum. I move chairs and small tables or accessories on the floor outside of the room; this makes the work much easier. Plug in your vacuum as close to your exit point as possible and begin vacuuming. Always keep the cord, hose, and canister behind you. Next, use any attachments to vacuum furniture, baseboards, or corners, then attach the right floor-care tool and do the floors last.

For floors with wall-to-wall carpet, first run around the perimeter of the room with the crevice attachment. For any hard-floored room with area rugs, start by vacuuming around those first, then vacuum around the perimeter of the rugs with the dust brush. Then switch to the attachment appropriate for your floor. Start at the corner opposite of the exit point of the room and place your vacuum at the corner of that section, as close to the baseboard as possible. Then, it's all W-pattern (see page 47).

Quick note for pet parents: I find it is most efficient when cleaning a space that has pet hair to vacuum before starting wave 2, then complete wave 2, then vacuum again. This is because pet hair floats around while you're cleaning and will land back on spaces you have already dusted. You get a much more thorough clean when you sandwich your wave 2 between two vacuuming sessions. I know it is more work, but you knew that was coming when you got little Fluffy or Fido.

HOW TO MOP

The most important thing when mopping is to use *just* enough product to cut the grease from your feet, sop up spills, and reveal the floor's natural shine. Have you ever walked on a sticky floor *after* it has been cleaned? That's from using too much floor cleaner. Plus, when it *is* sticky, it attracts dirt, making your floors dirtier, faster. Embarrassingly, I have written a one-line poem about mopping: *Less is more when mopping the floor.*

For tile, vinyl, and stone floors, use a twist mop and bucket or spray bottle and flat-head mop; for wood and laminate, use a flat-head mop with a spray bottle.

You'll mop a floor after it has been swept or vacuumed, which means it won't have anything that will get in your way. Then, mop section by section using the S-pattern, rinsing the mop head (if using a bucket) every minute or so or changing the flat-head mop pad when it gets dirty and too saturated, and mopping your way out of the room. For tiled surfaces (this goes for ceramic, porcelain, and stone), mop in the most convenient direction using the S-pattern, or for rectangular tiles, mop in the direction of the grout.

If your mop wasn't too wet, you can skip the next step: Take a dry microfiber cloth, attach it to the bottom of a flat-head mop, and quickly use an S-pattern to buff out any moisture and remove streaks. Your floors will sparkle.

Let me be the first to congratulate you for getting through this chapter. Whether you realize it or not, the transformation of how you think about cleaning has begun to take place. You'll never look at or think about cleaning the same, and that's a big win! This new knowledge will save you the time, tears, and frustration I went through to get here. Further, it'll make you extremely efficient and effective with your cleaning efforts (no matter how much time you plan to spend). No more wasting time—let's get cleaning!

CHAPTER 3

the entryway

What, *entryway*? Who cares—it's not even a room, right? For most people, when the home is upside down and in dire need of a clean, the entryway is one of the last places they think of. I beg to differ.

The entryway sets the mood for the entire *experience* of being at your home. But this notion doesn't just come from some Stepford-wifey thinking of wanting to please the neighbors with everything just-so. More important, how do *you* feel when you first walk in the door? Happy? Stressed? Excited? Calm? Annoyed? That's right, how your home receives you sets the tone for the remainder of your day. Case in point: if I walk in the front door and the entryway is tidy, uncluttered, and smells fresh, I feel good, calm, happy to be home. "Yessss! That traffic was nasty but it is so unbelievably good to be here. Let's cook dinner and have a drink." Contrast that with walking in after a busy day when the house hasn't been kept, and the first things that greet me are a gaggle of shoes kicked off every which way and a pile of mail, packages, and bags on the console. "Oh-em-gee. For real? Our house is such a sty. Now I have to deal with this, then cook dinner. Oy vey. I need a drink."

How do *you* want to be received each day? The entryway is most definitely one of my personal MIAs. I want it to smell beautiful, be clean, and feel bright and airy. Treat this space with great importance, and you'll notice a visceral difference the next time you come home.

Developing a Getting-Home Routine

Well, Mom, Dad, sorry. That wasn't me at my finest. The truth is, all they wanted me to do was create a new getting-home routine. I finally started to change . . . when I moved out of the house and into my own condo. (Did I say sorry?) Suddenly, my coat left lying about just seemed tacky. My shoes? I paid good money for them; I didn't want to kick them off where people could trip over them! It was like going through homeowner puberty—all these inner changes!

My getting-home routine is super simple. When I get home, I've usually got a bag or two, keys, a purse, a coat, and heavens knows what else. My first instinct is to just drop everything (old habits die hard!). But instead, my new routine stops this habit in its tracks. Try these five simple steps—they will take two minutes:

UPON ENTERING THE HOUSE

- Hang up your coat and put gloves, scarves, and hats away in a bin in the coat closet or area designated for coats (more on this below!). (Don't have a bin? Get one!)

- Line up your shoes neatly or place them—again, neatly—into the closet.

- Hang up your keys or place them in a bowl—you'll never lose them again if you always put them in the same place.

- Take your lunch bag or coffee thermos directly into the kitchen and empty it, tossing trash and placing containers in the dishwasher, leaving the bag in a designated spot for tomorrow's lunch.

- Take your bag or purse to a designated space.

Come on: even if you're stubborn, just try it. (I SAID TRY IT.) And if you want to get your kids to try a new getting-home routine, make it fun—maybe have them pick out their own kooky coat hooks (to be hidden on the inside of the closet door if they don't go with your décor, thank you). Explain to them why this is meaningful (they'll never lose anything, they can always scramble out the door without having to search all over for their other shoe, etc.—not to mention that tripping over book bags and jackets puts Mom and Dad a wee bit on edge). I lacked the understanding back then. I like to think that if I had truly *gotten* it, understood the emotional side (it makes me feel better and happier!) and not just the physical benefits (it looks better!), I would have tried harder to make my parents happy.

Equipping the Entryway

If you found that in your two-minute put-away routine you were caught wondering, *But where* do *I put this purse?* Or, *There's not really a good place to put my shoes*, then no wonder your entryway is tough to keep tidy! Your routine needs a support system, and that comes from organizational tools. You can work them into your décor (think: an occasional table or combo console/cubby, a beautiful coat rack) or outfit your closet (bins, cubbies, shelves, and plenty of hooks for each member of the family, hung where everyone can access them). Some solutions:

- Have ample hangers available for coats, and keep a bin or basket open and available for winter items.

- Have a small occasional table or cart in the front hallway where you can keep items like a reed diffuser, a deep bowl for keys and change, and somewhere you can leave items you need to remember on your way out the door. These are fun pieces of décor and the possibilities are endless!

- In wet or cold months, have a boot tray available to collect wet and snowy footwear.

- Determine if you wish to have shoes out or in a closet ahead of time—don't make that a game-time decision. Equip the closet or floor accordingly.

- Leave slippers at the door to remind you to change into them (and stop those outside shoes from tracking in dirt and debris).

- Have an established home for your schoolbag, briefcase, or purse, either right in the entryway somewhere or else walk it to your bedroom, desk, or wherever.

- Consider putting away out-of-season items and doing a purge at the end of each season so that you don't have to store anything you don't need anymore. This saves space—and an airy closet feels like a boutique!

- The main entryway is responsible for the majority of dust in your home. You track so much in with your shoes, and this brings dust and odors inside—not to mention that little pebbles and bits can scratch hardwood floors and shave down carpets. Having a three-mat system works well for me: an outdoor mat to wipe shoes, an indoor mat for collecting dirt or pooling water, and a boot mat or tray.

THE ENTRYWAY: EXPRESS-CLEAN (5 MINUTES OR LESS)

The objective is clean and calm, fresh smelling and welcoming.

Air it out. Open windows or crack open the door a bit, weather permitting, to let in fresh air.

Scent it. If you've got a reed diffuser, a candle, or something that smells nice, leave that at the front door on the occasional table or a ledge to help create a welcoming scent.

Whip shoes into shape. Put all the shoes where they belong, whether that's a shoe rack, a boot tray, the closet, or mudroom. Wait! We're in a hurry, but that doesn't mean you should just toss them in. Shoes should be paired up, all toes pointed in the same direction.

Corral the outerwear. Ensure coats and outerwear accessories are hung up or placed into a bin.

Tidy the floor. Clear the floor of any clutter and debris. Move anything that shouldn't be there, like bags or items for recycling.

Consolidate the console. The console table should be free of clutter. Place change and keys into a bowl and mail in the kitchen (of course you're going to read it while dinner's cooking!). Give the table a mighty-quick wipe-down with a microfiber cloth if you've got the gumption.

Sweep for the grand finale. Now, if you have time to spare and you're in the mood for earning extra points, you can sweep or dry-mop the floor—remember, it is a small space and won't take much effort. Okay, you're done. Good work!

★ **GOLD STAR! Ditch Your Kicks.** Consider instilling a no-shoes-in-the-house policy. If you have guests coming who like to wear shoes in the house, ask them to bring a pair of indoor shoes or supply them with fresh, clean, and comfortable guest slippers (not your stained old *SpongeBob SquarePants* pair).

ENTRYWAY: TOP-TO-BOTTOM CLEAN

PRODUCTS	TOOLS
All-purpose cleaner	Bin
Baking soda	High-dusting tool
Disinfectant (optional)	2 microfiber cloths
Glass cleaner	Flat-weave microfiber cloth
Rubbing alcohol	Paper towels
White vinegar	Vacuum
	Mop and bucket (for tile, vinyl, and linoleum floors) or flat mop and spray bottle (for stone, wood, and laminate floors)

Wave 1

TIDY AND ORGANIZE (5 to 15 minutes)

Choose your 12 o'clock starting point and work around the room from there. The goal is to tidy, remove garbage, and quickly organize the space. Place everything that doesn't belong in the entryway into the bin; place the bin right outside the space to deal with later.

Wave 2

We'll get into the meat and potatoes of the actual cleaning now. Let's start at the top and work our way to the bottom.

HIGH DUSTING (90 seconds)

Please note: Lights should be turned off during high dusting to avoid popping any lightbulbs.

With your high-dusting tool, head to 12 o'clock and position the tool right at the 90-degree angle, where the ceiling meets the wall. Now, walk around the room and go over ceiling corners, running over the moldings, tops of doorframes, and light fixtures. (Make sure you are gentle with light fixtures—you want to graze the surface to remove cobwebs, not knock them like a piñata.) You'll look like a crazed wizard; certainly not your finest selfie moment.

★ **GOLD STAR! Cleaning Light Fixtures.**

1. Make sure the light is turned off.

2. Using a stepladder if necessary, remove the outer fixture (where possible).

3. Take the fixture to a sink and give it a rinse in soapy water.

4. Buff dry. When it is completely dry, replace it. For parts of the fixture that are not removable, wipe with a damp cloth and buff dry.

CLEAN THE FRONT DOOR (2 minutes)

I don't clean the front door every time I clean my entryway, more on an as-needed basis. Give it a look-over and clean it if it is scuffed or marked with fingerprints.

1. Spray the door, locks, and knobs with all-purpose cleaner. (Don't spray any glass just yet.)

2. Starting from the top, wipe the door, locks, and knobs with a general-purpose microfiber cloth, working your way down to the bottom using the S-pattern. Treat the locks and knobs with disinfectant, if using, according to the bottle's instructions.

3. Any stubborn scuffs or fingerprints can be quickly treated with a pinch of baking soda applied to the surface, then rubbed in

with a slightly dampened cloth. Wipe well, and the marks should come right off.

4. Spray any glass with glass cleaner and wipe with a flat-weave cloth from top to bottom using an S-pattern.

MIRRORS AND WINDOWS (90 seconds per glass surface)

Again, this step is totally skippable if you don't see a reason to go for it.

1. Spray the glass lightly with glass cleaner.

2. Fold a flat-weave cloth into quarters (this way you have a few dry sides to use for buffing).

3. Using only one quarter of the cloth, start at the top left corner of the mirror and use the S-pattern motion to clean, going from top to bottom.

4. Flip the cloth to a dry quarter and repeat the S-pattern, retracing your steps from top to bottom. This helps dry the glass and finishes the job streak-free.

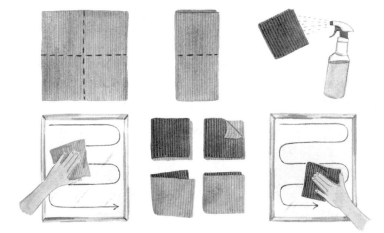

5. Using yet another dry quarter of the cloth, look for streaks and marks using the light, and gently buff them out as you see them.

✓ **PRO TIP: SCHMUTZ BE GONE!** For any mysterious sticky bits on your glass, dab with rubbing alcohol and wipe clean with a paper towel.

PICTURE FRAMES AND WALL ART (30 to 60 seconds per piece)

Please note: If the glass cover of a picture frame is not dusty, skip it. Just focus on the frame and tackle the obvious dust.

1. Use a dry microfiber cloth to dust the surface from left to right.

2. Repeat for each side of the frame.

3. If cleaning the glass, wipe clean with the flat-weave cleaning cloth dampened with water or a bit of glass cleaner.

4. Buff dry any wet spots to remove streaks.

✓ **PRO TIP: TWO HANDS:** Use your free hand to support the art while cleaning it. You don't want your original Picasso to drop on your toe! Ouch, I hate when that happens.

HORIZONTAL SURFACES (any furniture, like a console table; 1 to 2 minutes per piece)

1. Remove all items and place them safely on an uncleaned surface (generally, a surface to your right or the floor).

2. Fold a general-purpose microfiber cloth into quarters and dampen one side with all-purpose cleaner.

3. Wipe surfaces using the S-pattern.

4. Follow up by wiping with a dry quarter of the cloth.

5. Wipe each item as you pick it up, giving it a quick dust, then replace items where they belong.

★ **GOLD STAR! Clean Out Your Bag (10 minutes).** Once a month, clean out your purse, work bag, or knapsack, to keep things from getting gnarly in there. Dump everything out and use a lint roller or vacuum out the inside. Spot-clean stains, sort through the bag contents, tossing anything you don't need, and return what you need.

✓ **PRO TIP: EYE-PLEASING SURFACES!** When reordering items after cleaning, line them up parallel and perpendicular for a neat-looking surface.

POINTS OF CONTACT (2 minutes)

That's right, those gross places that we touch all day, spreading germs from here to there. In the entryway, that really means doorknobs and light switch plates.

1. For handles, knobs, and anything frequently touched (but not attached to electricity), spray with all-purpose cleaner and wipe with a general-purpose microfiber cloth. (For light switches or small handles, spray a cloth with the cleaner and wipe with the cloth.)

2. Treat with disinfectant according to the bottle's instructions.

CLEAN WALLS (10 seconds per mark)

Please note: Matte or flat paint may mark up if cleaned too vigorously. Please test this method in a small hidden area first.

1. Using a microfiber cloth dampened with all-purpose cleaner, give the stained area a quick wipe and buff dry. (Many times, a stain will come off with this treatment and you won't need to use anything more powerful.)

2. If the stain doesn't budge, sprinkle a pinch of baking soda on a small corner of your dampened cloth and begin to gently rub the stained area. Work gently, because anything too rigorous can actually remove the paint. Wipe well, then remove any remaining baking soda residue with a dry cloth.

CLOSET (10 minutes)

What? Really? But it's behind a door! Oh yes, my friend, because otherwise dust and dirt collect on the closet floor and make it that much harder to clean the rest of the space. You don't have to do this all the time, but when it looks a little disheveled back there, get to it.

1. Remove all items from the top shelf.

2. With all-purpose cleaner and a microfiber cloth, wipe the shelf surface clean.

3. Tidy and organize the items as you replace them neatly on the shelves. Get rid of any unused items in the process.

4. Hang up and straighten any coats hanging in the closet. Move all spare hangers over to one end.

5. Remove all shoes from the closet. Tap them well on the floor to remove dirt (you'll clean the floor last) and put them off to the side. With the vacuum cleaner, use the small-brush attachment to vacuum the floor, corners, baseboards, and tracks of the closet.

BASEBOARDS (2 minutes)

Baseboards also don't need to be cleaned every time. When you see dust building up—or scuffs or dirt marks—then that's how you know they need some attention. (I find that baseboards in the front entryway get dirty more quickly than those in the rest of the house.)

1. You want to use a dry cloth or *slightly* damp cloth to clean baseboards—a wet mop will cause dust to stick to them. Wipe sections from left to right. Alternatively, you can vacuum your baseboards using the small-brush attachment or use your high-dusting tool and flip it upside down to wipe the baseboards.

2. Remove any dirt or marks by sprinkling baking soda onto a damp cloth, then massaging into the area and wiping clean.

WELCOME MATS (5 minutes active time plus 30 minutes inactive time)

These hardworking mats are like the bouncers for dirt in the home. But they can't do their job when they're saturated with debris or start to stink. I like to have a three-mat system during the wet months (outdoor mat, indoor mat, boot tray), and two mats during the dry months (no boot tray!).

1. Take your outdoor and indoor mats to an area outdoors where it's safe to shake them out (I usually do this around the side of my house).

2. Shake well against the side of the house to beat out any debris.

3. Sprinkle baking soda onto the mats and gently pat it in. Let them sit for 30 minutes.

4. Shake the mats out again, then vacuum up the baking soda (ideally still outdoors).

5. Roll up the mats and carry them back to their homes (but don't put them back yet—we still have to clean the floors!).

6. Wipe salty boot trays with a cloth dipped in a solution of white vinegar and water. Rinse well and dry.

✓ **PRO TIP: BEST MATS!** For outdoor mats, I like those made of coconut (coir) fibers. Not only are these a more environmentally responsible option (biodegradable! Comes from a fruit!), the coarse texture helps to trap dirt, absorb moisture without harboring mold or mildew, and handle high-traffic zones with relative ease. For indoor mats, I prefer something that's got an industrial-carpet-like texture, which is rubber-backed for good grip.

★ **GOLD STAR! Stubborn Salt.** For salt stains on your indoor rug (bonus! This also works for carpet-style car mats), start by vacuuming up as much salt as you can. Then loosen the remaining salt with a soft-bristle brush and vacuum again. Sponge on a solution of equal parts white vinegar and water and allow it to sit for about 5 minutes. Blot well with a dry cloth and repeat this several times until the stains are lifted. Leave mats outdoors to dry.

Wave 3

VACUUM FLOORS (3 to 5 minutes)

Okay, we're in the home stretch. Start by checking that your vacuum bag or canister is empty, so that it works at full power.

1. Move all items that might be in the way of vacuuming out of the area temporarily. (Do not drag! Lift items that are easy to move, and only pull items out if they are on sliders or casters to avoid scratching the floor.)

2. Plug in your vacuum as close to the exit point of the room as possible.

3. Vacuum any upholstered items first, such as an occasional chair or pillows.

4. Vacuum the floor of the closet and the rest of the entryway.

★ **GOLD STAR! Don't Forget the Porch.** Whenever it needs it, you'll want to include sweeping the porch or front steps in your rotation.

MOP THE FLOORS (2 minutes)

See page 52 for details on how to mop.

Leave the room, let the floors dry, and then replace the shoes in the closet and replace the furniture and mats.

✓ **PRO TIP: MOP SMART!** Start mopping at the opposite corner to the most logical exit point of the room—that way you can mop yourself *out* of the room instead of into a corner.

The last step here, and for every room, is to deal with the contents of the bin full of items that need to be returned to their appropriate spots in the house—but don't forget to come back once you've done that and admire all your hard work.

CHAPTER 4

the living room and dining room

Why did I roll these two rooms into one chapter?

I find that people tend to fall in opposite extremes regarding the living room and dining room: they either use them *all the time*—or almost never.

Growing up, my family had a formal dining room that my parents spent several thousands of dollars decorating, with the help of an upscale interior designer. They chose only the most '90s modern furnishings, paint, and finishes. What we were left with was a wash of bright salmon walls (*"It's so now,"* the designer said), salmon carpets, and black and forest-green furniture and accents. Believe it or not, we used to host guests in that room—proudly! But if there were no guests, we never went in there. We ate in the kitchen. The dining room was attached to the living room—yet another space the designer's influence didn't escape. It was home to our piano, two couches, a coffee table, and other furniture that we were never really allowed to touch—unless, of course, guests came over. When we were alone, our family hung out in the family room right off the kitchen. It was as if the living room and dining room didn't exist without the presence of guests. Home to our family's most lavish dishes, cutlery, and décor, they absolutely did make a strong statement—one that said, "Keep Out." The feeling was mutual—we preferred to spend our time in the cozier rooms that we felt loved us back.

Today, I live in an 1,800-square-foot town house—and there are no spare, unused spaces. We eat at the dining room table up to three

THE LIVING ROOM AND DINING ROOM: EXPRESS CLEAN (10 MINUTES)

I generally clean these two rooms at the same time since they are almost always near each other and employ the same PTTs. Why take out the vacuum twice when you can zoom right from one room to the next?

Air it out. Crack open windows to freshen things up.

Mini wave 1: Walk around the rooms in a clockwise motion with a bin to collect anything that doesn't belong in the space. If you have the time after this cleanup, dump the trash and place the items in the rooms where they belong. Otherwise, find a temporary resting space for this bin. (Just to be clear, temporary means you'll deal with it later—today!)

Do the Scan 'n' Dust. Take a general-purpose microfiber cloth, all-purpose cleaner, and a small handheld broom and head to 12 o'clock (usually the doorway). Scan the space (physically moving your head up and down in a "yes" motion) and look for any dirt, scuffs, dust, or fingerprints. You're not doing a scrub-down—you're doing a touch-up. Anytime something catches your eye, deal with it—mist your cloth gently with the all-purpose cleaner, wipe the affected surface, and shine with a dry part of the cloth. Toss crumbs and dirt onto the floor, since you'll be dealing with the floor at the end.

Straighten as you go. As you do your quick-tidy, make sure each area looks organized, too. This means lining up all items parallel and perpendicular to the edges of the surface.

Brush off furniture. Head over to the chairs and sofas and use your handheld broom to brush off any crumbs, dirt, or debris onto the floor. Ensure the dining room table has been wiped and sparkles—after all, you're going to be eating there!

Finish up with floors. The floors set the stage for any space, and having them clean is key. The best possible tactic for a hard floor is to sweep or vacuum first and follow up with a quick mopping. But this doesn't have to be a floor-cleaning marathon; be strategic. Sweep or vacuum corners, around furniture, under tables, and around open spaces. Then, mop using the same general pattern. As always, I like to handle the perimeter of a space first, moving any obstructing pieces of furniture out of the way, and then vacuum the rest in the W-pattern, using the S-pattern for mopping.

Ditch the bin. Finally, grab that bin and deal with its contents. Take trash and dishes and glasses to the kitchen, books to the bookcase, and old papers and magazines to the recycling bin.

times a day. And since Chad and I often work at home, it also gets used as a conference table, craft table, think tank, and, heck, some days it is even my desk (I'm writing this sitting at my dining room table *right now!*). Our living room is no less used—it is often a hangout space for our team when they're over, and Chad's and my favorite bar for our cocktail hour (while we're cooking dinner, and then cleaning up after it). Your living room and dining room may be only occasional spaces; and if they are, bonus! You don't have to clean them as often. But if they're multipurpose spaces like mine, they've got to be cared for on the regular.

THE LIVING ROOM AND DINING ROOM: TOP-TO-BOTTOM CLEAN

Keep in mind how frequently you use these spaces will dictate the frequency and rigor of cleaning. I'll walk you through a general example here and then hit upon both permutations as we go.

PRODUCTS

Ammonia-free crystal-cleaning spray, such as Brillanté

Rubbing alcohol

Glass cleaner (see page 20)

Moisturizing leather cleaner, such as Leather CPR

Moisturizing wood cleaner (see page 27)

All-purpose cleaner (see page 16)

Disinfectant (optional)

Baking soda

White vinegar or dish soap

TOOLS

Bin and bucket

High-dusting tool (see page 31)

Clean towel

Plush microfiber cloth

White cotton glove (optional)

Flat-weave microfiber cloth

4 or 5 general-purpose microfiber cloths

Vacuum

Mop and bucket (for tile, vinyl, and linoleum floors) or flat mop and spray bottle (for stone, wood, and laminate floors)

Wave 1

TIDY AND ORGANIZE (5 minutes per room)

Remember, this first wave preps the space for cleaning.

1. Grab your bin and start at 12 o'clock. Work your way around the room clockwise and remove anything that doesn't belong in this room, such as garbage, misplaced items, or paper.

2. At the same time, straighten up items that *should* be in this room; for instance, line up knickknacks so they are parallel and perpendicular to the edge of the furniture or place items into a neat pile. It's much easier to clean a decluttered space.

Wave 2

HIGH DUSTING (90 seconds)

Please note: Any lights that you will be cleaning should always be turned off and cooled to avoid popping bulbs!

1. Head to 12 o'clock with your high duster and walk around the area, gently moving it around the ceiling moldings, getting into corners and the tops of doorframes. Remember to be gentle with light fixtures.

✓ **PRO TIP: DID THAT CRYSTAL GO HERE, OR THERE?** Is your light fixture particularly elaborate? Take a photo of it before you take it apart so you know how to reassemble it after cleaning.

★ **GOLD STAR! The Gentlest Light Fixture Clean.** Make like a butler and wear a white cotton glove when cleaning your light fixture. That way, fingerprints won't transfer onto your clean pieces.

HOW TO CLEAN A CHANDELIER
(1 to 20 minutes, depending on method)

Don't panic! You have my explicit permission to skip over this step if you're just not feeling it. But I'll remind you: you need to do this cleaning only once or twice a year. A sparkling light fixture dazzles. It's totally worth it.

For crystal, simply spray an ammonia-free crystal-cleaner directly onto the chandelier. Allow it to dry and you're all done (seriously). Can I get an amen?

For elaborate light fixtures or chandeliers you wish to clean by hand:

1. Lay out a towel or an old blanket on a flat surface (such as a table) as a buffer.

2. Remove each piece and place it gently on the towel.

3. Make a solution of one part rubbing alcohol to four parts water in a bowl or bucket.

4. Dip each piece into the solution and wipe clean with a plush microfiber cloth. Lay flat to dry. Alternatively, you can place this solution in a spray bottle and spray and wipe each piece. Whatever you prefer.

5. Take your cloth, now damp from all the cleaning, and carefully wipe the fixture itself to remove any dust or haze.

6. Replace all pieces carefully, one row at a time.

MIRRORS AND WINDOWS (90 seconds per glass surface)

Yay! Another optional step. Just do mirrors and windows when smears and streaks make an otherwise clean room look dingy.

1. Spray the glass lightly with glass cleaner and fold a flat-weave microfiber cloth into quarters (that way you have a few dry sides to use for buffing—see illustration, page 62).

2. Using only one side of the cloth, start at the top left corner of the mirror or window and use the S-pattern motion to clean, going from top to bottom.

3. Flip the cloth to a dry quarter and repeat the S-pattern, retracing your steps from top to bottom. This helps dry the glass and finish the job streak-free.

4. Using yet another dry quarter of the cloth, look for streaks and marks using the light and gently buff them out as you see them.

WINDOWSILLS (30 seconds per sill; see page 50)

CLEANING WINDOW TREATMENTS

These rooms tend to have the most formal window treatments in the whole house, which will need care about one or two times a year; blinds will need more regular attention. See page 50 for details.

PICTURE FRAMES AND WALL ART (30 to 60 seconds per piece)

1. Use a dry general-purpose microfiber cloth to dust the surface from left to right.

YOUR FANCIEST BELONGINGS
(PINKIES UP, EVERYBODY)

You know those precious wedding gifts and heirlooms? They don't need to be cleaned often because they are used infrequently. Curio cabinets or hutches with glass doors also keep out dust (a major plus if items are showcased here). Further, because they're usually costly, hard to replace, and sometimes delicate, cleaning them less is indeed best. The same goes for special furniture pieces: vacuum or brush upholstery only if they are visibly dirty, dusty, or lackluster. Anything fancy needs to be tended to two or three times per year. When you *do* decide to clean these items, I suggest doing them all at once and working your way clockwise around the room for an added "wave" of the 3-Wave system.

Fancy China and Crystal
For pieces that can be submerged in water:

1. Lay down a towel on an uncleaned surface (remember, we don't want to clean anything twice).
2. Place items gently on the towel.
3. Make a solution of one part rubbing alcohol to three parts water.
4. Dip one item into the solution and then buff with a plush microfiber cloth until dry.
5. Repeat with each item.
6. Before replacing the items, wipe the spot where they sit with a dry microfiber cloth first and a damp one second. Buff dry completely.
7. Replace each item neatly.

Expensive Showcase Accessories, like Fabergé eggs (seriously, you don't have any?) or Christofle punch bowls (naturally, I have one for every day of the week): lay down a towel and place the item on top of it to prevent breakage and clean with a dampened plush microfiber cloth while wearing a soft cotton glove, to prevent fingerprints.

Fancy Furniture

I know it's tempting to hit your leather and wood with their special cleaning conditioners all the time, but I find that using them frequently results in a buildup that can leave the furniture covered in dull residue. Instead, for your regular cleaning of leather or wood pieces, use a microfiber cloth dampened slightly with water to wipe clean (leather should get a quick vacuuming first with the dusting brush). That's it! When you notice the furniture looking a little thirsty—dull or dried out, in the case of leather, and not so shiny, for wood—use the cleaning conditioner.

For upholstered pieces, see wave 3, page 80: our goal is to bring out the vacuum once.

✦ **HANDY HABIT: Chair Sliders.** Place felt sliders on the feet of furniture to make pieces easy to move on hard-floor surfaces, or flat plastic glides to make them easier to move on carpet. When cleaning chairs, I flip the chairs up and lint-roll the felt sliders to remove debris and pet hair. (I've also been known to hot-glue my sliders right to the chair legs, since I find they fall off easily.)

✓ **PRO TIP: DETARNISH YOUR SILVER!** Don't waste time with that nasty pink silver polish. Try the trick below—a huge hit with my online readers.

SILVER CLEANER

1 tablespoon salt
1 tablespoon baking soda
1 cup boiling water
½ cup white vinegar

EQUIPMENT
basin (slightly larger than the silver to be cleaned)
aluminum foil
microfiber cloth

Line the basin with aluminum foil, shiny-side up. Add salt, baking soda, boiling water, and vinegar, and stir together until the salt and baking soda dissolve. Add the silver pieces, making sure that each piece directly touches the foil. Let sit 5 minutes.

Remove the silver pieces and use the microfiber cloth to buff dry and remove any remaining residue. The shine is amazing!

2. Check the glass for any spots or fingerprints and wipe clean with a dampened flat-weave microfiber cloth (just water or a bit of glass cleaner is fine).

3. Buff dry any wet spots to remove streaks.

HORIZONTAL SURFACES (1 to 2 minutes per piece)

1. Dampen one corner of a microfiber cloth with all-purpose cleaner, then fold it into quarters so that one side facing out will be wet and the other side facing out will be dry—one for wet work and one for dry work.

2. Remove items from the surface to be cleaned and wipe the surface in the S-pattern using the dampened side of the cloth. Dry with the dry side of the cloth.

3. Dust the items that live on top of these surfaces and reposition them.

POINTS OF CONTACT (2 minutes)

In the living room and dining room, points of contact are all the light switches. Clean first with all-purpose cleaner, then treat with disinfectant according to the bottle instructions, if using.

WALLS (10 seconds per spot)

Please note: Matte or flat paint may mark up if cleaned too vigorously. Please test this method in a small hidden area first.

1. Using a microfiber cloth dampened with all-purpose cleaner, give the stained area a quick wipe and buff dry. (Many times, a stain will come off with this treatment and you won't need to use anything more powerful.)

2. If the stain doesn't budge, sprinkle a pinch of baking soda on a small corner of your dampened cloth and begin to gently rub the stained area. Work gently, because anything too rigorous can actually remove the paint. Wipe well, then remove any remaining baking soda residue with a dry cloth.

BASEBOARDS (5 minutes per room)

You don't have to do them every time you clean—use your discretion!

1. With a slightly damp cloth or dry cloth, wipe a section of baseboard from left to right. Alternatively, you can vacuum your baseboards or use your high-dusting tool.

2. Remove any dirt or marks by sprinkling baking soda onto a damp cloth, then massaging into the area and wiping clean.

Please note: Don't use a wet mop! Dust will actually stick to baseboards. A dry cloth or slightly damp cloth is best. You can spot-clean baseboards to remove stains as you dust, using a damp cloth only as needed.

Wave 3

Time to break out the vacuum. Even if you have hard-floor surfaces, you need your vacuum; there are lurking food crumbs and dust bunnies that a broom can't capture. I start with all the upholstered pieces, from dining room chairs to sofas and occasional seating, move on to rugs, and then handle the flooring last (remember, go from top to bottom, so that we don't clean anything twice). When cleaning the floor, try to move furniture away from the wall where possible to access baseboards and areas underneath. When the floor has been vacuumed (and mopped for hard-floor surfaces), furniture can be replaced.

UPHOLSTERED PIECES (2 to 5 minutes per piece)

1. Lay a clean towel flat on the floor, and using the upholstery brush of your vacuum, vacuum all the small décor pillows, front and back, then place them on the clean towel.

2. Move on to the large removable cushions, front and back, again placing on the towel as you finish. Vacuum the upholstered base, now fully exposed, including the back as well as the seat. I like to work in an S-pattern for the back portion and use a W-pattern for the seat, breaking it into smaller sections for larger pieces.

3. Replace cushions and pillows neatly. (Now is the time to use that leather conditioner or wood polish, if necessary.)

AREA RUGS

Moveable rugs (ones without a ton of furniture on top of them): 40 minutes (10 minutes active time plus 30 minutes inactive time)

1. Take your rug to an outdoor area where it's safe to shake it out. Shake well, beating it against the side of your house to knock out debris. (Apartment dwellers: get creative! Take rugs into your building's courtyard, or do it on your balcony or fire escape—just make sure your neighbors aren't out enjoying cocktails directly below you.)

2. Sprinkle baking soda onto the rug and gently rub it in using a patting motion. Let it sit for 30 minutes.

3. Shake out the rug and vacuum it. Roll it up and bring it inside.

Unmoveable rugs (10 minutes; see page 82 for carpets)

1. Move any furniture, such as dining room chairs or relatively lightweight coffee tables, off the rug as best you can.

2. Using the appropriate vacuum attachment (for instance, use the dusting brush for a shag rug), vacuum the top of the rug following the W-pattern.

3. When done, work your way in sections around the edges of the rug. The area around a rug tends to get a nice little ring, or halo of dirt, to put it politely. So lift up a section at a time to reveal the underside of the rug and that dirt halo. Vacuum the floor well and replace the rug. (I don't recommend mopping under these rugs, since no one sees that floor and it will be hard to dry. Score.)

✦ **HANDY HABIT: Outsourcing.** Take your silk, Persian, or expensive area rug to a specialty rug cleaner every year. For broadloom or Berber, save cleaning these until you bring in a professional carpet and upholstery cleaner. Double up and bring in your fancy fabric window treatments at the same time!

✦ **HANDY HABIT: Stopping Stains from Sticking.** Keep a bottle of stain solution in your dining room to handle spills on rugs as they happen. Begin by blotting the stain well with several pieces of paper towel, then apply the stain product to the rug. Pat it in, and let it sit for 5 to 10 minutes. Rinse well with cool water to remove suds, and repeat as necessary until the stain disappears. Pat dry with a clean cloth.

✓ **PRO TIP: CHOOSING A RUG!** Choose a dark-colored or multicolored rug as opposed to a white one for the dining room. A spill or stain is much easier to clean and conceal. On the flip side, you have to be more attentive to food spills and crumbs since they can be harder to find. I've found that a low-pile rug works better than a high-pile in this space. If you can, get one that is stain-protected.

FLOORS: HARD FLOORS AND WALL-TO-WALL CARPETING

Almost done! I always vacuum the entire space before mopping a hardwood floor. Though you may want to skip this step in favor of sweeping, I already had you get out the vacuum to do the upholstery, so I would argue it's actually quicker and more efficient to just use the vacuum for everything. Vacuums are better at removing debris, too. No pressure, though.

TRUE STORY!

My sister and I were on a home-reno show in 2007 when we moved into a condo together in downtown Toronto. They kicked us out for two weeks and totally redid the living space, giving us a ton of new furniture; it looked gorgeous. While we adored most of it, the one thing they did that wasn't so brilliant was place a large black shag rug under the dining room table. While this looked fabulous for the camera, it was just awful in real life. Not only did it make the dining chairs nearly impossible to move (we often exchanged giggly, sisterly glances as we watched guests politely struggle with positioning their chairs at the table), but when food spilled, it was as though it fell into a spongy, seaweed-like abyss; there was no coming back. It was really hard to clean and, frankly, it felt gross to step on. Lesson learned: keep the shag rugs away from any place food is served and stick to low-pile for the dining room.

Vacuuming (5 to 10 minutes per room)

1. Move all items that can obstruct vacuuming out of the room temporarily to an adjacent room. Do not drag—lift items that are easy to move, and only pull items out if they are on sliders or casters to avoid scratching the floor.

2. Plug in your vacuum as close to the exit point of the room as possible.

3. Using the crevice attachment, clean the borders of the room (as in where the baseboard meets the floor).

4. Switch to the appropriate floor attachment and head to the opposite corner of the room from where the vacuum is plugged in. Vacuum the room using the W-pattern, breaking the room into sections as necessary.

If you have wall-to-wall carpeting, once you have vacuumed your way out of the room, replace any items you removed back to their original locations. Otherwise, if there is some (or all) hard flooring here, you will need to mop, so don't move anything just yet.

Mopping (3 to 5 minutes per room)

Please note: Check Chapter 2, "The Basics," for how to mop your particular type of hard flooring, and always use the appropriate product.

FINISHING TOUCHES

Look around for anything you might have missed and deal with the trash as well as the bin of stuff that you have to put away. Don't forget! After you've undertaken a Top-to-Bottom Clean, take a moment to go sit on your sofa and take it all in. Look around. Amazing, huh?

✓ **PRO TIP: FLIP THE DINING CHAIRS!** If you have time, for easiest access to the floor under the dining table, flip (carefully, gently) the dining chairs upside-down on top of the table and leave them there until you're done with all your vacuuming and mopping.

CHAPTER 5

the kitchen

I think the kitchen might be my most favorite

room. It's such a busy place, and for many people it's the most emotional, visceral space in the home.

I have so many memories of my childhood in the kitchen. I remember my dad teaching me how to cook some of his mother's famous holiday breakfasts, or when my mom and I would host a "cooking show" while making dinner (clearly I was starved for entertainment growing up). There were many arguments in the kitchen—some variation of "Samantha swept the broom over my foot!" or "Melissa dropped spaghetti sauce on me while she was clearing the dishes!" The kitchen table was homework central, despite the fact that I had a perfectly good desk in my bedroom and we also had a home office that anyone in the family could use. It was just more fun to work in the kitchen. It's even where my friends and I would hang out when they came over.

But even if you don't love the kitchen like I do, and cooking stresses you out, the fact is, kitchens get used and they need to be kept in check daily or else they become messy quickly (and *that's* stressful). Kitchens are the newborn babies of the home: high maintenance, emotionally intense, and requiring attention 24/7. The kitchen gets messy hour by hour, daily, ongoing—it's just like laundry. It's never done. The only way to keep it clean is to *clean it as you use it*. I'm going to tell you how to clean the kitchen, to get that gleaming room that we all want. But that is not enough for the kitchen. If you don't change your daily habits, you will never be able to keep it up, and it will always snowball into a big job.

THE KITCHEN: EXPRESS CLEAN (14 MINUTES)

When you're not looking to give your kitchen the royal scrub-down but still want to spruce it up, there's certainly a happy medium. You can fake it, just a little. Here's how to get your kitchen looking clean in about 14 minutes.

As always, we're going to work our way around the room, top to bottom, pretreating when we can to allow the product to do the most work for us.

Air it out. Open windows or crack open the door a bit, weather permitting, to let in fresh air.

Deal with the dishes. Start by unloading and reloading the dishwasher. Quickly hand-wash anything that needs it.

Clear counters and pretreat. Moving right along, spray down your counters and sink with an all-purpose cleaner that is safe for your countertops. If you feel extra sassy, sprinkle baking soda into the sink on top of the all-purpose cleaner (you're going to love the results). Do not wipe just yet!

Spot-clean. Quickly glance around your kitchen; are there any glaring grimy spots that you can quickly remove? Don't skimp on your scan: I want you to actually nod your head "yes" and really look top to bottom and find those grotty little spills, stains (like a dried smear of ketchup on the cupboard door), and fingerprints (all over your stainless fridge). As you see them, wipe them up with a microfiber cloth dampened with all-purpose cleaner, sprinkling with baking soda for extra abrasion as required (test first that it won't wreck the finish). Buff each area with a dry corner of the cloth to ensure you've removed all debris and moisture.

Clean counters. Now that the product has had time to soak, you can wipe the counters with ease. Use a microfiber cloth in an S-pattern, tossing crumbs onto the floor. Then take your sponge and agitate the baking soda around the sink a few times; this will help scrub out dirt and stains. Rinse well with hot water and buff dry with that same microfiber cloth. Wow, did you know your sink could look that good, that fast?

Deal with garbage. Empty the trash if needed and change the bag. There, that was easy.

Finish up with floors. Quickly sweep your kitchen floor or vacuum. Start at one corner and sweep like you were an Olympic curler all the way to the end of the room. Dustpan up that dirt and then guess what, you're done!

✓ **PRO TIP: SAVE THE SINK FOR LAST!** The kitchen requires "wet work," as we call it in the cleaning industry, so it is important to clean your sink *last* because you're going to use it again and again. For this reason, use the sink as your 12 o'clock starting point; you'll end here.

Fear not—I'll show you the ropes for making it easy as pie.

✦ **HANDY HABIT:** *Bon ap-PRE-TREAT.* Dinner is ready! I know, all you want to do is sit down and tuck in. But stop yourself: Do a quick kitchen assessment to see if there are any empty pots and pans that could use a pretreat. Fill them with soapy water NOW, and they will be a snap to clean up after dinner. Okay, now you can enjoy!

THE KITCHEN: TOP-TO-BOTTOM CLEAN

If I had to pick my favorite place to clean, I'd have to say the kitchen. I just love how clean and orderly everything looks when it's done. It just makes me want to cook in it and totally mess it up. My goal here is to teach you the methods I've used for years and trained my staff with. This way is really efficient and I recommend you follow closely and time yourself. You'll see how quick you become, and your results will be incredible.

PRODUCTS
All-purpose cleaner (see page 16)
Degreaser (see page 17)
Baking soda
Disinfectant (optional)
Enzyme cleaner (optional)
Stainless-steel cleaner (see page 20)
White vinegar
Glass cleaner (see page 20)
Dish soap

TOOLS
Bin or tray
Microfiber cloths
Sponge (one with a nonscratching side and a scrubber side)
Scraper
High-dusting tool (see page 31)
Cleaning toothbrush
Flat-weave microfiber cloth
Broom or vacuum
Paper towels
Mop and bucket (for tile, vinyl, and linoleum floors) or flat mop and spray bottle (for stone, wood, and laminate floors)

Wave 1

TIDY AND ORGANIZE

Decluttering the Space and Pretreating (5 to 10 minutes)

1. Starting at 12 o'clock (to the right of the sink!), carry a bin or tray with you and work your way around the kitchen, quickly tidying surfaces and collecting items that don't belong. As you're doing this, take note of any areas that are greasy and grimy that may require pretreating (we're talking backsplash, overhead exhaust, microwave, stove top, goopy jam spill, etc.).

2. Place the bin outside the kitchen door and deal with it later (as in, *really* deal with it once you're done; as in, put the stuff away in its rightful home).

3. Head over to any of those areas that require pretreating and spray them with either all-purpose cleaner or apply a degreaser for any heavily grimed-up spots. If you plan to clean inside your non-self-cleaning oven (covered on page 109), now's the time to pretreat the inside.

✓ **PRO TIP: PRETREAT!** When I first started my business, I learned the secret to cleaning a *really grimy* kitchen. As soon as I'd finish decluttering, I would practically hose down the kitchen with product—the countertops, cupboard doors, appliances, and backsplash. After a few moments, the product starts to penetrate the dirt and grease and I was left with very minimal work to do by the time I actually got around to the wipe-up. If you get to an area that you've pretreated and it's dried up, just re-spray the surface and keep working. You, too, will become a pretreating convert. (We meet Sundays at two.)

Wave 2

Okay, you've made it this far—you got this! Position yourself back at the sink and have a microfiber cloth in hand for wet work and drape one over your shoulder for dry work. Have a bottle of all-purpose cleaner ready, and also keep nearby something mildly abrasive, like baking soda. Don't forget the sponge and a scraper.

I am now going to walk you through the various components of a kitchen: counters, cupboard doors, appliances, etc. Every kitchen looks different, so follow along and envision this happening in *your* kitchen. If things are slightly out of order given your current layout, no worries, switch it up to suit you! So long as you're doing the techniques properly and working clockwise, the order will fall into place. Remember, you'll be dividing the room into slivers. So after high dusting, take position at your first section, remove all items from the counter, placing them adjacent to the surface you're cleaning (to the right if you're working clockwise), and prepare the space to be cleaned.

HIGH DUSTING (1 to 2 minutes)

With your high duster, go to 12 o'clock and walk around the area, gently moving the high duster around the moldings, into ceiling corners, and along the tops of doorframes and cupboards.

UPPER CUPBOARD FRONTS (5 to 7 minutes)

I'll explain how to clean all cupboards here, but start with only the upper ones for now.

The kitchen cupboards can get grease splatters and fingerprint buildup. Over time, these can create permanent stickiness (besides being very obvious on high-gloss surfaces like cupboards), so they should be regularly maintained.

1. Spray cupboard fronts and handles or knobs liberally with all-purpose cleaner if necessary.

2. Leave them to soak for a couple of moments if they weren't pretreated already.

3. With a damp microfiber cloth, wipe each cupboard and drawer front using the S-pattern, and make sure that you also get the handle with each wipe.

4. Pay particular attention to handles and areas around handles, as well as horizontal detailing, where a lot of grime tends to collect. If you notice a lot of buildup, get out your cleaning toothbrush. While the area is damp, brush the gunk out from the tiny crevices between the handle and the cupboard door. (You don't need to do this all the time, only when you have stubborn buildup.) Then, with a dampened microfiber cloth, wipe away. Shine up the surface with a dry cloth. Ahh, like new!

5. Treat knobs with disinfectant according to the bottle instructions, if using.

EXHAUST HOOD (5 to 10 minutes active time plus 10 minutes inactive time)

1. If the pretreat has dried up, reapply it.

2. Wipe down and scrub the inside and outside using a nonscratching sponge.

3. Rinse your sponge and the surface with clean water, then buff dry.

4. A few times a year, you'll want to go deeper: Remove the filter and pretreat the fan blades and accessible areas inside. Rinse with a sponge and buff dry. Replace the filter.

BACKSPLASH (5 minutes)

Please note: Be gentle. Some delicate backsplashes, such as painted walls, must be cleaned carefully so as to not ruin the paint. The same holds true for less-hardy finishes such as stone or glass tile. Always be sure to use the right product and material for the surface.

1. Assuming you've already pretreated this area, respray the backsplash with the appropriate cleaning product for the surface (all-purpose cleaner or even an enzyme cleaner works well here) if it has dried up. Let it soak for a few moments.

2. Any areas that are particularly stained should have some extra baking soda patted onto the stain, as long as it is safe for the surface.

3. Use a nonscratching sponge or dampened microfiber cloth and clean with an S-pattern. Pay extra attention to areas with heavier stains or soil.

4. With a damp microfiber cloth, retrace your work and wipe off the product.

5. With a dry microfiber cloth, buff the surface to remove streaks.

COUNTERTOPS (10 minutes)

Your countertop probably now has some fallout from the backsplash cleaning, which perfectly illustrates my point about always working from the top to the bottom.

1. Visually divide your counter space into sections.

2. If you haven't pretreated already, spray all-purpose cleaner onto the countertop and let it sit for a few moments to soak. If baking soda is safe for your counter surface, add it to those areas with more intense stains (this works quite well on laminate counters).

3. If your toaster and microwave stay on the counter, clean them now (see page 111). Otherwise, clean them in step 6.

4. Starting at one side, head back to the counter and wipe it clean with a damp microfiber cloth using an S-pattern. Use a nonscratching sponge to remove the grime that you treated with baking soda.

5. Follow that up with a dry microfiber cloth and buff the surface. Double-check for debris using the eye-level test (see page 94).

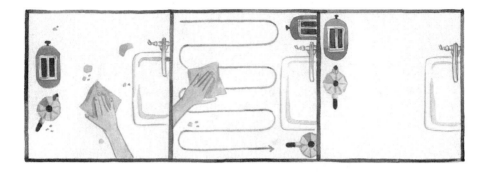

6. Clean each countertop item one by one, including emptying kettles and coffeemakers, wiping and shining exterior surfaces of these items with a damp microfiber cloth and buffing with the dry cloth. When cleaning these items, be sure to clean them either over the kitchen floor or on a section of counter that has yet to be cleaned—remember, you do not want to dirty up the clean area!

7. Replace all items neatly on the countertop.

LOWER CUPBOARDS AND DRAWERS (5 to 7 minutes)

I know, you already know how to do this (see pages 90–91)! But just a gentle reminder that since the counter is clean, now is the time.

✦ **HANDY HABIT: Drink Up.** Hey, this is a lot of work. Be sure to stay hydrated and have a tall glass of something delicious to drink while you clean the kitchen—I like to make a batch of fresh lemon water before I start. And don't forget the tunes. For the love of all that is good, you need music.

APPLIANCES

Cleaning the *outside* of the fridge, oven, and dishwasher is essential to getting a gleaming kitchen. Trust me—most laypeople don't think of this step, but it's one that my staff and I take seriously, because of the minimal time invested but maximum visual impact.

✓ PRO TIP! THE EYE-LEVEL TEST

Those of us in the biz know that freshly cleaned items can have a holographic horror-movie surprise: they can look clean when just looking down at them, but then squat so that the item is right at eye level and surprise! You'll see hidden grime that was lurking all along.

The Refrigerator Exterior (4 minutes)

1. Remove your jumble of magnets or anything else stuck to the fridge.

2. Spray the exterior fridge surface with an appropriate cleaner (all-purpose cleaner or glass and stainless-steel cleaner; see pages 16 and 20). Avoid electronic displays where possible.

3. With a damp microfiber cloth or the soft side of a sponge, wipe the fridge and freezer exterior using the S-pattern. Be sure to include the handles as well as the sides of the doors.

4. Should there be a stain or mark anywhere, try to buff it away (but do not use anything abrasive) using a circular motion and additional product. A spray of vinegar can help remove grimy marks quickly.

5. Rinse your cloth (with hot water, if possible) and repeat the same S-pattern to remove all product from the fridge surface.

6. Finish this up with a quick S-pattern wipe with a dry microfiber cloth to remove streaks.

7. Double-check the surface for streaks and marks, and remove with a dry cloth.

8. Replace any items that belong on the fridge.

Stovetop and Outside of Oven (5 to 10 minutes)

Your stovetop and the front of your oven might just be your kitchen MIA—they get dirty faster than just about anything else in the kitchen, so you'll want to stay on top of them to prevent their filth from diminishing the feel of your fresh and shiny kitchen. This is certainly a place you'll want to pretreat before you start wave 2; it greatly reduces your elbow grease expenditure (I'm pretty stingy with mine).

1. Remove all the non-stovetop items from the stove top (bottles, jars, pots, and pans), and place them somewhere that you haven't

cleaned yet. Also remove any grates and disks from above the heat elements. For coil cooktops, remove coils, rings, and drip pans; place the coils off to the side and the rings and drip pans into a sink full of hot, soapy water.

2. If possible, remove the knobs (they easily pop on and off) and spray the panel with all-purpose cleaner, avoiding electronic displays where possible. Dab some degreaser (see page 17) onto the greasy spots. Spray the stovetop and oven door again if the pretreat has dried, including the top of the oven door, but being mindful to avoid product dripping between the glass panes. Allow this to soak for a few moments.

3. Starting at the top, use the soft side of a damp nonscratching sponge and wipe the area clean using the S-pattern. For particularly greasy areas, use the scrubby side of the sponge and rub until clean, or gently scrape the area with the scraper. Buff with a dry microfiber cloth. (Be sure not to use an abrasive sponge on a cooktop!)

4. Scrub any grates or disks, rings, and drip pans clean in the sink using a nonabrasive sponge. Wipe any coils with a damp cloth.

5. Dry well using a large cloth or dish towel and replace in the appropriate orientation on the stove top. (If your stove top is gas, light each burner to make sure the cleaning hasn't put out the pilot light.)

6. Wipe down any bottles or items that you keep on top of the stove and replace them.

7. Spray the door and handles as well as the broiler or warming drawer with the all-purpose cleaner, again being careful not to get any liquid leaking in between those glass panes (man, those drip lines are pesky), wipe down with a damp microfiber cloth using the S-pattern, flip the cloth over, and buff with a dry section.

★ GOLD STAR! DEEP-CLEANING THE OUTSIDE OF THE FRIDGE (10 minutes)

Every six months or so, give your fridge some extra love. Carefully pull it out (make sure you don't scratch your floor or dent your wall) and unplug it. Clean the area behind it using a broom or vacuum—I often find cat treats, dust bunnies, and old blueberries under there. Then, take your vacuum with a brush attachment and quickly vacuum the vents and coils. This helps your fridge run more efficiently and reduces noise, too. Clean the top of the fridge using a damp microfiber cloth and water. It doesn't need anything fancy; you're just trying to remove dust. Finally, vacuum all gaskets—those rubber seals around the fridge doors—using the brush attachment to remove debris. Give the gaskets a wipe with a microfiber cloth by sticking your finger into the cloth, dampening it with gasket cleaner (see page 25), and rubbing the gaskets clean with your pointer finger. Dry the gaskets with a dry cloth, using the finger method below, to remove moisture (because, mildew).

8. Rinse your cloth with hot water and use the S-pattern to remove all product from the surface. Treat handles with disinfectant, if using.

9. Finish this up with a quick S-pattern wipe using a dry microfiber cloth to remove streaks.

10. Double-check the surface for streaks and marks and buff them out with a dry cloth by using the eye-level test.

11. The glass between the oven doors can get disturbingly dirty, I know. While I wish I could tell you how to clean it yourself, the fact is that you need to unscrew the oven door to clean it. In many cases, if you do this yourself, you will void your oven's warranty. Even I have to call in the pros on this one.

✓ **PRO TIP: GET UNDER YOUR OVEN!** Beware the visitor who peeks underneath the oven—gross. Employ a tiny ghost to clean it up! Pop a microfiber cloth over the bowl end of a wooden spoon and rubber-band it in place. Spray the cloth with some all-purpose cleaner and slide it underneath the oven. Move it from side to side and prepare yourself for everything it grabs.

Outside of Dishwasher (3 minutes)

1. Spray the exterior surface with all-purpose cleaner and allow it to sit for a moment. (Avoid electronic displays where possible.)

2. With a damp cloth or the soft side of a sponge, wipe the dishwasher exterior using the S-pattern. Be sure to wipe handles (then treat with disinfectant if using) and the sides of the door as well.

3. Should there be a stain or mark, buff away the stain.

4. Rinse your cloth with hot water and repeat the same S-pattern to remove all product from the surface.

5. If fingerprints are an issue, spray white vinegar onto the appliance surface. This can be used as a final wipe-down.

6. Finish this up with a quick S-pattern wipe with a dry microfiber cloth to remove streaks.

7. Double-check the surface for streaks and marks and remove any with a dry cloth.

WALLS (10 seconds per mark)

Please note: Matte or flat paint may mark up if cleaned too vigorously. Please test this method in a small hidden area first.

1. Using a microfiber cloth dampened with all-purpose cleaner, give the stained area a quick wipe and buff dry. (Many times, a stain will come off with this treatment and you won't need to use anything more powerful.)

2. If the stain doesn't budge, sprinkle a pinch of baking soda onto a small corner of your dampened cloth and begin to gently rub the stained area. Work gently, because anything too rigorous can actually remove the paint. Wipe well, then remove any remaining baking soda residue with a dry cloth.

KITCHEN TABLE (3 to 5 minutes)

1. Remove all items from the table.

2. Spray the table with an appropriate cleaning product (glass cleaner for glass, all-purpose cleaner, etc.).

3. If necessary, follow it up with a dry microfiber cloth to remove streaks. Do the eye-level test to catch any misses (there usually are a few on the kitchen table).

4. Wipe the table with a microfiber cloth using the S-pattern. If the table is large, divide it in half and work in smaller sections.

5. Wipe off chair seats quickly with a dry cloth to remove crumbs and debris.

6. Wipe and clean each item to go back onto the table using a damp microfiber cloth and replace.

PICTURE FRAMES AND ARTWORK (30 to 60 seconds)

That classic kitchen art—"Home," "Eat," or the print of a chef holding a bowl of pasta—often has actual food splatters on it.

1. Place one hand on the bottom corner of the frame to support it while cleaning.

2. Use a lightly dampened microfiber cloth and wipe the top of the frame from left to right.

3. Repeat for each side of the frame (left, right).

4. Check the glass for any spots and wipe clean.

5. Buff any wet spots dry to remove streaks.

MIRRORS AND WINDOWS (90 seconds per glass surface)

1. Spray the glass lightly with glass cleaner and fold a flat-weave microfiber cloth into quarters (see illustration, page 62).

2. Using only one side of the cloth, start at the top left corner of the mirror or window and use the S-pattern motion to clean.

3. Flip the cloth to a dry quarter and repeat the S-pattern. This helps dry the glass and finish the job streak-free.

4. Using yet another dry quarter of the cloth, look for streaks and marks using the light, and gently buff them out as you see them.

WINDOWSILLS AND BLINDS (see page 50)

POINTS OF CONTACT (2 minutes total)

You already got the cabinet knobs and appliance handles, so finish up with doorknobs and light switch plates.

1. Spray points of contact with all-purpose cleaner, then wipe clean. Exception: Do not spray directly on a light switch! Instead, spray your cloth and wipe the light switch plate.

2. Treat with disinfectant according to the bottle instructions, if using.

BASEBOARDS (5 minutes)

Kitchen baseboards can get pretty gross, as can the kickplates under your base cabinets and drawers. Include these areas in your baseboard cleaning for an absolutely sparkling space (now you can't unsee that area. Sorry!). Pretreat any splatters before you start wave 2 and this will be a speedy job.

1. With a slightly damp cloth or dry cloth, wipe a section of baseboard from left to right. Remove any splatters by wiping the area gently until it is clean.

2. Move furniture or items slightly, if possible, to access the baseboards and remove any dust bunnies before vacuuming.

3. Repeat for the next section until the entire room is complete.

Wave 3

Home stretch! Sink, sweeping, mopping. That's all you have left to do! As a reminder, you don't clean floors section by section as you clean in waves 1 and 2. In the third wave we clean the whole tamale, all at once.

FAUCET AND SINK (3 to 5 minutes)

Yay, you're done with your wet-work. Time to sparkle up your sink. Talk about redemption!

1. Rinse any debris down the sink, remove the sink strainer, and empty it into the trash.

2. Spray the sink, faucet, and drain area with all-purpose cleaner and sprinkle baking soda over the areas you have sprayed.

3. With a nonscratching sponge, scrub all areas of the sink, starting at the top and scrubbing the sides, base, and drain thoroughly.

4. Use a cleaning toothbrush or the corner of the sponge to get into the drain area where brown stains tend to build up. Scrub vigorously to break down stains. Clean the sink strainer this way, too. Remember to scrub in the direction of the grain of the stainless steel to avoid scratches. Avoid all temptation to rinse the sink until you've scrubbed the sink in its entirety. This saves water and you don't need to start at step 1 again with product.

5. Use the nonscratching side of the sponge to help preserve the finish, and clean the faucet.

6. Run the tap water hot, rinse your sponge, and use the hot water and sponge to rinse the sink well, getting all the product off the sides and faucet.

7. With a dry microfiber cloth, buff the sink and faucet area until it is both dry and shiny. It will make you happy, I promise. I'm convinced some joy-inducing chemical gets released into your body when you finish cleaning a sink.

HOW TO CLEAN STAINS ON AN ENAMELED SINK

Dry off the sink completely. Spray with hydrogen peroxide and let stand overnight. Respray the next day, and sprinkle baking soda all over. Add a squirt of dish soap to a dampened nonscratching sponge and squish it together to spread out the soap. Scrub the sink very well. Rinse and dry. Voilà! Your sink should be spotless.

FLOORS

Vacuuming (5 to 10 minutes)

1. Move all items that might obstruct vacuuming out of the room temporarily to an adjacent room.

2. Plug in your vacuum as close to the exit point of the room as possible.

3. Start with your dusting brush or crevice tool and get all the tight spots in the kitchen, including corners, any baseboards you earmarked for vacuuming, areas between appliances, seams between chairs, or tufting on upholstered pieces, etc.

4. When the perimeter of the room and the upholstery vacuuming is done, head to the opposite corner of the room and begin to vacuum—breaking the room into sections—using the W-pattern.

Mopping (3 to 5 minutes; see page 52)

TRASH AND TRASH CAN (5 minutes active time plus 10 minutes inactive time)

Skip this step and your newly sparkling kitchen will be foiled by the can's unpleasant aroma. This is best done in a garage or backyard. You don't want to clean the can in your freshly cleaned kitchen! Aim to treat your can to this spa-like experience monthly.

1. Empty the trash.

2. Spray the can with all-purpose cleaner and sprinkle a cup of baking soda inside, ensuring it sticks to the sides and lid.

3. Allow the can to sit for 10 minutes.

4. Shake out the baking soda (do this outside).

5. Respray the can if it is dry and wipe it with damp paper towels until gunk and residue are gone. Rinse well and wipe out with paper towels. Allow to air-dry.

6. Replace the liner when the trash can is fully dry.

And you're done! Seriously, can you believe you did it?

BONUS POINTS: CLEANING OUT YOUR APPLIANCES

When the insides of your appliances get completely ugh, it's time to clean them out. Here is my simple, fail-proof guide for the best way to do it.

Remember to unplug small appliances when cleaning them, and unplug larger ones when the manufacturer recommends doing so. On that note, be sure to keep your manufacturer manuals and review them. These are general guidelines, but every appliance is a little different and needs to be cared for according to the manufacturer's recommendations.

Inside of the Fridge (20 minutes)

You know how nasty it gets when you've gone too long without cleaning the inside of the fridge—food spills and spoils, sticky rings, and jars filled with prehistoric condiments. Plus, you start to get that not-so-fresh smell every time you open it. Be sure to give the inside of your fridge some attention every few months—or anytime it gets sticky or stinky.

1. Unplug the fridge.

2. Remove all items from the interior of the fridge, including food, shelves, and drawers, and place them on a surface that has yet to be cleaned. You can even lay out a towel on the floor if you are short on counter space. Keep a trash can and recycling bin handy. As you remove items, toss any old food as well as bottles and jars, and make a list of anything you need to replace. For condiments, a good rule of thumb if you can't find an expiration date on the bottle or jar is to smell for freshness, or toss anything after six months of opening. Place shelves and drawers by the sink.

3. Your fridge should be an empty cavity now, so spray the interior of the fridge with all-purpose cleaner and sprinkle baking soda over any areas that are stained or discolored. Pretreat the shelves and drawers the same way.

4. With a nonscratching sponge and damp microfiber cloth, head back to the fridge and begin to wipe the interior walls with the sponge first, then use the damp cloth. Start at the sides, then head to the top and work your way down the back. Finish up with the base, then buff dry with a clean, dry cloth.

5. Now, head back to the shelves and drawers. Clean each by spraying it down with all-purpose cleaner and agitating the product with a sponge. (Any stubborn stains like old jam can be soaked for a few moments before scrubbing.)

6. Rinse well and dry with a cloth.

7. Replace shelves and bins as each one gets cleaned, then replace all food, wiping bottles and jars with a dampened cloth as you go (buh-bye, sticky bottoms). Plug the fridge back in.

8. Remember to change your baking soda box out for a fresh one!

TRUE STORY!

When we first moved into our new house, I bought some pre-made cabbage rolls as part of that first grocery shop, when even what we put in the cart was exciting. I love cabbage rolls. I crave them. And admittedly, I am way, way too lazy to ever make them myself. I had wonderful visions of eating them in our new dining room and enjoying every single bite. I can't tell you why, but I never got around to actually pulling them out for dinner. I always thought, *Oh, I'll save those for that one night I really don't want to cook.* I think I threw that box out six months ago—meaning, I had that box in my freezer for almost six-and-a-half years. GROSS. Lesson learned—don't stockpile just because you can toss it into the freezer! Just buy what you know you'll use within the month.

HACK: MY ICE TASTES BAD!

You know what I'm talking about: you kick back on a Friday night and eagerly take your first sip of your favorite drink on the rocks, only to discover, uh-oh, it tastes like the inside of your freezer. What a buzzkill! There are a number of reasons why your fridge might start making bad-tasting ice and a number of steps you can take to remedy the situation.

First off, hopefully I don't need to tell you that a freezer that's too full of ice buildup on the walls or old, freezer-burned food will start to transfer its flavor to the ice. The first step is always to make sure your freezer is clean, fresh, and organized. And hey, even a stinky fridge can transfer flavors to the ice, so make sure you stay on top of keeping your fridge cleaned out, too.

Dump out the ice bin and give it a good wash in hot, soapy water and ½ cup of baking soda to fight those odors, then replace it. Since the bins are porous and made of plastic, sometimes if bad-tasting ice is a persistent problem, it's best to get a new bin and dump out the ice cubes any time they start to taste bad.

If you've done all this and your ice still has a bad taste, the problem may lie in the ice maker itself and the tubes that carry the water. Check your manual instructions for options for replacing the water filter and/or cleaning out the ice maker, or call your repair person if you don't know how to access these parts yourself.

Freezer Cleaning (5 to 10 minutes)

This is something you can do on an as-needed basis or even once a year. It's a good idea to get rid of debris and old, freezer-burned food and make space for the good stuff. If you live in a cooler climate, do this during the winter so that you can place frozen items outside. As with the fridge, this is the perfect opportunity to sort through old stuff and get rid of it.

1. Unplug the fridge.

2. Remove all items and store them in a cooler or in an area where the food can stay frozen.

3. Toss anything that is old or has freezer burn (generally anything older than a year has to go—I'm talking to you, cabbage rolls!).

4. Scoop out any large debris or crumbs with a dampened paper towel, then toss the paper towel into the trash.

5. Don rubber gloves and fill a bucket with hot, soapy water. Dip a sponge into the water and wring it out well.

6. Scrub the base and sides well, lifting away stains and debris. (You likely won't be able to buff it dry.) Wipe well with a damp cloth.

7. Replace all items in an orderly fashion.

8. Plug the fridge back in.

Inside of the Oven

This is one of the scarier household cleaning tasks, but it's a valuable one. And once we break it down, you'll see that it's nothing but a sheep in wolf's clothing. The oven takes a lot—splatters, drips, bubble-overs. That begins to carbonize at the base of the oven and becomes blackened, stinky, and increasingly more challenging to remove. I recommend cleaning the inside of your oven every three to six months depending on how often you use it. Speed up the time line if you smell burning or even see smoke coming from the oven as you cook at normal temperatures.

Self-cleaning ovens have a special coating on the interior that allows it to be heated up to nearly 1,000 degrees, singeing off any food remnants. After running an intense and smelly self-clean cycle, all you're left with is white ash, which can be easily wiped up once the oven has cooled. Keep in mind, using the non-self-cleaning method in a self-cleaning oven will ruin the special coating and void your warranty, so remember not to try it! (Yes, you still have to do just a little work!) Here, I'm going to give you the best techniques for either a self-cleaning or non-self-cleaning oven.

TRUE STORY!

In 2006, when I first started Clean My Space, my cleaning service, I did a lot of the cleaning myself. I was at a client's condo one day and the inside of her oven was caked with carbonized spills and splatters. She asked me to clean it out. *No problem, I've got this.* I took everything out and set it to self-clean. In about an hour, the smoke alarm went off. Neighbors started knocking at the door to see if everything was okay. I threw open the windows, but the unit was so full of smoke I could barely see anything! I was just about ready to Stop, Drop, and Roll. Finally, though I managed to clear the house of visible smoke (or maybe by that point I was so intoxicated by those fumes that I just ceased to perceive it), the house still smelled as if it were burning. I don't believe that lady ever called us back again. Wise lesson learned: it's a good reminder to always remove the extra debris from your oven before you start the self-cleaning cycle.

Self-Cleaning Oven (10 minutes active time plus 3 to 4 hours inactive time)

1. Remove everything from your oven—coils, grates, oven racks (yes, these are NOT self-cleaning), anything from the warming drawer, and anything that sits on top of the oven.

2. Remove any large and easily moveable debris with a damp paper towel and a dull edge, such as a scraper—this makes the oven-cleaning process less smoky.

3. Crank the exhaust fan, open windows, and set your oven to self-clean mode. (Check out your operating manual for your oven's specific instructions.) You'll hear a loud click—that's your oven door locking, to keep you from opening it while it's cleaning. (It's protecting you from reenacting that last scene in *Raiders of the Lost Ark.*)

4. Your oven will need about 3 hours to work and about 30 minutes to cool down. Once it cools, wipe the interior with a damp paper towel and toss (this includes the warming drawer).

5. Replace accessories.

Non-Self-Cleaning Oven (20 to 45 minutes active time plus 10 minutes inactive time)

I'll just put it out there right now. It's one of the longest cleaning tasks you'll have to do in the house. But it will be worth it, I promise. And afterward, I highly recommend treating yourself with something extra special (I'd vote for wine).

1. Remove everything from your oven—coils, grates, oven racks (these get in the way), anything from the warming drawer, and anything that sits on top of the oven.

2. Remove any large debris with a dull edge, such as a scraper—that leaves less for you to scrub at the end.

3. Wearing rubber gloves, sponge the interior of the oven down with hot, soapy water.

4. Create a paste of equal parts baking soda and dish soap (one of my all-time favorite cleaning scrubs—this is like an exfoliant for your oven) and spread it evenly over the interior of the oven. Allow this to sit for 10 minutes. I've also had really great results with enzyme cleaners for this task.

5. Take a superfine steel-wool pad and begin to scrub the interior, working section by section. This should lift off most of the carbonized grease. Use the Scraper to remove any stubborn bits while the product is still slathered on the surface.

6. To clean a glass door, sprinkle a product like Bon Ami onto the surface and rub it in with a damp sponge.

7. Allow to soak, then scrub with a nonscratching sponge.

8. Rinse well, ensuring that no product seeps into the glass door, and buff dry with a clean cloth.

9. Rinse the interior several times with a clean sponge and warm water until all traces of product are gone and then buff dry with a rag (not a pretty cleaning cloth!).

10. Replace accessories and items as required.

Oven Racks (up to 10 hours; don't worry, only 10 to 20 minutes active time!)

I can hardly think of a less exciting thing to do than clean oven racks. And frankly, I'm okay with mine looking less than perfect. That said, about once a year, they do need a good scrubbing to remove greasy buildup. You'll be using your bathtub for this, and the racks soak for quite a while, so make sure to plan around when everyone is done showering and bathing for the day!

1. Lay a towel along the bottom of your bathtub—this is going to protect the surface of your tub from being scratched by the oven racks or powdered detergent.

2. Place dirty oven racks on top of the towel.

3. Plug the drain of the tub and start filling it with the hottest water possible. This is really important because it will help break down the grease and activate the detergent. Fill the tub until the water completely covers the racks.

4. Finally, add a cup of laundry detergent or automatic-powdered dishwasher detergent dissolved in hot water.

5. Good news: that's it! Now we let the detergent do its thing for the next 6 to 10 hours. I like to just leave it overnight and give it enough time to really loosen all that caked-on grease and grime.

6. Remove the racks and gently wipe with a damp sponge. The grime will come off like magic. Rinse, dry, and replace.

Inside of the Dishwasher (one cycle plus overnight; 15 to 20 minutes active time)

Despite what we may think, the dishwasher isn't self-cleaning. You may start to notice debris clinging to your plates and glasses, glassware coming out spotty with film, and odors wafting up whenever you open the door. There are a few simple steps to returning your dishwasher to its out-of-the-box-shiny state. Remember to quickly rinse or scrape dishes to remove food debris before loading up—this helps keep the filter clear, which ultimately affects how well the dishwasher will work.

1. Empty the dishwasher.

2. Remove the filter and soak it in hot, soapy water. Get a wad of paper towels and sop up any of the crud hanging around the filter area (careful, you may find broken glass here).

3. Squirt dish soap on the filter and scrub it clean with a nylon bristle brush, then rinse and replace in the dishwasher.

4. Pour a cup of white vinegar into a dishwasher-safe glass and place it upright on the top rack of your dishwasher. Turn the dishwasher on and run it on the hottest possible cycle. This breaks down grease, grime, and mineral deposits.

5. When that cycle is done, sprinkle 1 cup of baking soda into the bottom of the dishwasher, close the door, and leave the dishwasher to sit overnight.

6. In the morning, run the dishwasher again, empty on the hottest possible setting. The baking soda will help deodorize and scrub the surface clean.

7. Load and use as normal.

Microwave, Toaster, and Small Appliances

These small appliances can get just as gross inside as a full-size oven, so don't forget them!

Microwave (5 Minutes)

1. Take a microwave-safe bowl and fill it halfway with water. Slice a lemon in half, squeeze both halves into the bowl, and drop them into the bowl.

2. Microwave for 3 minutes.

3. Carefully remove the bowl with an oven glove (it will be boiling hot) and dump it out.

4. Wipe the top, sides, bottom, and rotating plate of the microwave with a soft sponge or damp cloth to remove buildup and debris.

5. Dry with paper towels (don't skip this step—it also acts as your insurance to wipe up any remaining debris).

6. Close the microwave and spray the exterior with all-purpose cleaner. Do not spray the electric panels—simply wipe these clean.

7. With a damp cloth, wipe the exterior, including the top, sides, and handle.

8. For anything sticky or goopy, apply vinegar and allow it to sit for a moment before wiping off.

9. With a dry cloth, wipe the exterior dry, ensuring no streaks or marks are left behind.

Toaster (5 to 10 minutes)

1. Unplug the toaster.

For a Pop-Up Toaster

a. Remove the crumb tray if possible and rinse it in the sink, then wipe dry.

b. Invert the toaster over the sink and shake well, loosening crumbs (this is really all you can do).

c. Clean the exterior of the toaster using all-purpose cleaner for plastic or a paste of equal parts cream of tartar and lemon juice for stainless steel. Replace the crumb tray.

For a Toaster Oven

a. Remove trays, racks, and the crumb tray and place them in a sink filled with soapy water to soak. Add baking soda if there are heavy stains.

b. With a damp cloth, wipe out the interior of the toaster, including the top, sides, and elements.

c. For glass, sprinkle a nonscratching sponge with Bon Ami and spread it onto the glass. Scrub well, rinse the glass with a damp cloth, and buff dry.

d. To remove any streaks inside and out, use some vinegar and a paper towel to shine it up.

e. Sponge the racks and trays clean in the sink.

f. Rinse well and towel-dry, then replace in the toaster, being careful not to scatter more crumbs.

2. Wipe the exterior of the toaster with a dry cloth to remove streaks and marks.

3. Plug it back in.

A clean, sparkling kitchen: a dream for practically everyone, and now you have made it a reality!

CHAPTER 6

the den

Let's talk about one of the most exploited rooms in your house, whether you call it the den, the media room, the TV room, the living room (for those of you without a separate room), the family room, the rec room, whatever. For our purposes, I'm just going to say den, but you get what I mean: that place where you kick back to watch some TV; or the place where your friends or family hang out on movie night; or where you might gather around the coffee table on game night. Dens tend to be cozy—a room for sweats and pajamas.

But—have you gotten *too* comfortable? Don't wait until guests are coming to address the obvious: that dirty coffee cup, the piled-up newspapers under the coffee table like some weird litter box liner—on some level, they interfere with *your* ability to really relax here, too. What about that throw blanket (when was the last time you washed it? Do you dare—brace yourself—take a sniff and see if it might be a little stinky?).

Keeping your den in good shape will mean only that it's always welcoming—you won't have that nagging feeling about how awful it looks while you binge-watch your next series. And you'll never cringe about any mess when it's time to move a party in here for a movie or a round of Settlers of Catan—you'll just say, "Come on in."

THE DEN: EXPRESS CLEAN (10 MINUTES)

For the den, our goal is to make the space comfortable and cozy. This tidy-up should take you 10 minutes or less.

Air it out. Crack open windows to freshen things up.

Mini wave 1: Grab a bin and a tray and start at 12 o'clock (typically the doorway). Working clockwise around the room, collect all items that don't belong there, placing plates, cups, and kitchen items onto the tray and anything else into the bin. You'll deal with the contents at the end.

Straighten as you go. As you go around the room, also straighten items on surfaces, lining them up parallel or perpendicular to the edges. Shake out and fold up blankets and fluff pillows (you do this by literally beating the pillows—consider it anger management) and replace them neatly on the sofa. As you come across magazines and books, DVD cases, game cases, consoles, and remotes, replace all CDs in appropriate cases and line up or stack neatly on shelves or tables.

Do the Scan 'n' Dust. Take a microfiber cloth sprayed with all-purpose cleaner, a lint roller, and a handheld broom, and quickly work your way around the room, starting at 12 o'clock and moving section by section. You're just going to look for obvious areas that need cleaning at eye level only—leave the high and low stuff for your full cleaning. If you see a goopy stain, fingerprints, or marks, whether on the wall, furniture, or a point of contact, give it a quick wipe with your dampened microfiber cloth. But on the whole, don't worry too much about detail—just get anything that immediately catches your eye. When you get to the sofa and cushions, use the handheld broom to bring crumbs and debris on upholstery to the floor, and use the lint roller to zip up any pet hair or obvious debris. (This should take about 5 minutes or less—any more and you're getting too caught up in details. Remember, this is an express clean!)

Finish up with floors. Floors are really a choose-your-own-adventure situation—how dirty are they, and how much time do you want to spend on them? If you are in a big rush, you can quickly vacuum the floor and that's all (clearly the case for carpet, but even for hard-floor surfaces). Don't worry about moving furniture or getting out the crevice tool; just do the main floor area, working section by section using the W-pattern. If you want to earn extra points for hard floors, get out your mop and give the floor a quick once-over. For these quick floor cleans, I like to use a flat-head mop and spray bottle filled with the appropriate floor cleaner. It takes less than 2 minutes, and the end result looks great. Remember to always clean in the direction of the grain of the wood, to minimize streaking.

Ditch the bin. Finally, grab that bin and deal with its contents. Take trash, dishes, and glasses to the kitchen, books to the bookcase, and old papers and magazines to the recycling bin.

THE DEN: TOP-TO-BOTTOM CLEAN

PRODUCTS

All-purpose cleaner
(see page 16)

Electronics cleaner (see page 124)

Glass cleaner (see page 20)

Baking soda

Disinfectant (optional)

Compressed air

Leather cleaner (as needed; see page 21)

Wood polish (as needed; see page 27)

Floor cleaner of choice (see pages 18–19)

TOOLS

Bin

Tray

2 general-purpose microfiber cloths

High-dusting tool

Flat-weave microfiber cloth

Cotton swabs

Cleaning toothbrush

Vacuum with brush and crevice attachments

Mop and bucket (for tile, vinyl, and linoleum floors) or flat mop and spray bottle (for stone, wood, and laminate floors)

Wave 1

TIDY AND ORGANIZE (5 to 15 minutes)

I enjoy doing the first wave (I can't believe I just said that) because it's easy and I feel I've accomplished so much (a third!) of the work in mere minutes. My den always has plenty of trash and recycling and other stuff lying around. I'm not saying I live in a Dumpster—but you know, package wrappers, old magazines, empty soda cans, socks . . . all of this piles up.

1. Grab your bin and your tray and place them somewhere central. Then head to 12 o'clock and work your way around the room, collecting any garbage, recycling, or dishes (the former two go in the bin, the latter on the tray to take to the kitchen when you're done cleaning).

2. As you work your way around the room, straighten up any items that *do* belong in the den but that are out of place, like coffee-table books, DVDs, whatever, lining them up parallel and perpendicular to the edge of the surface. Fold blankets, too.

3. One other thing to do while going through wave 1: quickly observe any areas where there may be a dusty buildup (think: behind the TV, under the sofa cushions, etc.). Since the den gets used *a lot*, if you can squeeze in a quick visual inspection of these spaces during the tidy-up, you'll have a mental map of what really needs your attention and what you can skim over in wave 2. (This is something I try to teach my staff when I'm training them to be cleaning ninjas. The more prepared you can be going into your next task, the faster and more efficiently the work can get done.) So, if you see a hot zone (and by that I mean hot mess), you now know what to spend more time on in wave 2.

Wave 2

Start back at 12 o'clock and have your all-purpose cleaner and two general-purpose microfiber cloths with you. In the center of the room, place the high duster, electronics cleaner, flat-weave cloth, cotton swabs, and glass cleaner in an accessible spot—the floor or a table.

HIGH DUSTING (90 seconds)

1. Head to 12 o'clock and walk around the room, gently moving the high duster around the moldings and getting into ceiling corners as well as any other high areas. Search for cobwebs and dusty ledges and quickly swipe those clean. Graze the surface of (turned-off) light fixtures gently. If you have recessed lights, ensure they have cooled and use your high duster to zip around the edges to get any cobwebs.

2. Run the tool along the top of any doorframes and across any air vents. If you notice the vents are super dusty, make a mental note and vacuum the vents when you've got your vacuum out in wave 3, using the brush attachment.

MIRRORS AND WINDOWS (90 seconds per surface)

1. Spray the surface lightly with glass cleaner.

2. Fold a flat-weave microfiber cloth into quarters.

3. Using only one side, start at the top left corner of the glass and use the S-pattern to clean the surface.

4. Flip the cloth to a dry quarter and repeat the S-pattern, retracing your steps from top to bottom.

5. Look for streaks and marks using the light, and using yet another dry quarter of the cloth, gently buff them out as you see them.

✓ **PRO TIP: HI-YAH!** To get that perfect dimple in the top of a decorative pillow, make like the home stagers do and follow up the fluffing with a nice, centered *karate chop.*

SPOT-CLEANING WALLS (10 seconds per mark)

Please note: Matte or flat paint may mark up if cleaned too vigorously. Please test this method in a small hidden area first.

1. Using a microfiber cloth dampened with all-purpose cleaner, give the stained area a quick wipe and buff dry.

2. If the stain doesn't budge, sprinkle a pinch of baking soda on a small corner of your dampened cloth and begin to gently rub the stained area. Wipe well, then remove any remaining baking soda residue with a dry cloth.

CLEANING A GLASS-TOP SURFACE (SUCH AS A COFFEE TABLE)

1. Remove all items from the surface.

2. Spray the surface with glass cleaner.

3. Fold a flat-weave microfiber cloth into quarters and wipe using an S-pattern.

4. Buff dry with a dry quarter of the cloth.

5. If you still notice streaks, that means the underside of the glass is dirty. Clean the underside by either repeating steps 2 through 4, moving the S-pattern in the *opposite direction*, or by taking a damp cloth and spot-cleaning, using the light as your guide to finding steaks and marks. If you still see streaks, the direction of the S-pattern will tell you whether the mischievous marks are on the top or the bottom side of the glass.

PICTURE FRAMES AND ARTWORK (90 seconds per piece)

Please note: The glass cover of a picture frame does not need to be cleaned unless it is visibly dirty or dusty. Otherwise, just focus on dusting the frame (horizontal surface).

1. Place one hand on the bottom corner of the frame to support it while cleaning.

2. Use a general-purpose microfiber cloth lightly dampened with all-purpose cleaner to wipe the top of the frame from left to right.

3. Repeat for each horizontal edge of the frame (left, right).

4. If dusty, wipe the glass with a dry flat-weave microfiber cloth.

5. Check the glass for any spots or fingerprints. If dirty, spray glass cleaner onto the glass and wipe clean with the flat-weave microfiber cloth. If there's just a spot that's noticeable, simply spray the cloth with glass cleaner and wrap the cloth around your pointer finger, then buff the spot out. Don't clean any more than is needed!

6. Buff any wet spots dry to remove streaks.

HORIZONTAL SURFACES (1 to 2 minutes per piece)

Please note: In general, I always want you to focus on dusting and cleaning horizontal and angled surfaces, since vertical surfaces don't get as dusty or dirty. But in the den, splashes and splatters do land on vertical surfaces, so it is important to do a quick visual inspection for these. Recently, I found a long, sticky Grand Marnier stain on my wall (someone was clearly a little overzealous when pouring a drink).

Section by section, here's what to do:

1. Remove all removable items from a given surface.

2. Use either your dry or your slightly dampened cloth to dust and clean (removing both debris and marks) using an S-pattern.

3. Pick up any item that belonged on that surface, and holding it securely with one hand,

   a. Dust and wipe with a damp cloth,

   b. Buff dry to remove streaks and replace the item (make like a burglar and hold the item with a dry cloth while cleaning to avoid getting new fingerprints on it).

4. Move down to the next surface or item and repeat the steps.

POINTS OF CONTACT (2 minutes)

Points of contact in the den require some TLC, just due to how much time we spend in here. I consider many electronics points of contact, but I'll cover that separately (see below). In this case, let's consider light switch plates and doorknobs.

Please note: Light switch plates connect to an electrical source, meaning they cannot be sprayed directly. Please spray a cloth with all-purpose cleaner to clean a light switch plate, then treat with disinfectant according to the bottle's instructions, if using.

1. While cleaning, visually identify your points of contact.

2. Spray the point of contact with all-purpose cleaner and wipe clean, scrubbing where possible to remove visible debris or marks.

3. If you notice any blackened buildup in the grooves of the light switch, use a dry cleaning toothbrush to loosen the dirt, then wipe up as usual.

4. Treat with a disinfectant, if using.

CLEANING ELECTRONICS

Television (2 to 3 minutes)

I'm going to take a shot in the dark here and assume you have a flat-screen TV. Here's how to clean one.

1. Use your dry flat-weave cloth and quickly dust the exterior frame and TV screen (moisture would cause the dust to stick).

2. Fold your flat-weave microfiber cloth into quarters and lightly spray one quarter with electronics cleaner.

3. Starting at the top frame, give a quick horizontal wipe, then move on to the left- and right-side frames, too.

4. Clean the screen starting at the top left, going over to the top right corner and working your way down to the bottom using the S-pattern. For any areas with a stubborn mark, stick your pointer finger in a damp part of the cloth, and apply gentle pressure while using a circular buffing motion to get the spot out. Use a little more spray on your cloth as needed.

5. When you're done with the screen, quickly flip the cloth around to a dry section and follow up with a dry wipe, to remove any streaks or moisture.

6. Give the bottom frame and the base of the TV a wipe with the same cloth.

ELECTRONICS CLEANER

This recipe is simple and inexpensive—the water extends the cleaning properties of the alcohol, and the alcohol helps all the moisture evaporate quickly, so it won't damage your electronics.

———

1 cup rubbing alcohol
1 cup water

Mix together in a spray bottle.

✓ **PRO TIP: FLAT-WEAVE CLOTHS FOR ELECTRONICS!** Flat-weave microfiber cloths are designed to pick up dirt and marks as well as dust, without taking any scratchy debris along for the ride. Because of its design, general-purpose, terry-style microfiber cloths can scratch your shiny surfaces and leave those tiny scratches nerdily referred to in cleaning lingo as *spider webbing*. Instead, flat-weave cloths are super soft—just right for those delicate electronics.

Remote Control and Game Controllers (30 to 60 seconds each)

I've seen homes with several remotes—one for the TV, one for the cable box, a universal remote (so why all the others, then . . . ?), one for the DVD player, one for the window coverings . . . you name it. Remotes are a dirty part of the home.

1. Use a can of compressed air to quickly blast out any debris from buttonholes. Make sure to do this (or any compressed-air cleaning) over a surface that you have yet to clean, like the floor. Do you really want to redust the coffee table when you're done?

2. With your dry cleaning toothbrush, work your way around the item, brushing crevices and those tiny grooves. (Brush outward so that you aren't redepositing the dirt back into the electronic item.) If the toothbrush isn't working well, take a piece of paper and fold it in half and then into quarters. Use the strongest point in the fold to sneak into that crevice and move the paper around. The gunk will start popping out. You'll feel like you're having a National Geographic moment, but just roll with it.

3. Spray a cotton swab with electronics cleaner and use this to get in and around the buttonholes—there are usually splatters and stains between buttons, and that can jam them up (not to mention, it is *repulsive*).

4. Fold your flat-weave microfiber cloth into quarters, and spray one quarter with electronics cleaner.

5. Wipe the remote from top to bottom, ensuring you get off all debris. Envelop the remote in the cloth and wipe vigorously, getting in between the buttons.

6. Return to a clean surface.

HOW TO CLEAN A CD OR DVD

Your favorite song starting to hiccup? The first line of defense is always to clean the CD, since any oils from your fingers or other smudges can get transferred to the player and make everything all wonky. Hold the disk by its edges and use a soft cloth to wipe it in strokes from the center outward to the edge. Should any extra-stubborn spots not come out this way, a gentle soap-and-water solution on a cloth should get the job done, still applying and then cleaning off from the center outward. Buff dry, again from the center outward.

DVDs and Video Games (30 seconds to 20 minutes)

Every so often, the media and their shelves need to be cleaned and, more often, organized. If you are feeling rather lazy (I approve!), just dust the ledge of the shelf where dust collects; but every so often you'll have to go full-force and take everything off.

1. Remove all cases and discs. If they are not matched up, do this now (sometimes we "forget" to replace them in their appropriate case).

2. Wipe the shelf with a dry general-purpose microfiber cloth to remove dust.

3. Only if needed (think: visible dirt and debris), wipe the shelf with a damp cloth.

4. Wipe each case with a damp cloth and replace when dry (cases can have dirt and dust stuck on them).

Game Consoles, Stereo, Cable Boxes, and DVD/Blu-ray Players (60 seconds per item)

These get so dusty—their vents that are designed to allow air to circulate actually attract the stuff. If we don't get rid of the dust, they can eventually overheat. So give them some love.

You don't have to do a thorough clean of these each time you clean. Just give it a quick wipe-down with a damp general-purpose microfiber cloth. But every now and again (as in, when you notice a visible layer of dust), get out your vacuum. Note: It is not advisable to clean *inside* any console.

1. Remove the console from the shelf and unplug it.

2. Fit your vacuum with the brush attachment and gently vacuum the exterior of the console, getting the top, grooves, sides, and back vent.

3. Use a general-purpose microfiber cloth dampened with all-purpose cleaner and wipe the exterior of the surface.

4. Follow up with a quick wipe to remove excess moisture, using a dry general-purpose microfiber cloth.

5. Ensure that the shelf or surface is clean and free of dust, then replace the console.

Speakers and Sound Bars (60 seconds per item)

Similar to consoles, speakers, sound bars, and stereos get used a lot and have little holes or grooves in their grilles that get dusty over time. Most of the time, I don't bother cleaning my speakers, aside from giving the touch pad a quick wipe with a damp cloth. However, if your speakers are getting dusty:

1. Remove the speakers from the shelf.

2. Use a dry general-purpose microfiber cloth and remove as much dust as possible.

3. For delicate speakers, use a paintbrush to brush away dust, always working from top to bottom and flicking the brush in a downward motion. A lint roller can help dislodge any stubborn lint.

4. For more durable speakers, use a handheld vacuum with the brush attachment and gently remove dust from the speaker grilles (always check manufacturer's instructions to make sure that your specific speakers can be vacuumed).

5. Using a general-purpose microfiber cloth folded in quarters and dampened with all-purpose cleaner, wipe the exterior of the speaker, also cleaning any buttons as well as exposed areas that may have stains or marks.

6. Give the item a once-over with a dry portion of the microfiber cloth.

7. Return your speaker to a clean shelf.

TRUE STORY!

Chad and I had saved up for close to two years to purchase our dream sofa. It was an extra-deep one, to accommodate Chad, who is 6 foot 4. It banged up our wall getting to the upstairs den, but it was so worth it. The couch was glorious. Comfortable, visually stunning—we just adored it.

Not six months in, though, unbeknownst to us, Paislee, one of our cats, got a urinary tract infection, and started to pee outside her litter box. There are literally thousands of spots she could have peed on to let us know. But the brand-new sofa that we were constantly sitting on? That was the place.

After the first time, we panicked. We cleaned it very thoroughly with a cat-urine remover and hoped she wouldn't do it again. Well, cats like to pee wherever they smell their scent, and so, Paislee turned our new sofa into her own executive bathroom. We treated Paislee's infection, of course, but by then, it was too late. There was nothing left to do—but get a new (cheaper) sofa. Now, there's no more peeing. Paislee's in perfect health. We just can't have nice things.

WINDOWS, WINDOWSILLS, AND BLINDS

You know my philosophy: windows don't have to receive your undivided attention every time you clean. Just inspect them and focus on the tracks and sills, as well as any noticeable smudges, and use your judgment for when to dig deep (see page 50).

BASEBOARDS (5 minutes)

Because of all the dust the electronics generate, you will want to pay some extra attention to the baseboards in the den.

Wave 3

We've made it! We're so close to TV time, it's not even funny. I like leaving the upholstery to wave 3, because we typically want to vacuum it, and it is most efficient to just get all the vacuuming done in one shot. Crack out the vac, and let's get going.

UPHOLSTERY (2 to 5 minutes per piece)

Crumbs really collect on and in den upholstery. So does money, jewelry, pet toys, old candy, cereal, you name it. I find it important to clean *under* cushions occasionally as well. But I always clean the exterior cushions, because if I don't, the schmutz literally transfers itself onto me when I stand up. Here's what to do:

1. To vacuum under the cushions, lift them all up and place them on the floor (on top of a clean towel if you prefer).

2. Use the upholstery attachment (or dust brush for leather) and begin to make long strokes, top to bottom, on the upholstery base.

3. Vacuum each cushion top and side.

STAINS ON UPHOLSTERY

Upholstery stains are inevitable. Even the most careful family will end up with them. I have found over the years that having a couple of tools on hand has been critical to saving my upholstery. First, a carpet *deep-cleaning system* is a good idea. Mine cleans carpets and has a small unit that detaches and can be used for upholstery. In this case, it is important to use the appropriate cleaner and not make your own, since the cleaner is designed to lift out the stain and work properly with the machine.

I also like *enzyme cleaners* (see page 25), because often the stains that happen on upholstery are challenging ones like blood, urine, juice, or vomit. These cleaners work by "digesting" protein stains, and they help remove odors, too. After blotting up the stain as best you can, dampen the stained area with the product, then allow it to sit for a few moments. Blot up and remove the product, adding water and blotting as necessary until all stains and soapy residue are gone. When your cat or dog is the culprit, get a specialty enzyme cleaner specifically for pet stains.

Finally, if all else fails, I strongly recommend *bringing in a professional* to perform extraction cleaning or steam cleaning on badly stained upholstery or carpets. It's expensive, but it is worth it, especially since we don't buy new furniture all that often.

CLEANING MICROFIBER UPHOLSTERY

Full disclosure: I am not a fan of microfiber upholstery. I find it fussy and hard to keep clean if you live in a stain-prone home. That said, if you love it and have it, you have to know how to care for it, so here are the basics.

Use the upholstery attachment to vacuum your microfiber when needed, going in straight strokes for that pretty striped look. For more thorough cleaning, you will have to locate the cleaning codes on the upholstery tags. *W* means that you can use water, whereas *S* indicates that you need to keep water away and use solvent. *S-W* means either can be used, and *X* means neither can be used. Upholstery with a *W* code can be hand- or machine-washed (gentle cycle, please) and hung to dry, then replaced on the furniture; otherwise it can be spot-cleaned with a gentle soap and water solution, then brushed when dry. If the furniture has an *S*, blot gently with rubbing alcohol, then blot clean and brush until dry, to even out the nap.

4. Replace each cushion appropriately, zippers facing in.

5. As pillows are replaced, beat each pillow until it is fluffy, plump, and even looking.

6. Replace blankets and straighten them out.

7. If possible, move the item away from the wall and see if the baseboard or area underneath requires a cleaning. Leave here until you vacuum floors.

CLEANING A LAMPSHADE

Especially if they're fabric, lampshades cling to dust and look dull over time. To remove the dust, use the upholstery brush on your vacuum and gently vacuum in quick top-to-bottom strokes; or for a quick cheat, use a lint roller to dust instead.

LEATHER UPHOLSTERY (5 to 10 minutes per piece)

Leather upholstery should be vacuumed with a dusting brush on a regular basis and spot-cleaned with a water-dampened cloth as needed. From time to time, if you notice your leather has stains, marks, or looks a little lackluster, by all means, condition it!

1. Remove anything from the surface (blankets, remotes, pets, your spouse, magazines, etc.). Shake out items over the floor to remove any extra debris. You'll vacuum that up later. Vacuum the piece well.

2. Wipe the upholstery down with leather conditioner using the S-pattern. I like to work cushion by cushion.

3. Buff in to further remove melted dirt and to polish up to a nice, consistent finish.

4. Allow to dry and replace items.

CLEANING A FIREPLACE (20 minutes active time plus 5 minutes inactive time)

My fireplace gets flicked on and off and leaves no dirt behind. While gas fireplaces are certainly convenient, there's something absolutely charming about wood-burning fireplaces. But maintaining them is one heck of a job.

Start by using a broom and dustpan to remove as much of the ashes and soot as possible. Make a thin paste of—you guessed it—baking soda and water, or dish detergent, for a little extra cleaning power. Apply the paste to all the sooty areas both inside and outside, and let sit 5 minutes. Then use a large cleaning brush or cleaning toothbrush as needed to scrub up some of the stains. Rinse with clean water and repeat as needed.

If you use your fireplace regularly, you'll want to get it cleaned by a professional chimney sweep at least once every two years, to keep it in safe working order.

CLEANING PLANTS (1 minute per plant)

You are probably thinking, *Seriously, I have a million better things to do than clean a plant.* And you'd be right—99 percent of the time. But there will be that 1 percent where you'll walk by your plant, fake or real, and notice it's rather dusty. At that time, give it a quick clean and you'll see the leaves will look brighter and shinier. And in the long run, your plant will be healthier, since it won't have all that dust clogging its pores, so to speak.

Dampen a microfiber cloth with water and gently hold chunks of the leaves in one hand while you lightly wipe, almost in a quick slapping or beating motion (obviously, don't do this with a cactus). Be gentle to avoid damage to the leaves. If the plant is very small, use a dry paintbrush to dust the plant leaves.

HOW TO CLEAN A RADIATOR

Radiators gather dust and may look complicated to clean, but good news: they're not. A dusty radiator can't circulate as much heat as a clean one (a big fail, especially on chilly winter nights). Here's the fix:

You'll need an ostrich-feather duster and a radiator cleaning brush (these can also be used to clean fridge coils and dryers!), which is a soft-bristle brush that looks like a giant mascara wand. You can find them online or at a big–box home store.

Starting above the radiator, dust the wall or ledge, which often builds up dust, thoroughly with the feather duster. If you notice any remaining dirt, then you can wipe away with a general-purpose microfiber cloth dampened with all-purpose cleaner.

Lay down a towel underneath the radiator to catch flying dust. Starting at the top of one section of the radiator and working your way down, carefully push the brush in and start to move it in and out vigorously (like you're pumping a tube of mascara); this will swipe out all the dust and force it to fall onto the towel. Do this a few times per section, and if you come across a bar in the radiator while cleaning, spend a few seconds brushing around that bar to shake out anything that's settled on the horizontal surface. Repeat for each section until done.

Now, if you want to give the radiator the ol' spit-and-polish, well, don't use spit. Instead, use a well-wrung-out sponge dipped in soapy water to wipe each section, then buff dry with a plush microfiber cloth.

Remove the towel and toss remnants. When vacuuming the floor, be sure to vacuum up any additional dust under the radiator, using whatever attachment you can to get as far underneath the unit as you can.

WASH THOSE BLANKETS (AND PILLOWS)!

Laundering blankets and pillows that are used in the den is something you can do on an as-needed basis (read: stains, odors), but do it at least once a year. Whenever I wash mine, I say to myself, *Ahh, I should have done this sooner.* As always, check the fabric-care label on blankets and pillows. Many blankets are machine washable. However, if the blanket is wool or another material that doesn't seem like it would be machine washable, take it to be dry-cleaned.

For décor pillows and sofa cushions with a removable, machine-washable covers, simply remove and launder them (no dryer!). If not, consider taking these to a dry cleaner. If the pillow does have a stain, spot-clean by blotting up the stain with a damp paper towel, then using a tiny dab of stain remover. Rub it in gently and agitate with a cleaning toothbrush. Use fresh water and a clean cloth to blot up the soapy residue. Continue doing this until the stain and soap are gone. Remember to always test this in a hidden area first, since you never know if water or soap can permanently ruin your fabric.

FLOORS

Vacuuming (5 to 10 minutes)

Please note: Use the appropriate vacuum attachment and settings and ensure that the bag or canister is empty to provide you with the best vacuum possible.

1. Move all items that might obstruct vacuuming out of the room temporarily to a location adjacent to the room you are in.

2. Plug in your vacuum as close to the exit point of the room as possible.

3. Vacuum the perimeter of the room using the crevice tool.

4. Head to the opposite corner of the room with the appropriate attachment for the floor and begin to vacuum using the W-pattern.

5. Once you have vacuumed your way out of the room, replace any items you removed back in their original locations (if you need to mop, do not replace the items yet).

Mopping (where required; 2 to 5 minutes)

See page 52 for full mopping instructions.

Oh, swoon. A clean den. When was the last time it looked this good? Last time it *smelled* this good? It's a little like falling in love all over again, isn't it?

CLEANING TOYS

Proceed with caution; you don't want to deal with what happens when Froggy is unavailable at bedtime, due to a nasty accident with the clothes dryer.

Plush: Most plush toys come with a care label that should be reviewed to determine the appropriate cleaning procedure. Pay attention to toys that say their filling cannot get laundered—these can become moldy inside or not dry properly (due to organic fillers like husks); spot-shampoo these as necessary. You can vacuum dust off of any plush toy by fitting pantyhose over a vacuum brush. To machine-wash, throw toys into an old pillowcase or lingerie bag, zipped closed. Use cool water to prevent melting any eyes or noses. Dry by hanging them in the sun.

Plastic, rubber, or silicone (without batteries): Add a squirt of dish soap to a sink or bucket with warm water and add the toys. Wipe with a soft cloth or cleaning toothbrush.

. . . and with batteries: These simply cannot be immersed in water. Remove batteries prior to cleaning. Dip a cloth in soapy water and wash the exterior, being careful not to get any moisture near the battery box. Make sure no moisture gets into gaps between moving parts.

Wood toys: Though wood is naturally antibacterial, you can give it a wipe-down with white vinegar if necessary.

CHAPTER 7

the bathroom

A bathroom is such a funny space; it's a microcosm of our best and worst habits. We use it as a place of solitude (shower) and deep thought (toilet), we are our most sick there, and on the opposite end of the spectrum, it's where we get clean and beautiful each day. Emotions can run high in the bathroom, yet when it comes to cleaning it, we generally shudder and want to avoid it at all costs. When I was growing up, I shared a bathroom with my sister, Samantha. We had one sink between us and about a foot of counter space each. If, heaven forbid, she left a hairbrush even a millimeter over the halfway point on the counter, I'd find some passive-aggressive way to let her know she crossed the line, literally. She'd do the same. And being that we were two girls with long hair, we saw our share of stray hairs (it was only ever hers, of course, never mine), not to mention used dental floss and all the bathroom trappings that come with being a woman. It was one contentious hot zone in our house, let me tell you.

Fast forward to when I moved in with Chad. You learn so much about a person when you share a bathroom—sometimes more than you'd like to know. I think my relationship with Chad deepened immensely one night *because* of a bathroom, when we were on vacation in Miami. Chad ate something rather, shall we say, experimental that afternoon while enjoying the local flavors. Later that night as I slumbered peacefully, he got up and went to the bathroom. We'd been living together for over three years at that point and I knew that he never, ever got up to use the bathroom during the night; something was wrong. Chad's interest-

THE BATHROOM: EXPRESS CLEAN (3 TO 5 MINUTES)

This is the perfect touch-up for before guests arrive; it's quick and punchy and I promise, you won't break a sweat.

Air it out. Open windows or crack open the door a bit, weather permitting, to let in fresh air.

Mini wave 1: Gather anything that doesn't belong in the bathroom and get it out. Any countertop clutter, such as extra bottles, containers, hair tools, or cosmetics, can go into a bin and be stored under the bathroom sink.

Wipe and shine. Use a light spritz of all-purpose cleaner on a general-purpose microfiber cloth and spot-clean any splatters on the mirror and quickly move to the vanity top, wiping the surface clean using the S-pattern. Finish up with a quick wipe and shine of the faucet, then finish up by wiping out the sink.

Speedy swish. Squeeze in some toilet bowl cleaner and give the toilet bowl a 30-second swish with the toilet bowl brush. Flush well, and wipe the lid, seat, and exterior bowl with fresh paper towels dampened with all-purpose cleaner.

Towel service. Change up the towels and fold them neatly over the towel rack—you'd be surprised how much cleaner a bathroom looks with fresh, neat towels.

ing afternoon snack had transformed into a raging case of food poisoning, and we were in a tiny hotel room with one bathroom. Let's just say that I experienced his food poisoning totally, but vicariously. I spent time with him the next day and got him drinks and whatever else I could get my hands on at the gift shop to quell his discomfort. But though he was sicker than I'd ever seen, he was, all the while, somehow able to be concerned about the bathroom between his visits—he wanted it to be somewhat clean for me to use should I need it. I couldn't believe that at his weakest time, after using every inch of the toilet in every possible position, he would then spend time to quickly clean the space up just for me. That, my friends, is true love. Chad gets the value of a clean bathroom—and for that, I am eternally grateful.

Keeping the bathroom clean is so important; it demonstrates self-care and self-respect, as well as respect and care for others. But most of all, a clean bathroom is so achievable and looks great! Rather than be grossed out by stray hairs and other assorted signs of bodily functions, you'll have that serenity that you get when walking into a spa. You'll love your bathroom like an ally, not a foe, one that allows you to focus on what you need to do in a bathroom: care for your body. Give it a try; once you get a taste of a bathroom in all its gleaming glory, you won't want to go back.

THE BATHROOM: TOP-TO-BOTTOM CLEAN

Things are a little different in the bathroom, you might notice. We don't do formal waves here, and rather than follow the traditional clockwise path, I start in the bathroom by pretreating the particularly grimy areas that require soak time, then move my way to the easier-to-clean areas, and finally head back to those grime bombs. The sink area gets cleaned last, since that's the area that gets used (and splashed) the most while cleaning, and seriously, don't we have better things to do than clean the sink seven times in fifteen minutes?

PRODUCTS	TOOLS
Tub-and-tile cleaner (see page 22)	High-dusting tool (see page 31)
Baking soda	Double-sided nonscratching sponge
Glass cleaner (see page 20)	Rubber squeegee
All-purpose cleaner (see page 16)	2 general-purpose microfiber cloths
Toilet bowl cleaner (see page 22)	Paper towels
Disinfectant (optional)	Toilet bowl brush
White vinegar	Flat-weave microfiber cloth
	Cleaning toothbrush
	Vacuum with brush attachment
	Fresh trash can liner

THE BATHROOM TIMELINE

I'll explain how to clean each item from start to finish, in case you're focusing on one thing. But when you're doing everything, clean the bathroom in this order:

1. Pretreat the shower tiles (remove all bottles, soap, and other shower accessories before treating).

2. Pick up and remove everything on the floor in the bathroom— (clothes, hampers, rugs, magazine racks, toilet paper cozies, etc.); place them just outside the door.

3. Pretreat the toilet.

4. Dust the moldings, corners, wall fixtures, and the exhaust fan.

5. Clean the mirror.

6. Clean the vanity top and accessories.

7. Clean the shower tiles and pretreat the tub.

8. Clean the toilet.

9. Clean the tub, then rinse and dry the tub and tiles.

10. Pretreat the sink area.

11. Dust and straighten, clean points of contact, change the trash bag, and wipe the baseboards.

12. Clean the sink.

13. Clean the floors.

14. Replace remaining clean items back into the bathroom.

TO GLOVE, OR NOT?

If you want to preserve your hands from getting dry and covered in cleaning products, consider rubber gloves. For the toilet, I'd recommend using disposable gloves, or else wear the same gloves and simply wash your gloved hands thoroughly with soap and hot water prior to cleaning a new area.

EXHAUST FAN AND HIGH DUSTING (3 to 5 minutes)

Gauge how much dust has built up. When something looks fuzzy, it's time to dust. Thankfully, these jobs are incredibly simple to do—and help a space look super sparkly.

Remember: Lights should be turned off during high dusting to avoid popping any bulbs!

1. Head to 12 o'clock with the high-dusting tool and walk around the room, gently moving it around the moldings and getting into ceiling corners. Dust light fixtures gently. Work your way around the room in a clockwise direction to ensure you cover all areas.

2. Use your vacuum to quickly zip the bathroom exhaust fan and remove dusty buildup.

3. For really dusty vents, get out the ol' stepladder and a screwdriver, remove the vent cover, and wash it out in the sink. Vacuum the fan and replace the cover when dry. It will help your

exhaust fan run more efficiently and quietly—and avoid you having a rude awakening when you're relaxing in the tub, staring up at the ceiling.

HANDY HABIT: BEFRIENDING YOUR SQUEEGEE

Squeegee the walls dry every time you shower (get one of those squeegees with a convenient suction cup). This way, the dirty shower water that carries soap, body oils, and dirt will never hang out on shower walls, and you'll never have to scrub away soap scum! It's a quick habit that has a big impact on reduced bathroom cleaning time.

The squeegee really is the best line of defense, but some people hate it, for some reason. If that's the case for you, a daily postshower spritz with a daily shower spray can work wonders.

DAILY SHOWER SPRAY

1 cup white vinegar
½ cup water
20 drops tea tree oil

Mix well in a clean spray bottle and spray down the tiles and tub after each shower with this solution. Do not wipe off.

CLEAN THE SHOWER AND TUB (10 to 15 minutes active time plus 5 to 10 minutes inactive time)

Most people think this is one of the hardest places to clean. We're tackling mold, mildew, dead skin cells, body oils, hard water, soap scum . . . so yeah, I hear you. But with this new way of cleaning, you're going to be a tub-and-tile-cleaning rock star in no time.

1. Start by removing all items from the tub and shower—shampoo bottles and soap, loofah, razor, etc. Place them somewhere out of the way.

2. Liberally spray tub-and-tile cleaner all over the tiles, working your way from top to bottom. You want them soaking wet. (Notice that we're not pretreating the tub just yet; we do that to keep the tub dry in the event you need to stand inside it while scouring the tiles. Smart, right?)

3. Move on to your next item until it's time to return to the tiles (see the timeline).

4. In 5 to 10 minutes, rewet the tile surface if needed with product. Start scrubbing with the sponge, scrubby-side down, using the S-pattern, working your way from top to bottom, section by section, until you reach the opposite end. If you encounter a stubborn area, scrub additionally with baking soda or a heavier tub-and-tile product as required (but don't rinse just yet).

Please note: Though most tub-and-tile cleaners work great on glass shower doors (beware of etching), do not use the abrasive side of the sponge on shower doors—clean using only the soft side. Once you've finished rinsing product off the glass, finish up with a glass cleaner to remove streaks. Stubborn streaks can be treated with lemon juice or full-strength vinegar and wiped away with a microfiber cloth.

MOVING ON TO THE TUB

1. **Pretreat:** Liberally spray tub-and-tile cleaner all over the tub, working your way from top to bottom and around the corners.

2. **Clean:** Using the scrubby side of a wet sponge, wipe the sides and base of the tub using the S-pattern, working section by section, removing soap scum and scrubbing more thoroughly where required. You'll know it is clean when you feel a smooth surface with no resistance.

3. Run the water very hot. If you have a removable shower head, lift it off before turning your water on. Otherwise, get a tall, narrow container and fill it with hot water. Rinse the shower walls and tub very well, removing all soapy residue, until tiles and tub feel squeaky clean.

4. Dry both the tiles and the tub with a squeegee or a dry plush microfiber cloth. Working section by section, remove excess liquid until a clean, streak-free shine is revealed. Ensure your chrome pieces are cleaned as well during this process (see next page).

5. Wipe and replace bottles, caddies, and any other bathroom accessories.

WARNING! WARNING!

If you stick with my homemade products, you should be golden; but if you're using store-bought, be sure to check labels before applying one product soon after another. Some have incompatible chemicals that can release toxic fumes. (Are you convinced yet to go with my homemade products?)

✓ **PRO TIP: MILDEW TAMER!** For areas with mildew that just don't come clean during your regular scrub session, level up and use a powerful mold-and-mildew cleaner on your grout and caulking. To learn more, see page 23.

✦ **HANDY HABIT: Keeping the Air Circulating.** Leave your bathroom fan on during a shower and 30 minutes after—and leave your bathroom door open, too. You want to get rid of as much moisture as possible to help prevent the growth of mold and mildew.

✓ **PRO TIP: CARE FOR YOUR CADDY!** Shower caddies are convenient but often become grimy. Look for a caddy that you can easily remove and soak in a solution of one part vinegar to one part water every month or so to help remove grime and mold.

★ **GOLD STAR! Don't Forget to Wash.** Remove your shower curtain, shower curtain liner, nonslip bath mat, and any bathroom rugs if you have them, and launder them every few months. They can all be placed in the same load—plastic, too!—assuming they are all safe to launder according to their care instructions. Add regular laundry detergent plus a cup of white vinegar to the load, which will help get rid of mildew and odors, and toss in a towel to help scrub off any buildup. Hang all items to dry when done—your shower curtain and shower curtain liner can go right back on their hooks; they'll dewrinkle as they dry.

CHROME BATHROOM FIXTURES (1 minute per fixture)

This small step has a high impact on how clean your bathroom can look. A streaky faucet looks dirty, even if it was just cleaned. The key is to clean it first and remove the streaks second—that's what makes any bathroom look photo-worthy.

1. Spray tub-and-tile cleaner onto the fixture and let it soak for a minute. (For quick cleanups, you can even use a squirt of vinegar or lemon juice—both are great at breaking down soap scum and water marks.)

2. With a damp microfiber cloth, wipe the area and scrub off any spots (an abrasive sponge may scratch the metal).

3. Use a clean, dry microfiber cloth to do a final wipe and shine.

THE TOILET (I know, you're excited about this one; 3 to 7 minutes active time plus 5 minutes inactive time)

I have a girlfriend who grew up in a beautiful home; we lovingly called her mom Susie Homemaker because she kept a perfect house and knew how to do everything (she also worked!). But guess what: not long after moving out on her own, my girlfriend confessed to me, "I can clean just about anything, but cleaning a toilet makes me gag!" See? Even Susie Homemaker's daughter struggles with the toilet.

So once and for all, let's break it down and see how simple (and un-gagworthy) it is!

1. To pretreat, spray the toilet with all-purpose cleaner in the following order: the toilet lid, flusher, tank, seat lid, hinges, underside of the lid, top of seat, bottom of seat; inside the bowl, use toilet bowl cleaner by squirting it under the rim and inside the bowl (see recipe on page 22). Then spray the base and surrounding area of the toilet with all-purpose cleaner (you know, where all the mystery splashes end up—this helps eliminate that "pee" smell from the bathroom).

2. To clean, spray down the toilet quickly with the same product if the product has dried and begin to wipe each zone using the S-pattern with a dry paper towel, retracing your spray pattern and wiping all areas clean. Change the paper towel as it becomes soggy and dispose in the trash (not down the toilet).

3. Take the toilet bowl scrub brush and scrub underneath the perimeter of the rim, then spiral your way down toward the chute with the brush, scrubbing rigorously to ensure grime is brushed off. Clean the chute a few times by inserting and removing the brush quickly. Flush the toilet to drain product and rinse the bowl while holding the brush in place to clean it off. Place the brush under the toilet seat lid to drip-dry while you finish the rest of your cleaning.

4. Wipe any excess moisture off the toilet exterior with a paper towel and double-check for any hair or grime left behind.

HACK! CLEANING IN YOUR SLEEP

For smelly or stained toilets, dump a cup of Borax into the toilet bowl before bedtime. (The Borax works overnight to break down stains, odors, and bacteria.) Scrub the toilet quickly the next morning and flush. Done!

★ **GOLD STAR! Get Classy Like.** Having guests over and want to really impress them? Fold your toilet paper into a point (toilet paper origami) by taking the last square of paper and folding one corner under toward the middle, stopping at the base of the perforation. Then fold the other corner in the same manner. Crease well and voilà, a toilet paper point (you're so fancy!).

★ **GOLD STAR! Make Guests Comfortable.** Toilets can be so. Utterly. Awkward. At the most inopportune time, they'll clog. Do your guests a favor and leave a proper plunger out. I have personally been in situations where there hasn't been a plunger, and, well, I'll spare you the details, but it got ugly and sweaty. Also, leave ample toilet paper available for guests. I have a rule that as soon as I get down to the last roll in my basket, I grab three more.

★ **GOLD STAR! Scents and Scentsibility.** Want to cover up that number 2 smell? Make your own "Poo Pourri" to keep the bathroom smelling fresh even in the most challenging times. In a small spray bottle, mix ½ cup water, 3 tablespoons vegetable glycerine, 2 tablespoons rubbing alcohol, 40 drops essential oil, and 20 drops blue food coloring (it's optional, but it helps you ensure full bowl coverage). Shake well. Quickly spritz into the toilet bowl before getting down to business!

DON'T FORGET THE TOWEL BAR AND TOILET PAPER HOLDER (30 seconds)

Most people forget about these areas, but they get dusty, too. With a slightly damp cloth, wipe the towel bar and toilet paper holder.

★ **GOLD STAR! 5-star Tip.** Ever wish your bathroom could have that pristine look, like a fresh hotel bathroom? Fold your towels this way: Lay the towel flat on a surface, tag-side facing you. Imagine your towel is divided into quarters lengthwise. Fold the outermost quarter in toward the center, then repeat on the opposite side so the edges meet in the middle. Fold it in half over the towel bar, leaving the front end sitting slightly longer than the back end to hide any sloppy edges.

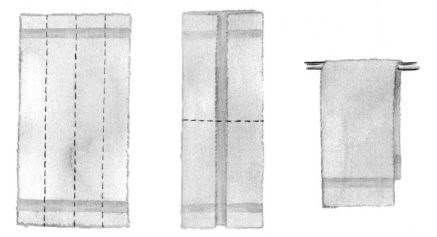

WALLS (10 seconds per mark)

Please note: Matte or flat paint may mark up if cleaned too vigorously. Please test this method in a small hidden area first.

1. Using a microfiber cloth dampened with all-purpose cleaner, give the stained area a quick wipe and buff dry.

2. If the stain doesn't budge, sprinkle a pinch of baking soda on a small corner of your dampened cloth and begin to gently rub the stained area. Wipe well, then remove any remaining baking soda residue with a dry cloth.

MIRRORS, MEDICINE CABINET, AND WINDOWS (5 to 7 minutes total)

You want to look gorgeous. Especially at six in the morning or before a night out. But it's hard to look your best when you're squinting your way through a splattered and messy mirror. Let's get it clean and see you, you sexy animal!

1. Spray the mirror lightly with glass cleaner. Fold a flat-weave microfiber cloth into quarters. Using only one side of the cloth, start at the top left corner of the mirror and use the S-pattern to clean the mirror, going from top to bottom.

2. Flip the cloth to a dry quarter and repeat the S-pattern, retracing your steps from top to bottom. This helps dry the glass and finish the job streak-free.

3. Do that dancing cross-check to make sure streaks are gone from every angle. Look from the left, right, and squat down to make sure they're all gone.

✓ **PRO TIP: MIRROR PRETREAT!** For any stubborn marks on a mirror, such as hairspray, first use a dab of rubbing alcohol on a cloth to remove the muck. Then, clean your mirror as above.

WINDOWSILLS AND BLINDS (see page 50)

VANITY TOP (5 to 8 minutes)

Your bathroom counter (if you are fortunate enough to have one) is a veritable catchall for products, stray hairs, toothpaste, makeup, and spills, and oh my goodness, does the list go on. If you happen to share this bathroom with other people, it is one of the most territorial spaces in the home, too. Cleaning and caring for this high-value real estate will help your bathroom feel and look cleaner and may even keep the peace.

1. Remove all items from the vanity top (you may want to divide it into sections depending on how large the counter is) and place them in an uncleaned area nearby (the floor!).

2. Spray the countertop with the appropriate countertop cleaner (remember, marble, granite, or stone requires a safe, nonacidic product; see page 19) and let it soak for a couple of minutes.

3. Wipe the counter with a microfiber cloth using an S-pattern, ensuring you wipe all debris off the counter. For any stubborn stains, use a touch of baking soda to help lift off the gunk.

4. Flip your microfiber cloth over onto the dry side and repeat the S-pattern really quickly to remove any left-behind hair, debris, or streaks.

5. Style it! Pick up each item and wipe it as you replace it on the vanity where it belongs. Line everything up parallel and perpendicular to the edge of the vanity, stacking where possible to save space.

✦ **HANDY HABIT: Divvying up Bathroom Space.** When multiple people share a bathroom, create sections or areas on the vanity for each person. Have a communal area for items such as hand soap and toothpaste, and distinct areas for personal items, such as face wash and shaving cream. There are many alternatives available at organization stores, home stores, and even furniture stores, where you can find storage solutions aplenty.

SOAP DISH AND TOOTHBRUSH HOLDER (1 to 2 minutes per item active time plus 5 minutes inactive time)

1. Remove all items from the toothbrush holder and the soap from the soap dish.

2. Spray and soak the holders with all-purpose cleaner and leave for a couple of minutes.

3. Using a cloth liberally treated with all-purpose cleaner, wipe items until scum and marks are gone. If you really need to get

in there, use a cleaning toothbrush or add some baking soda for extra abrasion.

4. Rinse well under running water. Dry each piece with a dry microfiber cloth. Replace each item, wiping them clean as you put them away.

✓ **PRO TIP: GET YOUR TOOTHBRUSH HOLDER CLEAN!** Place your toothbrush holder and soap dish into the dishwasher if they are porcelain or plastic, and let the machine do the dirty work for you. If you're not getting them clean, soak them in vinegar overnight and then try again. The vinegar will help break down super-difficult stains and tackle mildew.

★ **GOLD STAR! Clean Your Tubes and Pumps.** You know how gunky the toothpaste and soap pump can get! Wipe your toothpaste tube and cap, along with the soap pump, with a dampened piece of paper towel. If the soap pump gets grimy, soak it in a bowl filled with hot water for 10 minutes, pump several times to rinse the system, and then replace.

POINTS OF CONTACT (2 minutes)

1. For handles, knobs, and anything frequently touched (but not attached to electricity), spray all-purpose cleaner on the area and wipe clean. For light switches, treat a cloth with all-purpose cleaner and wipe with the cloth.

2. Treat with disinfectant according to the bottle's instructions, if using.

THE SINK (2 to 3 minutes)

The sink is the bathroom workhorse—it really takes a beating. Cleaning it requires a bit of scrubbing and a bit of shining.

1. **Pretreat:** Spray all-purpose cleaner all over the sink. If you notice any extra-crusty areas, sprinkle some baking soda over the top.

Saturate your faucet with white vinegar, to break down any hard-water stains or scum.

2. Use the scrubby side of the sponge to work your way from top to bottom, and scrub the sink in a clockwise motion. Spend extra time scrubbing any areas that are dirty or stained, especially around the drain. If you notice a grimy "border" around the drain, break out the cleaning toothbrush and get right in there to give it a good scrub. Wipe down the chrome with the damp microfiber cloth as well.

3. Rinse the sink well and wipe the faucet to a beautiful shine, then wipe the rest of the sink down with the same dry microfiber cloth, ensuring you pick up any stray hairs along the way.

✦ **HANDY HABIT: Quick-clean in Between.** It's sort of gross to stare at a hair-and-toothpaste-splattered sink while you're brushing your teeth and washing your face. Keep a cloth and spray bottle filled with all-purpose cleaner under your sink and give these areas a quick wipe between cleans when it's looking unsavory.

BASEBOARDS (2 minutes)
Hit 'em with the high duster, flipped over!

THE FLOOR (3 to 5 minutes)
Your floor will have just caught the brunt of your cleaning fury—and that's on top of what it has *already* been subjected to. A quick clean of the floor gets your bathroom gleaming in no time.

Using a damp microfiber cloth (one that you've already used, say, on the mirror or to polish your chrome), spray the floor in sections and wipe using the S-pattern. With this movement, you'll notice you collect all kinds of extra hair and debris and shine the floor at the same time. While asking you to get down on your hands and knees may sound like an evil-stepmother move, unless you have a relatively large bathroom, I find it less work to wipe the floor by hand than to mop. If you choose to mop, make sure you sweep or vacuum first.

REPLACING ALL ITEMS

It is finally time to put the bathroom puzzle back together. Hang up fresh towels, ensure your trash can has been emptied, fitted with a new liner, and replaced where it belongs. Put bathroom rugs and other accessories back in their rightful places. This final straighten-up makes the bathroom look complete and ready for you to enjoy (even if only for a few moments!).

CHAPTER 8

the bedroom

My bedroom has always been important to me, and I always saw the bedroom as an extension of myself and my own taste. Growing up, I proudly chose my wall color, a bubblegum *purple*, along with a comforter and pillow set that was blue, yellow, purple, and pink. Was it gorgeous? I sure thought it was. Tacky as it may have been, that purple room was *mine*. In that room, I came into my own slobbery, too. I would rarely make the bed. *Why bother? I'm just getting back into it later.* Fast-forward to moving in with a partner: that's when the situation gets real. Your shtick and your partner's shtick about room cleaning collide head-on, and you've got to figure it out, fast. Negotiating the state of the bedroom is something that most couples can attest to working through, as Chad and I have.

The bedroom is an extension of who we are, and thus, keeping it clean is the ultimate way to treat ourselves well. I'm not trying to impress any guests. I want it to be our sanctuary from everything else we deal with all day long, and having it clean and orderly means that it will be just that. At the end of my day, whatever I've been doing, it's just divine to have a clean room to flop into.

THE BEDROOM: EXPRESS CLEAN (10 MINUTES)

Even a quick cleanup in the bedroom is supremely gratifying. You can get a ton accomplished here in just 10 minutes. It might inspire you to devote an extra 2 minutes a day each morning before you leave for work just to get it how you like it. This one's just for you, so consider it a small investment of time in your day for a big impact on your emotional well-being when you come home.

Air it out. Open windows or crack open the door a bit, weather permitting, to let in fresh air.

Mini wave 1: Grab a bin and work your way around the room clockwise, starting at the door. Pick up anything that's out of place and pop it into the bin. Dishes, books, garbage, you name it. If it's not at home, in it goes. Clean and dirty laundry can go into a pile in the middle of the floor. As you go around, straighten anything that's out of place, lining up items parallel and perpendicular to the edge of a surface, closing boxes, etc. Put the bin aside.

Make the bed. It doesn't have to be Marines-perfect, but even a two-minute-made bed will totally make your day. First, rip the comforter and flat sheet off the bed. Place the pillows right at the head. Grab the flat sheet and snap it over your bed a couple of times to get the wrinkles out, then lay it flat over your mattress, shaking it back and forth as necessary to get it to lay properly. (For extra points, tuck the bottoms of the sheet under the mattress.) If your bed is up against a wall, allow the sheet to crumple up along that edge; you'll deal with it in a moment. Next, do the same with your comforter as you did with the flat sheet. If your bed is up against the wall, hop on the bed and push both the flat sheet and comforter between the wall and bed as best you can. Smooth

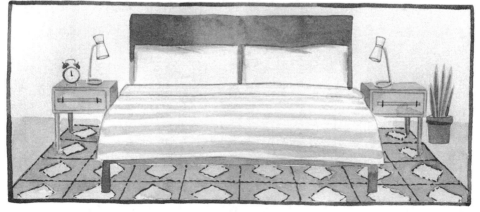

out the bedding so it looks neat. Fold down about a foot of the comforter and flat sheet back over itself, for that neat and tidy fold. Done.

Hit the laundry pile. What's clean? Toss it onto the bed. What's dirty? Place it into the hamper (if you don't have one, I really recommend you get one; they make an enormous difference in keeping a clean room). Fold or hang the clean stuff—it takes so little time. Just trust me on this.

Finish up with floors. How dirty are the floors, and how much time do you want to spend on them? If you are in a big rush, you can quickly vacuum the floor and that's all (clearly the case for carpet, but even for hard-floor surfaces). If you have time, get out your mop and give the floor a quick once-over.

Ditch the bin. Finally, grab that bin and deal with its contents. Take trash and dishes and glasses to the kitchen, books to the bookcase, and old papers and magazines to the recycling bin.

And you're done. The bedroom clean is a breeze, and to come home to a clean bedroom is one of the best feelings. Enjoy it!

THE BEDROOM: TOP-TO-BOTTOM CLEAN

Cleaning your room can feel overwhelming, especially if it's been a mess of late. But it's a really gratifying job, and the way I break it down makes it simpler. I promise you that.

PRODUCTS

All-purpose cleaner (see page 16)

Glass cleaner (see page 20)

Disinfectant (optional)

TOOLS

Fresh sheets if you're changing the bed

Trash bag

Recycling bin

Bin

High-dusting tool (see page 31)

2 general-purpose microfiber cloths

Flat-weave microfiber cloth

Vacuum

Mop and bucket (for tile, vinyl, and linoleum floors) or flat mop and spray bottle (for stone, wood, and laminate floors)

Wave 1

TIDY AND ORGANIZE (7 to 20 minutes)

Start by making your bed. Change your sheets, if desired.

Make Your Bed (2 minutes [making the bed] to 10 minutes [changing the linens])

This is one of the nicest things you can do for yourself. A freshly made bed is absolutely heavenly—your room smells nicer and just feels cleaner and crisper. I always feel as if I'm spending the night at a hotel when I get into a freshly made bed.

1. When placing fitted sheets on the bed, make sure the sheets are stretched out so that all sides of the mattress fit into the sheet pocket corners properly.

2. Tuck each elastic corner under the mattress corner until you have a tight fit.

3. Add your flat sheet; lay it print-side or flat-seam-side down.

4. Tuck in the corners at the foot of the bed so that they are not hanging sloppily (this is called hotel or hospital corners). To do this:

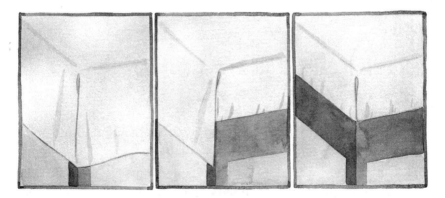

   a. Gently lift the bottom of the mattress at the foot of the bed and tuck overhanging sheets under the mattress snugly.

b. Let the mattress sit back down on its base.

c. Move to the left end of the bed, lift and fold back the sheet overhang on that side of the bed, then tuck in any sheet still hanging over the edge of the mattress and fold back the sheet that you lifted up, almost as if you are "gift wrapping" the mattress. The corners should look very neat.

d. Repeat on the right side of the bed.

5. If needed, pull and fix the bed skirt.

6. Now, place the comforter on the bed, making sure all corners and edges fall over the mattress and sides neatly and evenly. Smooth around the bed.

7. At the head of the bed, take the comforter and the flat sheet in your hands and turn both back to create a neat fold about a foot long across the top of the bed. Now you can see the pattern of the flat sheet appear neatly over the comforter.

8. Place the pillows standing up against the back of the headboard, then fluff and straighten them, making sure the open end of the pillowcase is facing outward and the edges are folded in.

9. Place any sham or decorative pillows in front of those, fluffing and straightening them as well. Karate chop pillows as you see fit.

Do everything you can to resist flopping into the bed at this point—the urge will be strong!

LAUNDRY IN THE BEDROOM

Whether or not you keep a clean bedroom and the question of how you deal with laundry are at least, in my estimation, 90 percent linked. One of the first tenets of keeping a clean bedroom: laundry must be dealt with immediately. It cannot go into that purgatory holding place on your bedroom chair (we all know *that* chair), which soon becomes piled up with sweaters, pants, and dress shirts. Laundry must immediately go into a hamper or be put back in a drawer or the closet. I strongly recommend keeping a hamper right in your bedroom, closet, or bathroom (or wherever you change) so that you eliminate temptation to leave worn clothing where it doesn't belong. Don't clutter up your bedroom by leaving this "unmade decision." Decide whether laundry is clean—put it away—or dirty—into the hamper—instead of leaving it to be dealt with later.

Time to Tidy (5 to 10 minutes)

Now that the bed is made, it sets the stage for the rest of wave 1. Set your trash can, recycling bin, and bin for misplaced items in the center of your room. Starting at 12 o'clock, walk around the room and collect items that are out of place and put them where they belong: Granola bar wrapper? Garbage. Soda cans and old newspapers? Recycle. Dirty clothing? Floor. Clean clothing? Bed. Dry cleaning pile? Bin. You'll deal with all those items after the cleaning takes place, but this is a cursory sorting, which makes later placing everything where it belongs infinitely easier. As you go around, straighten up items that *do* belong, lining them up parallel and perpendicular to the edge of the surface that they're on. Once you hit the door, you're ready to do the second wave: cleaning a really tidy bedroom.

Wave 2

Place all your products and tools at the 12 o'clock starting point so that you never have to chase them.

HIGH DUSTING (90 seconds)

Please note: Lights should be turned off during high dusting to avoid popping any lightbulbs.

1. Head to 12 o'clock with your high-dusting tool and gently move it around the moldings and get it into ceiling corners, as well as light fixtures.

2. Run your tool along the top of any doorframes and across any air vents.

TRUE STORY!

Even from a young age, I was a budding slob. I remember once getting my hands on one of those large, multicolored lollipops that was about the size of a personal pizza. It had every color in the rainbow and fulfilled most of my childhood aspirations. I treasured that lollipop. I'd enjoy some of it and then leave it on my dresser, all wet and sticky, and pick it up again a little later and give it some more licks. Not surprisingly, my dresser developed a sticky, gooey residue that locked the lollipop in place when I wasn't eating it. I didn't care that it may have attracted dust and hair or that it sat out and made my dresser continually grosser. I don't remember much else about that lollipop, like if I ever finished it. But I do remember that I had no regard for how utterly disgusting I was making my room.

CLEANING AND DUSTING

Now, head back to 12 o'clock and work your way around the room, section by section, with your all-purpose cleaner and glass cleaner, completing the tasks as required by the layout of your space. As I get myself ready for this cleaning, I carry two general-purpose microfiber cloths and one flat-weave cloth with me, the latter of which is usually draped over my shoulder (it's a *really* edgy look). One general-purpose cloth is used for wet work I do, such as spraying the cloth and wiping, and the dry one is used for buffing and polishing up.

Mirrors and Windows (90 seconds per item)

1. Spray the mirror lightly with glass cleaner.

2. Fold a flat-weave microfiber cloth into quarters to keep a few dry sides for buffing.

3. Using only one side of the cloth, start at the top left corner of the mirror and use the S-pattern to clean the mirror, going from top to bottom.

4. Flip the cloth to a dry quarter and repeat the S-pattern, retracing your steps from top to bottom. This helps dry the glass and finish the job streak-free.

5. Using yet another dry quarter of the cloth, look for streaks and marks using the light, and gently buff them out as you see them.

Picture Frames and Artwork (30 to 60 seconds per piece)

Please note: The glass cover of a picture frame does not need to be cleaned unless it is visibly dirty or dusty. Otherwise, just focus on dusting the frame (horizontal surface).

1. Place one hand on the bottom corner of the frame to support it while cleaning.

2. Use a microfiber cloth lightly dampened with all-purpose cleaner and wipe the top of the frame from left to right.

3. Repeat for each horizontal edge of the frame (left, right).

4. If dusty, wipe the glass with a dry general-purpose microfiber cloth.

5. Check the glass for any spots or fingerprints. If dirty, spray glass cleaner onto the glass and wipe clean with the flat-weave microfiber cloth. If there's just a spot that's noticeable, simply

spray the cloth with glass cleaner and use your cloth wrapped around your pointer finger to buff out the spot.

6. Buff dry any wet spots to remove streaks.

✓ **PRO TIP: WHEN IT'S REALLY, REALLY DUSTY!** If the dust is very thick on any surface, start with a dry microfiber cloth and dust the surface first, then finish up with a damp cloth as you normally would, using an S-pattern. Otherwise the dust sticks like glue to the surface, and you get a truly obnoxious film left behind. Similarly, when you are cleaning surfaces that don't require product (such as wood or leather), just use a dry cloth, and a dampened cloth to remove fingerprints or marks. If after you dust the surface it has a filmy residue, marks, or anything warranting further cleaning, go for it. Otherwise, just stick with a dry cloth and save your time.

Walls (10 seconds per mark)

1. Using a microfiber cloth dampened with all-purpose cleaner, give the stained area a quick wipe and buff dry.

2. If the stain doesn't budge, sprinkle a pinch of baking soda on a small corner of your dampened cloth and begin to gently rub the stained area. Wipe well, then remove any remaining baking soda residue with a dry cloth.

Horizontal Surfaces (1 to 2 minutes per piece)

Please note: Focus on dusting and cleaning horizontal and angled surfaces, since vertical surfaces don't get as dusty or dirty.

At 12 o'clock, start at the top of the room and pick the highest surface you need to clean, and work your way down. Section by section, here's what to do:

1. Remove all removable items from a given surface, keeping them in a safe area.

2. Use your dry, or wet then dry, cloth to dust and clean (removing both debris and marks) using an S-pattern.

3. Pick up any item that belongs on that surface, hold it securely with one hand, and dust and wipe with a damp cloth.

4. Buff dry to remove streaks and replace the item where you found it (I usually place the item back neatly using the dry cloth to avoid getting fingerprints on it again, crime-scene style).

Points of Contact (2 minutes)

1. Identify your points of contact while cleaning (switch plates, door handles, and knobs).

2. Spray points of contact (unless it is a light switch) with all-purpose cleaner and wipe clean.

3. Treat with disinfectant according to the bottle's instructions, if using.

4. For a light switch, simply spray your cloth, wipe the light switch plate, and ensure all marks are removed.

Windowsills and Blinds (see page 50)

You don't have to do them every time. While you're cleaning, take an honest assessment. If they don't look so bad, keep rolling!

Baseboards (5 minutes)

As with windowsills, check them as you clean. If I notice they need a cleaning, I'll do what is required to get them looking right. You can do baseboards the same way we did corners and the ceiling at the beginning of wave 2—with the high duster.

Wave 3

Guess what, you're in the home stretch now, baby! All we'll do here is clean the floors and move on!

FLOORS

Vacuuming (7 to 10 minutes)

Please note: Use the appropriate vacuum attachment and settings and ensure that the bag or canister is empty to provide you with the best vacuum possible.

1. Move all items that might obstruct vacuuming out of the room temporarily to a location adjacent to the room you are in.

2. Plug in your vacuum as close to the exit point of the room as possible.

3. Vacuum all upholstered items first (remove cushions, vacuum, replace properly).

4. Vacuum the perimeter of the room using the crevice tool.

5. Head to the opposite corner of the room with the appropriate attachment for the floor and begin to vacuum using the W-pattern, breaking the room into sections as necessary to maintain the pattern.

6. Lift up the bed skirt and vacuum under the bed. (Isn't it good feng shui to have it free of dust bunnies under there?)

7. Once you have vacuumed your way out of the room, replace any items you removed back in their original locations (if you need to mop, do not do this yet).

Mopping (where required; 3 to 5 minutes)

Please note: Use a little product when mopping the floor to reduce stickiness underfoot. The mop must always be very well wrung out to avoid streaks and damage. See page 52 for details about how to mop. Replace furniture when you're done!

And there you have it. A clean bedroom. It yields the most wonderful and relaxed feeling. Enjoy it!

CHAPTER 9

the home office

The home office is a space that's either work-ing hard or hardly working. Many of us are working from home these days—at least 50 percent of the U.S. workforce works from home at least some of the time—and work arrangements are quite different from what they were fifty years ago.

"Organized chaos" is something I hear about a lot when I talk to peo-ple about their home offices. *"Oh, I know where that important document is. It's under the pizza coupon and the pile of magazines, to the right of the half-chomped pens and that nest of receipts from last year."* Well, let me be clear. I'm not going to scold you. Certain parts of my life could well be described as organized chaos. I get it. My space can get a bit messy or scattered, but I know where everything belongs and where I can find it. However, when we get to the point where we can't find things, then we're no longer living in organized chaos; then, it's just chaos. So let's be hon-est with ourselves and stay on top of this space.

Your home office may be where you work, where your kids work, or where your family accounting and administration is done. Regardless, there are a few home office maxims: The office must be arranged for func-tion; it must be pleasant to spend time in, since, let's face it, some of the tasks that take place here can be a little boring or soul sucking; and it must be clean and free of that dust that loves to build up on office gadgets.

THE HOME OFFICE: EXPRESS CLEAN (10 MINUTES)

The office has three main features we need to think about in the Express Clean: the desktop (not on your computer—your real, physical desktop!) and all the papers and tchotchkes included in that, the electronics, and the floor. Everything else can wait until you do a thorough office clean.

Air it out. Open windows or crack open the door a bit, weather permitting, to let in fresh air.

Mini wave 1: Grab a bin, and starting at 12 o'clock, which should be the doorway, collect all the items that don't belong in the space and place them into the bin. Trash and recycling need to be placed in the appropriate containers, and personal or business paper trash should go into the shredder.

Straighten as you go. As you go around, quickly straighten up items—books, papers, office supplies—by piling them neatly (organized chaos!) and lining them up parallel and perpendicular to the edge of the surface. This makes your office look and feel much more productive. Meanwhile, take note of areas that are super dusty or grimy.

Quick-clean electronics. Now, take one flat-weave microfiber cloth with a corner dampened with water or my electronics cleaner (see page 124) and one general-purpose microfiber cloth dampened with all-purpose cleaner. Starting back at 12 o'clock, quickly spot-clean any areas that look grimy, dusty, or dirty. For sticky spots, run the general-purpose microfiber cloth over the area a few times and the muck should lift off. If it's a stubborn sticky stain, apply a bit of all-purpose cleaner to the surface and let it sit for a moment while you do other things, then wipe it away. Any time you encounter an electronic item that doesn't have a monitor or touchscreen, hold up the item over the floor and wipe it quickly with the dampened flat-weave microfiber cloth. (A good rule of thumb is to make sure your electronics are off while cleaning. Never spray the electronic directly, and always have your flat-weave cloth handy to do a quick follow-up dry.) For your keyboard, pick it up, give it a few long swipes and a good tap or two over the floor (prepare for a potential snowfall!). Your mouse, cordless phone, and most other office electronics can also handle this kind of cleaning. For any electronics that do have monitors or touchscreens, give a quick dry-wipe with the flat-weave cloth; and only if you notice a fingerprint or stain should you use a tiny spritz of electronics cleaner on your flat-weave cloth to quickly wipe away that mark. Follow up with a quick buff to dry it.

Finish up with floors. Finally, the floors. If you have a hard floor, you can certainly clean the floors with a dust mop. But if you want to do things right, I'd still recommend using a vacuum here with the appropriate floor attachment, since offices tend to get really dusty. And who wants to be working in a dusty and depressing office all day? No one I know. Start at the area farthest from the door and vacuum or mop your way out.

Ditch the bin. Finally, grab that bin and deal with its contents. Take trash and dishes and glasses to the kitchen, books to the bookcase, and old papers and magazines to the recycling bin. Just like that, your office is clean!

THE HOME OFFICE: TOP-TO-BOTTOM CLEAN

Offices aren't really complex to clean at all. The most important things to focus on here are keeping on top of dust, keeping your electronics cleaned, and keeping some sort of organization system in place.

Dust management is important. It can gather and look and feel gross, of course, but also, working in a dusty space isn't healthy; it can exacerbate allergies or asthma. Plus, eventually dust will clog up the air-intake vents of your electronics and overheat them. Dust circulates a lot in offices because we have tons of machines whirring, sucking in cool air and pushing out hot air via tiny vents. And electronics also have lots of tiny crevices that dust loves to settle in.

Your electronics should be kept clean also; while their life-spans do seem to get shorter and shorter, keeping them clean will help them work well until their final days. And keeping your office organized, at least somewhat, will not only give you a supportive space to work in, but you'll have the ability to find what you need when you need it. All right, let's tackle the home office and make it work . . . for work!

PRODUCTS

Glass cleaner (see page 20)
Baking soda
Compressed air
Rubbing alcohol
Electronics cleaner (see page 124)
All-purpose cleaner (see page 16)
Disinfectant (optional)

TOOLS

Bin
High duster (see page 31)
At least 2 general-purpose microfiber cloths
Flat-weave microfiber cloth
Feather duster
Cleaning toothbrush
Cotton swabs
Vacuum cleaner with attachments
Mop and bucket (for tile, vinyl, and linoleum floors) or flat mop and spray bottle (for stone, wood, and laminate floors)

Wave 1

In the first wave, we'll do the same as we always do: collect stuff that doesn't belong and straighten up the space in preparation for the second wave—where we'll *actually* clean. Now beware: in the office, the first wave can suck you into a bit of an organizing rabbit hole. You may get spontaneously inspired to file, shred, organize, or declutter. I know, *not me*, you're thinking. But I've seen it happen—*especially* in the office, so be prepared. Now, if this does happen, you might be surprised to hear me say this: I want you to go off-track like a wild stallion and genuinely embrace this moment. Inspiration like this is a golden opportunity not to be missed. When it happens to me and I go on an organizing spurt in my office, I don't question it; I just focus and ride the wave for as long as it carries me. The efforts can really pay off. But promise me this: once you're done with your spontaneous organizing rampage, just get back to the rest of the office cleaning, and you'll be doubly thrilled. It's very exciting. Okay. Let's get to wave 1.

TIDY AND ORGANIZE (5 to 10 minutes)

Grab a bin and place it in the middle of the room. Starting at 12 o'clock, work your way around the space and start to collect items that don't belong in the room. You may notice that you need to find a home for certain items, like a backpack (an over-the-door hook is a great solution) or piles of mail (how about a physical in-box?). While you're going around and doing this, straighten piles of paper and try to make the piles make sense. Group like items together; for example, all letters together, all receipts together, all magazines together. Then straighten up the piles neatly; stagger-stack them and line them up parallel and perpendicular to the edge of the surface. Depending on how cluttered your office space is currently, you may spend as much time in wave 1 as you will in wave 2, but it's worth it.

Wave 2

Here's where the rubber meets the road for office cleaning. We've got a good amount of ground to cover; but it's simple work, and once you know how to do it, you'll be able to do it efficiently. And the more you clean your office, as in, the more you stay on top of things, the less dust you'll have to deal with. Also, as you go around and clean, think about the actual stuff in the office—what can you organize? What can you get rid of? This is your time! We'll work our way from top to bottom, as we do, paying special attention to those dusty areas and electronics.

HIGH DUSTING (90 seconds)

You know the drill. We always want dust to fall to the bottom—we'll catch it when we're vacuuming!

1. Head to 12 o'clock with your high duster and walk around the room, gently moving it around the moldings and getting into ceiling corners, as well as any other high areas.

2. Run your duster along the top of any doorframes and across air vents. If you notice the vents are super dusty, make a mental

note and vacuum the vents when you've got your vacuum out in wave 3, using the brush attachment.

3. Here, or in any other room with books and bookshelves, run your high duster along the exposed top of the bookshelf.

CLEANING AND DUSTING

Now, head back to 12 o'clock and work your way around the room, section by section, looking up and down, cleaning as you go with the steps outlined below. Complete each task listed according to the layout of your space. Remember to use one general-purpose microfiber cloth for any of the wet work and the dry one for buffing and polishing up (the plush microfiber cloth works great for this!). Your electronics will be cleaned using the flat-weave cloth.

Mirrors and Windows (90 seconds per glass surface)

1. Spray the glass lightly with glass cleaner.

2. Fold a flat-weave cloth into quarters (this way you have a few dry sides to use for buffing).

3. Using only one quarter of the cloth, start at the top left corner of the mirror and use the S-pattern motion to clean the mirror, going from top to bottom.

4. Flip the cloth to a dry quarter and repeat the S-pattern, retracing your steps from top to bottom. This helps dry the glass and finishes the job streak-free.

5. Using yet another dry quarter of the cloth, look for streaks and marks using the light, and gently buff them out as you see them.

Windows and Window Coverings (see page 50)

I hope you have a window in your office. And if you do, you know how important it is to bring that natural light in and look at the view. While you don't need to do windows all the time, cleaning them every now and again will help keep the space light, fresh, and inspirational (even if you're doing taxes!). See page 50 for details on how to handle windowsills and blinds and their coverings.

DUST: WHAT IS THE DEAL?

We release two billion dead skin cells—which amounts to about a handful of breakfast cereal—each day. Gross. That just lingers around; dust mites feed on that delicious dinner and then poop out their business, which then becomes part of the dust as well. Add to that anything that comes in from the outside, plus tiny food crumbs and pet dander and hair. And I'm sure other foul things, too—I haven't spent time in a lab evaluating dust bunny contents, but it's easy to use your imagination. Dust contributes in large part to so-called sick building syndrome, the headaches, nausea, itchy eyes, and more serious respiratory illnesses that can plague those who work in offices with too little fresh-air circulation and too much dust and other indoor air pollution. So for real. Let's take it seriously.

Picture Frames and Artwork (30 to 60 seconds per piece)

College degrees, kids' artwork, treasured photos of a beach you'd rather be on, beautiful prints, and everything in between—the office is a great space to hang nice things. I mean, we need something nice to stare at while we work, right?

1. Place one hand on the bottom corner of the frame to support it while cleaning.

2. Use a microfiber cloth lightly dampened with all-purpose cleaner and wipe the top of the frame from left to right.

3. Repeat for each horizontal edge of the frame (left, right).

4. If the glass is dusty, wipe it with a dry general-purpose microfiber cloth.

5. Check the glass for any spots or fingerprints. If dirty, spray glass cleaner onto the glass and wipe clean with the flat-weave microfiber cloth. If there's just a spot that's noticeable, simply spray the cloth with glass cleaner and use the cloth wrapped around your pointer finger to buff out the spot. No use in cleaning more than needed!

6. Buff dry any wet spots to remove streaks.

Walls (10 seconds per mark)

Please note: Matte or flat paint may mark up if cleaned too vigorously. Please test this method in a small hidden area first.

1. Using a microfiber cloth dampened with all-purpose cleaner, give the stained area a quick wipe and buff dry. (Many times, a stain will come off with this treatment and you won't need to use anything more powerful.)

2. If the stain doesn't budge, sprinkle a pinch of baking soda on a small corner of your dampened cloth and begin to gently rub the stained area. Work gently, because anything too vigorous can actually remove the paint. Wipe well, then remove any remaining baking soda residue with a dry cloth.

Horizontal Surfaces (1 to 5 minutes per piece)

The surfaces in offices tend to be mostly wood, laminate, or glass for the desk, and metal and plastic filing cabinets and organizing bins. However, if you have a beautiful wood desk with a leather blotter, you're going to clean it the same way as any other surface in the office. It's a simple move: remove items, clean the surface, clean the items properly, and replace.

1. At 12 o'clock, start at the top of the room and pick the highest surface you need to clean. Work your way down to lower surfaces (as in, do the tall cabinet before the waist-high desk in the same section). Section by section, here's what to do:

a. Remove all removable items from a given surface (including electronics), keeping them in a safe area. Items such as monitors and printers can stay where they are. If you wish, you can remove these once or twice a year, but they are okay to just stay put most of the time (no one's really checking!).

b. Spray the surface where possible using an all-purpose cleaner (or for a glass surface, use a glass cleaner). Areas with grimy buildup and food stains can soak for a moment or two before wiping. If the area can't be sprayed because of the proximity to electronics, liberally spray your general-purpose microfiber cloth instead. Wipe the surface using an S-pattern. Remember, if the area is super dusty, start by dusting the surface with a *dry* general-purpose microfiber cloth; this will help make the wet cleaning significantly easier and you won't have any of that sticky dust residue left behind.

c. Follow that up by quickly buffing dry the surface with a dry general-purpose microfiber cloth (you don't want to put anything back on a damp surface, as it can warp wood; also, buffing it dry helps remove any remaining debris and moisture, giving you that gorgeous, streak-free shine).

d. Clean and replace items and piles:

   i. Pick up any item that isn't papers or electronics (such as an accessory or décor item) that belongs on that surface and hold it securely with one hand.

   ii. Dust and wipe clean with a damp cloth.

   iii. Buff dry to remove streaks and replace the item— thankfully you have already tidied, so you know where this is going to go. Remember to line the item up neatly, parallel or perpendicular to the edge of a surface.

   iv. For piles of papers, assemble the pile neatly and tap it on a flat surface a few times to make it nice and even. Group like items together and then stagger-stack to keep things sorted and tidy.

HOW TO CLEAN AN OFFICE CHAIR (2 TO 10 MINUTES)

Remember to always spot-check methods in an inconspicuous spot to avoid surprising color changes. For leather, wipe down weekly with a dry microfiber cloth. If it needs a little more attention, wipe with a cotton cloth moistened with leather conditioner (see page 21) according to the package instructions; buff dry with a dry cloth. For mesh, vacuum the chair regularly (remember to do this part in wave 3!), and spot-clean any dirt or stains with a cloth dampened with soapy water, then blot with a water-dampened cloth, and then a dry cloth to soak up as much moisture as possible.

For fabric, check the label to see if it bears a *W* (for water-based cleaner), *S* (for solvent cleaner), *SW* or *WS* (for either), *C* (for Crypton cleaner), or *X* (for professional cleaner). For *W* upholstery, vacuum first, dab on a mild soapy solution over stains or dirt, then blot dry. For *S*, dampen a cloth with your solvent and gently blot over the stain. For *SW/WS* fabrics, I recommend starting with the gentlest option (the water method) and working your way up as necessary. Crypton fabric can be cleaned with water methods or with specialized Crypton cleaner, but not with solvents. You can scrub the soapy water or cleaner into the stain with a brush, allowing it to soak into the fabric, and rinse well to remove residues. Use a clean towel to blot out as much moisture as possible.

Books and Bookshelves (2 to 10 minutes per shelf, depending on how in-depth)

1. As part of your regular cleaning routine, you'll want to wipe down the exposed parts of bookshelves like any other horizontal surface.

2. When you want to dust the tops of books, a feather duster will be your best bet. Wipe the shelf in front of the books after; the duster will have pushed a significant amount of dust forward.

3. Several times a year, you'll want to slide out the books and fully dust the shelves with a dampened microfiber cloth. Make sure to buff any moisture completely dry before returning the books to the shelf.

ELECTRONICS

News reporters just love writing about how dirty office electronics are. And it's true, our electronics harbor a ton of bacteria, dirt, dead skin cells, old food, and oil. Seriously, I just played with my hair and scratched my ear while writing this very paragraph. Now, most of the time the bacteria is harmless. But over time, this stuff builds up. And if I was sick, I would transfer my germs onto the keyboard and voilà, there they would be, founding a new colony. A U.K. consumer organization reported in a 2008 study that the average computer keyboard is generally up to five times dirtier than the average toilet seat (hello!). To keep your workspace healthy (not to mention, this stuff really bungs up your electronics over time), let's take a few and learn how to clean and care for our electronics properly.

Remember, each time you clean an electronic item, turn it off first!

Keyboard (3 minutes)

This will be one of the most disgusting, and thus gratifying, cleaning jobs you'll take on. Once you attack it with compressed air, you'll see heaps of stuff fly out, as if a blizzard were happening.

1. Turn off the keyboard and unplug if it is wired.

2. Tilt the keyboard straight up on its side onto an uncleaned surface; this will help the debris fall right out instead of right back into the keyboard.

3. With your can of compressed air, begin blasting the gaps between the keys in short strokes, working your way from top to bottom (and don't blow toward you—eww. Blow toward the surface!). The can might get super cold; if so, give it a break (don't shake it!).

4. Use a dry cleaning toothbrush and brush the areas between the keys as needed—do this if your keyboard still looks a bit grimy after the compressed air. Wipe the pile into the garbage—it

will probably be substantial. (You can even take a picture of your keyboard crap and put it on your social media accounts—#sogross.)

5. Lay the keyboard flat and take a cotton swab dampened with rubbing alcohol (not soaking, just damp); clean the areas between the keys and those tiny crevices. If the cotton swab turns brown or black (try not to faint), change it up as needed.

6. Spray a general-purpose cloth lightly with electronics cleaner (spraying away from the keyboard) and wipe the keyboard, ensuring the key tops and plastic panels are being cleaned. Clean the back, too; just the other day I flipped over my keyboard and I saw a bunch of buildup on the bottom from sliding around my desk. I'm always discovering new places to clean.

Mouse (1 minute)

A mouse is quite simple to clean as well—it's an easier version of the keyboard.

1. Unplug the mouse or turn it off.

2. Use a dry cleaning toothbrush to gently brush away debris from the crevices and small openings where plastic parts meet up (typically where you can click a mouse button).

3. Lightly spray a general-purpose microfiber cloth with electronics cleaner and wipe down the mouse, top and bottom.

4. Pay particular attention to the area around the small nubs at the bottom that allow the mouse to slide around—these tend to build up dirt over time. If needed, use a cotton swab dipped in rubbing alcohol to remove this grimy buildup.

5. Use a cotton swab dipped in rubbing alcohol to get into the small crevices of the mouse if there is still remaining gunk; simply trace the crevice with the cotton swab and you'll get that stuff out.

Monitor (2 minutes)

Monitors need to be treated in a particular way, but once you know how to do it, it's easy-peasy. Many times, I have heard of people using cleaning wipes or glass cleaner to clean their monitors, and they're left with awful streaking and spotting. Flat-panel monitors are not designed to be cleaned with any products. Here's the right way to do it:

1. Use a flat-weave microfiber cloth to dry-dust the entire monitor, base, and frame—wipe from top to bottom using an S-pattern. Oftentimes, this will be sufficient. While dusting, take note of any spots or fingerprints that need additional cleaning. Look at the monitor in various angles, catching the light, to check for these.

2. Lightly spray a corner of your flat-weave microfiber cloth with water—as in, spritz it once or twice with water. Tap the cloth quickly on your hand to remove excess moisture.

3. Stick your pointer finger into the dampened corner and gently buff out any fingerprints or marks with your finger. Be gentle— use the same pressure as you would to rub your eye. By buffing a small area, you will concentrate your efforts and quickly lift off the stain or mark. Continue to do this until the mess is gone.

4. Wipe the area dry with a dry corner of the cloth.

Computer Speakers (1 minute per speaker)

Speakers rarely need more than a good wipe-down with a dampened microfiber cloth. Just pick up each one (being careful not to move them around too much and disrupt the funky wire setup), wipe it gently, and re-place. However, if your speakers are super-duper dusty, here's what to do:

1. Unplug the speakers.

2. Vacuum the grille of each speaker using the brush attachment, paying particular attention to dusty buildup.

3. Fold a general-purpose microfiber cloth into quarters and dampen

one side with all-purpose cleaner. Give each speaker a quick wipe-down with the damp side.

4. Finish up by buffing dry the speaker with a dry portion of the cloth.

Printer (1 minute)

Printers can get dusty on top, plus they can have small ink leaks internally that over time clog up all the gears (*that's not annoying*). Luckily, many printers these days have a self-cleaning setting that takes care of internal maintenance; if there is stubborn ink buildup on the print heads, you may need to dampen a paper towel with some alcohol, then rub it gently over the staining until it lifts away. A cotton swab dipped in alcohol can help get ink out of any crevices. While you have the printer open, use some compressed air to get any dust out of the guts.

Computer Tower (2 minutes)

If you speak to a tech wizard, they'll tell you to unscrew the back panel of the computer and vacuum the fans. I'm not going there with you, because I wouldn't take that on myself. Vacuuming the back vent occasionally will keep most of the dust out of a computer. If you find that your computer's fan is roaring like a steam engine and your computer gets hot and starts to slow down, consider taking it to get professionally cleaned at a computer shop, where they will take apart your computer, clean the components, and replace them.

To clean the exterior of your computer tower, here's what to do:

1. Start by unplugging the computer and various components (speakers, mouse, keyboard, LAN cable, monitors, printer).

2. Fit your vacuum with the brush attachment and begin to gently vacuum the entire backside of the computer. Pay special attention and be extra gentle around any vented areas.

3. Lift up the computer and clean the area where it sits; it will likely be insanely dusty. If the computer is sitting on a carpet, you will

likely want to use a regular vacuum attachment for this or even a rubber broom, as the dust will be practically cemented into the carpet.

4. Fold a general-purpose microfiber cloth into quarters and dampen one side with all-purpose cleaner. Give the plastic parts of the exterior tower a quick wipe-down with the damp side, avoiding the back panel.

5. Finish up by buffing dry the tower with a dry portion of the cloth.

Telephone (1 to 2 minutes)

If you still have a landline, you probably have a phone in your home office. You know, for calling the bank and staying on hold for thirty-four minutes. The phone especially needs love—not only does it have buttons, but it's got an earpiece *and* a mouthpiece. Oh mother. The mouthpiece is millimeters away from our dirty, dirty mouths and that mouthpiece is a museum of your and your family's oral bacteria. Now again, don't sweat it, because most of the time it's NBD, but every now and again, this bacterial Smithsonian needs a cleaning.

1. Stand up the phone over an uncleaned surface so that it is sitting 90 degrees to the ground. Using a cleaning toothbrush, brush out any debris from between the keys.

2. Dip a cotton swab into rubbing alcohol (it shouldn't be dripping) and use it to clean the small holes and area surrounding the earpiece. Brace yourself: the swab will turn brown.

3. Use the other side of the cotton swab and do the same for the mouthpiece.

4. Fold a general-purpose microfiber cloth into quarters and spray one quarter with all-purpose cleaner.

5. Wipe the phone exterior thoroughly with the cloth, paying attention to the receiver, earpiece, and mouthpiece. Be sure to lift up the phone and clean underneath as well.

6. Using a dry portion of the cloth, buff dry the phone.

7. If you have a charging base for the phone, clean the base by repeating steps 4 through 6.

Tablet (30 to 60 seconds)

A tablet is basically a walking point of contact; we're touching it all the time! Thankfully, a microfiber cloth with a touch of water can remove bacteria and grease effectively, or if there's more than a fingerprint or two, feel free to swap out water for electronics cleaner. Using products on touchscreens isn't advised; there are specialized coatings on your electronics that can come off over time if a product is used. Microfiber will take care of most of the bacteria and grease for you. I clean my touch-screens weekly, just because I can. It's easy and convenient; especially because I leave a flat-weave cloth at my desk! The same method can be applied to a smartphone.

1. Fold a flat-weave microfiber cloth into quarters and lightly spray one quarter with water. Tap the cloth on the back of your hand to remove excess moisture.

2. Remove the tablet from a case, if any.

3. Lay the tablet on a flat surface and secure it with one hand, and with the other hand wipe the tablet from top to bottom in an S-pattern using moderate pressure.

4. Flip over the tablet and repeat on the backside.

5. For any remaining streaks, marks, or dirt, spray a bit more water onto a small corner of the cloth and place your pointer finger in the cloth, then buff out the spot.

6. Flip over your cloth to a dry quarter and repeat the S-pattern wipe to buff it dry and remove any moisture or remaining streaks.

YES, REALLY, JUST WATER!

I know what you're thinking: I give my blessing that a swipe of the microfiber will remove bacteria? Well, don't take it from me, take it from the *Wall Street Journal.* They reported in 2014 that water-dampened microfiber cloths were enough to remove viruses and bacteria in many cases. So when protecting delicate coatings on screens are an issue, I reach for nothing more than just that.

Laptop (2 to 5 minutes)

My laptop and I spend almost every day together. I eat in front of it (I know, I know), I shop on it, I am writing this book on it, I interact with the Clean My Space audience on it, and I run my businesses from it. Despite my best efforts to keep it clean, my laptop gets covered in food splatters, fingerprints, cat hair, crumbs, and stains. And I know yours does, too. I happen to have a hard-shell case for mine, which protects it from scratches and damage, and I think it was a wise investment, especially given how easy it is to keep clean. Cleaning your laptop and case is something that you should do every so often, especially if you use your laptop as much as I do. If you notice your keys sound or feel funny and have dark spots between them, the screen is practically blurred, and the plastic or metal components look dull, that's a good sign it is time to clean your laptop. Clean it on top of a yet-to-be-cleaned surface.

1. Always consult your user manual first, to learn of preferred techniques, along with dos or don'ts.

2. Shut down and turn off your laptop and unplug anything in the ports.

3. Use compressed air to blow dust out of any fan vents.

4. Spray a general-purpose microfiber cloth with electronics cleaner until just barely damp; tap the cloth on your hand to blot off excess moisture.

5. Wipe down the exterior of the laptop, over and under; buff dry.

6. Use the compressed air to blast out as many crumbs from the keyboard as possible.

7. Use the general-purpose cloth slightly dampened, then wrung dry, to wipe away the finger oils and splatters on the keyboard (use gentle strokes that touch only the keys here—no mashing the cloth into the crevices). Find a dry corner of the cloth and buff everything dry. Clean the track pad in the same manner.

8. Wipe the screen with a dry flat-weave microfiber cloth.

9. Use compressed air (or a pipe cleaner!) to remove dust from ports.

POINTS OF CONTACT (2 minutes)

We've covered the most pertinent points of contact in the office, the electronics. There are still the standard ones we need to take into consideration, but boy, won't those seem like a breeze now that we've been going crazy with the compressed air?

Please note: Light switch plates connect to an electrical source, meaning they cannot be sprayed directly. Please spray the cloth, then wipe.

1. Spray the point of contact (unless it is a light switch) with an all-purpose cleaner and wipe clean.

2. Treat with disinfectant according to the bottle's directions, if using.

BASEBOARDS (5 minutes)

In the office, especially close to the computer, your baseboards are going to get *dus-tay*. And while I know that most wires are buried underneath a desk and can be practically impossible to access, every now and again, do what you can to sneak under the desk with a vacuum and a crevice tool just to clean things up around there. There is a slight risk to having a bunch of cords hanging around dust; if a power cord's protective rubber coating is frayed or loosened, the metal wire, when plugged in, can become exposed to dust and lead to fires (hey, the more you know . . .). So every now and then, perhaps monthly, vacuum that area and keep the cords and baseboards as dust-free as you can.

1. As you complete each section of the room, the last place you'll check before moving clockwise to your next section will be the baseboards. Eyeball the area quickly. No dust? Move on. Dust? See below.

2. For areas with furniture and cables, clean the baseboards by simply running the vacuum fitted with the crevice attachment along the edge. Be careful to not suction up any cords or components.

3. For areas that are free and clear of cords, use a microfiber cloth slightly dampened with all-purpose cleaner and wipe a section of baseboard from left to right.

4. Slightly move furniture or items if possible to get to the baseboards and remove any dust bunnies before vacuuming.

Wave 3

Yay! Have you come to love those words—*wave 3*—as much as I do yet? We're just about done. So grab yourself that iced macchiato you stashed in the fridge and keep moving.

FLOORS

Vacuuming (7 to 10 minutes)

Please note: Use the appropriate vacuum attachment and settings and ensure that the bag or canister is empty to provide you with the best vacuum possible.

1. Move all items that might obstruct vacuuming out of the room temporarily to a location adjacent to the room you are in.

2. Plug in your vacuum as close to the exit point of the room as possible.

3. Vacuum all upholstered items first (remove cushions, vacuum, replace properly).

4. Vacuum the perimeter of the room using the crevice tool (if the room is carpeted wall-to-wall).

5. Head to the opposite corner of the room with the appropriate attachment for the floor and begin to vacuum using the W-pattern, breaking the room into sections as necessary to maintain the pattern.

6. Once you have vacuumed your way out of the room, replace any items you removed back to their original locations (if you need to mop, do not do this yet).

Mopping (where required; 2 to 3 minutes)
See page 52 for details on mopping.

And that's it! If your cleaned home office isn't the coziest spot you've ever seen to get work done in at this point, then I don't know what.

CHAPTER 10

hallways, staircases, and other passageways

I think the whole reason I absolutely, positively despise vacuuming has to do with the bitter memories I have of vacuuming our main staircase as a kid. That was one of my chores. I recall struggling with that beast of a 1990s extra-large canister vacuum on our salmon-pink staircase. Carrying it up the stairs, resting it on a stair, trying to maneuver the nozzle just so, occasionally allowing the vacuum to tumble down the stairs (I suppose it speaks to the durability of vacuums—it kept on working), and having to repeat this thirteen, yes, thirteen times—once for each step on that staircase. Needless to say, by the time I was done vacuuming the stairs, I was a puddle of sweat and rage.

Well, there is a better way, and once you put it into action, cleaning these spaces becomes downright satisfying.

We'll still use the basic tasks you've learned how to do so well in the other spaces in your home. Talk about transferrable skills! The main points of focus will be scuffs and marks on the walls, dust, cobwebs, and clutter. It's easy stuff, I promise!

THE HALLWAY AND STAIRCASE: EXPRESS CLEAN (5 TO 10 MINUTES)

The Express Clean won't vary much from the actual clean here. We'll leave out some of the heavier work, but really, cleaning a hallway or a staircase takes mere minutes.

Air it out. Open windows or crack open the door a bit, weather permitting, to let in fresh air.

Mini wave 1: Starting on the top floor, collect anything that doesn't belong. Repeat on the staircase and then the bottom floor. (All stray items can be put away at the end.)

Finish with floors. Do a quick sweep or vacuum. Mop, if you have time. Start at the area farthest from the door and vacuum or mop your way out.

Ditch the bin. Finally, grab that bin and deal with its contents. Take trash and dishes and glasses to the kitchen, books to the bookcase, and old papers and magazines to the recycling bin.

THE HALLWAY AND STAIRCASE: TOP-TO-BOTTOM CLEAN

I'd suggest keeping your products and tools in a fairly central spot and doing all hallways on the same floor at one time instead of breaking them up. I also like to do my staircase before I clean the lower floor it is connected to; that way, any dust that falls from the staircase can be easily caught by the vacuum instead of getting sprinkled all over my clean floors. (It's really just a giant, house-wide version of my motto of cleaning from the top down.)

PRODUCTS	TOOLS
Glass cleaner (see page 20)	Bin
All-purpose cleaner (see page 16)	High-dusting tool (see page 31)
Baking soda	Ostrich-feather duster plus an extender pole
Disinfectant (optional)	Handheld vacuum or rubber broom
	Flat-weave microfiber cloth
	General-purpose microfiber cloths
	Vacuum
	Mop and bucket (for tile, vinyl, and linoleum floors) or flat mop and spray bottle (for stone, wood, and laminate floors)

Wave 1

TIDY AND ORGANIZE (3 to 5 minutes)

This wave is going to be lightning-fast, because these areas tend to not get very cluttered. But just in case, get a bin or tray and walk around these areas quickly in a circular pattern starting on the top floor, then the staircase, and finishing with the lower floor, picking up anything that doesn't belong. If anything is out of place, straighten it up and move on.

Wave 2

Pick the top of the stairs as your 12 o'clock starting point and work your way around that floor until you get back to your starting point, then move on to the staircase, then the lower floor, making the bottom of the staircase your starting point for the lower level.

CLEANING A HIGH-UP CHANDELIER (5 TO 10 MINUTES)

Once or twice a year, you'll want to clean even those way-up-there chandeliers. The easiest thing is to get it clean with an extendable feather duster.

Remember to do this before you clean the staircase or the bottom floor. Turn the chandelier off and allow it to cool. Make sure you stand somewhere you feel safe and secure and begin gently dusting at the top of the chandelier; work your way down to the various tiers and components. Your dominant hand will be on the top part of the pole and will gently twist the pole to get the feathers to shake off the dust as you guide the pole with your nondominant hand. Be sure to get any cobwebs you see along the way.

HIGH DUSTING (2 to 5 minutes)

I love how so many two-story homes have open stairwells with high ceilings. Airy. You know who else loves high ceilings? Spiders. And they show their affection for the space by practically knitting hammocks up there. High dusting these areas will shake out those webs. When you're picking up, just pay attention to this area. If you see the spiders getting their patio furniture out, you'll know it's time to do some high dusting.

Please note: Lights should be turned off during high dusting to avoid popping any lightbulbs.

1. Head to your 12 o'clock starting point with your high duster or extended ostrich-feather duster and walk around the area, gently moving the high duster around the moldings, ceiling corners, and any other high areas. (If you are doing this by a staircase, choose a location and position that you feel safe and stable in, and stand in a static location while you move the duster around to pick up cobwebs. Ostrich-feather dusters are particularly good at capturing dust and cobwebs.) Tap it vigorously when you're done to shake off any goodies.

2. Repeat this for any air vents high up on the wall or in the ceiling.

MIRRORS AND WINDOWS (90 seconds per glass surface)

1. Spray the glass lightly with glass cleaner.

2. Fold a flat-weave cloth into quarters (this way you have a few dry sides to use for buffing).

3. Using only one quarter of the cloth, start at the top left corner of the mirror and use the S-pattern motion to clean the mirror, going from top to bottom.

4. Flip the cloth to a dry quarter and repeat the S-pattern, retracing your steps from top to bottom. This helps dry the glass and finishes the job streak-free.

5. Using yet another dry quarter of the cloth, look for streaks and marks using the light, and gently buff them out as you see them.

WINDOWSILLS AND BLINDS (see page 50)

PICTURE FRAMES AND ARTWORK (30 to 60 seconds per piece)

1. Place one hand on the bottom corner of the frame to support it while cleaning.

2. Use a microfiber cloth lightly dampened with all-purpose cleaner and wipe the top of the frame from left to right.

3. Repeat for each horizontal edge of the frame (left, right).

4. If dusty, wipe the glass with a dry general-purpose microfiber cloth.

5. Check the glass for any spots or fingerprints. If dirty, spray glass cleaner onto the glass and wipe clean with the flat-weave microfiber cloth. If there's just a spot that's noticeable, simply spray the cloth with glass cleaner and use the cloth wrapped around your pointer finger to buff out the spot.

6. Buff dry any wet spots to remove streaks.

CHALK IT UP

Another great move for removing fingerprints on the walls, if these methods don't work, is to run a piece of white chalk over any greasy areas; the chalk will absorb the grease. A few moments later, brush away the dust and wipe the area with a cloth dipped in soapy water.

WALLS (10 seconds per mark)

Please note: Matte or flat paint may mark up if cleaned too vigorously. Please test this method in a small hidden area first.

1. Using a microfiber cloth dampened with all-purpose cleaner, give the stained area a quick wipe and buff dry. (Many times, a stain will come off with this treatment and you won't need to use anything more powerful.)

2. If the stain doesn't budge, sprinkle a pinch of baking soda on a small corner of your dampened cloth and begin to gently rub the stained area. Work gently, because anything too vigorous can actually remove the paint. Wipe well, then remove any remaining baking soda residue with a dry cloth.

STAIRCASE (5 to 15 minutes)

Staircases get really dusty in their own special ways. Carpeted staircases that rarely get cleaned properly will have darkened edges where the tread (the flat part that you step on) meets the riser (the vertical part). And the areas around the bannister also get darkened from dust being absorbed in the crevices, too. This is no classy ombré look—it's a problem. Generally, vacuuming is ideal for carpeted stair maintenance; however, there are so many tight spots that are hard to reach with the vacuum, plus schlepping a vacuum up and down stairs is practically an *American Gladiators* challenge. I don't think it's reasonable to use a full-size vacuum, upright or canister, on a staircase.

A handheld vacuum is ideal for cleaning carpeted stairs. Look for one that comes with an automated brush attachment, similar to the beater bar on your regular vacuum (which is great for driving down into pile and bringing up ground-in debris; it also helps to reinvigorate your carpet). If you don't have a handheld vacuum, investing in a simple rubber broom will help drag out dirt, debris, and hair from the carpet on the stairs, which can be quickly vacuumed up at the bottom of the stairs.

Cleaning Hardwood Stairs with a Feather Duster

I recommend using an ostrich-feather duster. I've not found anything better for cleaning hardwood stairs. Otherwise, use a handheld broom.

1. Start at the top stair. Have an ostrich-feather duster in one hand and a general-purpose microfiber cloth dampened with floor cleaner in the other.

✓ PRO TIP! START AT THE TOP (AGAIN)!

When cleaning stairs, always start at the top stair and work your way to the bottom. And clean your stairs before you clean the lower floor—in other words, before the third wave of the lower floor. If you have a runner on your steps, you'll need to do a combo move of cleaning hardwood stairs and cleaning carpeted stairs—see pages 195 and 197 for details.

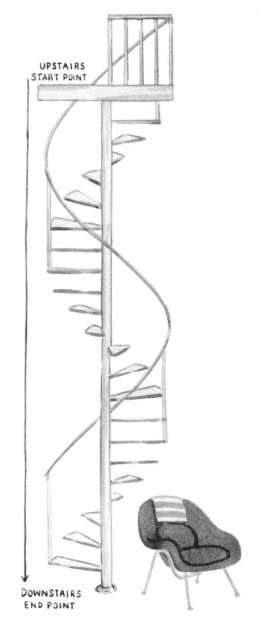

UPSTAIRS
START POINT

DOWNSTAIRS
END POINT

2. With the feather duster, start dusting in long strokes from left to right, getting into each crevice around the bannister spindles and bringing the debris and dust to the center of the stair. When you get to the side with the baseboard, ensure you dust that as well. Push all the dust down to the next stair.

3. Quickly wipe the step you have just dusted with the dampened cloth. You can also wipe the riser or clean up any marks on the baseboards or wall as you go, if you see any.

4. Move down a step and repeat steps (ha!) 2 to 4.

5. When you get to the bottom, leave the dust pile in an obvious space so that you can easily vacuum it up when you're cleaning the floor.

6. On your way upstairs, take a clean microfiber cloth sprayed with all-purpose cleaner and wipe the bannister. Then treat with disinfectant according to the instructions on the bottle, if desired.

Cleaning Carpeted Stairs with a Handheld Vacuum

Use the appropriate brush attachment and keep the crevice tool handy to get into the areas around the spindles. Here are the "hard-core" cleaning instructions (steps 1 and 2), which you can do every month or so, and the light cleaning (steps 3 through 7) you can do in between.

1. Start at the top stair and use the crevice tool to strategically clean the "borders" of the step. This includes areas around each spindle, the seam where the riser meets the tread, and then the baseboard and the area where the stair meets the wall (if it is up against a wall). Don't worry about the rest of the step right now—we'll get to that in step 3. Just focus on anything you can do with the crevice tool. It's much easier to do this all in one shot, rather than having to keep changing your tools out.

2. Repeat this task for each step.

3. Head back up to the first step and change out your vacuum head to a roller-brush attachment, size permitting. Otherwise use a brush attachment.

4. Vacuum the riser first (that's the part that is vertical on a stair) in a left-to-right pattern.

5. Then vacuum the tread using a front to back stroke (I find you can get more coverage this way than left-to-right strokes, but seriously, no one's awarding style points here).

6. Repeat until each step is complete.

7. On your way upstairs, take a clean microfiber cloth sprayed with all-purpose cleaner and wipe the bannister as you go. Treat with disinfectant if desired.

Cleaning Carpeted Stairs with a Rubber Broom

Rubber brooms on carpets pack a surprisingly powerful punch. Rubber creates friction and helps draw out ground-in hair and debris, and the bristles really dig into the fibers, while also helping to even out and fluff up the pile. This requires a bit of getting used to, but once you do, it's sort of addicting to see how much crap you can rake out of your carpets. It's gross, but you can't look away. If you want a little more power, slightly dampen the rubber bristles for major friction.

1. Head to the top stair. In one hand, have a microfiber cloth lightly dampened with water, and in the other, have a rubber broom.

2. Place the rubber broom on the tread. Using firm pressure, use short strokes starting at the back of the tread and pulling the rubber broom toward you.

3. Repeat this motion several times as you move from left to right on the tread, and you'll see debris and hair start to come up. Pick up the clump and place it in a bag, or toss it down into a large general pile that you'll vacuum up later.

4. Get into the small crevices with the rubber broom as best you can: the area where the tread meets the riser, the area with spindles, etc.

5. Wipe the baseboard with the damp cloth.

6. Repeat steps 1 through 5 for each stair (it takes less time than it sounds like).

7. When you get to the bottom, remember to vacuum up that crusty pile when you're cleaning the floor.

8. On your way upstairs, take a clean microfiber cloth sprayed with all-purpose cleaner and wipe the bannister as you go. Treat with disinfectant, if desired.

✓ **PRO TIP: TOUCH UP PAINT!** If you keep a little can of touch-up paint on hand and cover up any nicks as they happen, your walls will always look fresh and clean, as opposed to strong contenders for a "before" shot in a home makeover TV show. Every three months, take out your can of paint and a brush and give yourself 10 minutes to scan the house and touch up nicks. You'll be maintaining your paint with next to no time spent, and your walls will look great.

HORIZONTAL SURFACES (1 to 2 minutes)

Unless you're living in a European castle, I'm doubtful that you have very much furniture in your hallways. And even if you do have some, I'm doubtful that it will need much by way of cleaning, since it is likely occasional furniture. As you see fit, take a few moments to dust the furniture and keep it looking good.

Please note: Focus on dusting and cleaning horizontal and angled surfaces, since vertical surfaces don't get as dusty or dirty. Also, ensure you are using the right tools and products for a given surface to avoid damage.

1. Have two general-purpose microfiber cloths and all-purpose cleaner handy.

2. Remove all removable items from a given surface, keeping them in a safe area and remembering where they should be replaced.

3. Use your dry, or wet then dry, cloth to dust and clean (removing both debris and marks) using an S-pattern. Buff dry if necessary.

4. Pick up any item that belongs on that surface, hold it securely with one hand, and

    a. dust and wipe it with a damp cloth, then

    b. buff dry to remove streaks and replace it where it belongs.

    c. Now, move down to the next surface or item and repeat steps 2 through 6.

POINTS OF CONTACT (switch plates, door handles, knobs, locks, and rails; 2 minutes)

Please note: Light switch plates connect to an electrical source, meaning they cannot be sprayed directly. Please spray a cloth, then wipe clean.

1. Spray the point of contact with all-purpose cleaner and wipe clean.

2. Treat with disinfectant according to the bottle's instructions, if desired.

BASEBOARDS (5 to 10 minutes)

Your baseboards in the hallway will get quite dusty, being a high-traffic zone. I know I don't always say pay attention to these, but in this case, pay attention to these! They are not generally obstructed by furniture, so they (and their dusty fur coats) are super visible. You want them sparkling. If they are just a tad dusty, use your high-dusting tool. If the baseboards are quite dusty, use the vacuum with a brush instead. And, if the baseboards require some actual cleaning (i.e., dirt or splattered food—what were you doing with that smoothie in the hallway, anyway?), use a microfiber cloth dampened with some all-purpose cleaner to wipe them instead. Who knew there were so many options when it came to baseboard cleaning? Me. I did. I knew that. And now you do, too.

1. Trace the baseboards with the low-dusting tool as you walk around the room. Have a dampened general-purpose microfiber cloth along with you as you do this.

2. Note any areas with stains or marks, and clean those as you go with your dampened cloth—just give the area a quick spot-clean.

3. Slightly move furniture or items if possible to reach the baseboards and remove any dust bunnies before vacuuming.

For very dusty baseboards:

1. Wait until wave 3, and use a dust-brush attachment on your vacuum to clean the baseboards.

2. Work your way around the room using the tool, just focusing on baseboards.

3. Take a general-purpose microfiber cloth dampened with all-purpose cleaner along with you and wipe any stains or marks that might be revealed after vacuuming.

TRUE STORY!

I was recently at a girlfriend's house when she bashfully pulled me upstairs to her hallway. She asked me, *"Why are my carpets gray right up against the baseboards?"* I tried to be as delicate as possible; I crouched down and ran my finger along the edge of the carpet where it met the baseboard. To her amazement and horror, a huge ball of dust came up. I told her all she needed to do was vacuum the edges before she vacuumed the rest of the space and the problem would be solved. We then went back downstairs to rejoin the rest of the girls and never spoke of the incident again.

Wave 3

By this time, your hallway is looking pretty fabulous. Floors are the only thing left to do! And you're on wave 3, so, you know, time to (almost) celebrate.

VACUUMING (not including stairs; 7 to 10 minutes)

Depending on whether you have hard floors or carpets, this may be the last stop for you. If you have rugs, refer to the section in the dining room (on page 80). Paying particular attention to the area where the floor meets the baseboard is key here, since hallways and staircases accumulate a lot of dust. Even if you have hard floors in your hallways, I still recommend vacuuming, since it removes dust and debris that will easily get tracked into other parts of the house if not removed.

1. Move all items that can obstruct vacuuming out of the way temporarily to a location adjacent to the space you are in.

2. Plug in your vacuum as close to the exit point of the space as possible.

3. If you have anything upholstered, vacuum this first using the upholstery attachment.

4. Now, attach the crevice tool and vacuum the area where the floor meets the baseboard and any corners you find, including those around the top or bottom of a staircase—these are tricky areas that rarely get cleaned. If you come across any vents, vacuum these as well.

5. Assemble the vacuum with the appropriate floor tool—one with a beater bar for carpets or one with a hard-floor brush.

6. Head to the opposite corner of where you've plugged in the vacuum and begin to vacuum sections of the hallway using the W-pattern. Each completed section should bring you closer to the outlet, until you vacuum yourself out of that space.

7. Once you have vacuumed your way out, replace any items you removed back in their original locations (if you need to mop, do not do this yet).

MOPPING (where required; 3 to 5 minutes)

I prefer to clean hard-floor stairs by hand, as I have explained on the previous page, so I'm only talking about hallways here, not the steps. (See pages 18 and 19 for details of cleaning solution and technique.)

Woo-hoo! Now your hallways and staircases are fit to be passed through a million times a day. Happy travels.

CHAPTER 11

storage spaces:
garage, laundry room, basement, attic, unfinished pantry, etc.

I don't know about you, but until I was an adult, I was terrified of my basement. I was positively convinced that it was haunted and that if I went down there, the horrifying ghost that waited only for me would materialize. Though things improved marginally once my family finished the basement (they painted the walls salmon, naturally), I still had to shake the Stephen King script playing in my head whenever my mother sent me down for a can of beans.

Though most adults have outgrown fears of a paranormal experience in the basement, many of us still on some tiny level dread these unfinished storage areas for their sheer unpleasantness. First off, basements and attics become black holes for our garbage—er, collectibles. And on top of that, they can get damp, dusty, and dirty.

Sure, these spaces aren't stylish or interesting, and we don't host friends and family in them, but keeping them clean is a good idea. So instead of just closing the door and forgetting about them, here's what you can do to maintain them from time to time, perhaps one to four times per year. You'll note that I broke this chapter's cleaning into two sections: one for unfinished spaces and one for finished spaces, so skip ahead accordingly.

UNFINISHED STORAGE SPACES: EXPRESS CLEAN (ESTIMATED TIME: 5 TO 15 MINUTES PER SPACE)

For unfinished spaces, it is really about cleaning the floors and dealing with clutter. Keep in mind, since these spaces aren't connected, they need to be done one at a time. While the needs of each space will differ, we'll cover some general moves and then go into more specifics for each space.

Air it out. If you have windows or a door to the outside in this space, open them, weather permitting, to let in fresh air.

Mini wave 1: Start at 12 o'clock with your bin and work your way around the room collecting anything that doesn't belong. Meanwhile, straighten or tidy anything that requires it.

Speed-sort. If you are cleaning a cellar pantry area, consider quickly organizing cans and packages to look neater. If you're in a laundry room, line up and tidy bottles and packages of product, and place any dirty clothing in a dirty clothing pile, and clean clothing in a clean clothing pile (baskets are best). Place the basket of clean stuff by the door, so that it's out of the way and will remind you to deal with it when you leave the room.

Line up storage bins. If you have storage bins, stack and pile them neatly—line the perimeter of the room with these and leave the center of the floor clear as best you can.

Finish with floors. Use a natural-bristle broom for a basement or cold cellar, a larger push broom for a garage, or a vacuum for a laundry room. Start at one corner and vacuum or sweep vigorously, forming a pile of debris and taking it along with you toward the door or exit point. Then sweep up in a dustpan.

Don't forget. For extra points in the laundry room, vacuum the dryer lint trap, too: remove the trap and use the crevice tool to get as much of the dust out of the slot as you can.

Ditch the bin. Finally, grab that bin and deal with its contents. Take trash and dishes and glasses to the kitchen, books to the bookcase, and old papers and magazines to the recycling bin.

UNFINISHED STORAGE SPACES: TOP-TO-BOTTOM CLEAN

Since we don't spend oodles of time in these spaces, we can breeze through them. They are also a little grosser and dirtier, so prepare!

PRODUCTS

Glass cleaner

Mold inhibitor (see page 23)

All-purpose cleaner (page 16)

Baking soda

Mild dish soap

TOOLS

Work gloves with a rubber grip

Face mask for very dirty areas

Protective eyewear

Drop cloth

Shop vacuum, including the dust-brush attachment, filter, and vacuum bags

High-dusting tool (Instead of a microfiber cloth this time, flip an old sock inside-out to make one—the terry material is quite grippy for cobwebs and is easier to wash, plus the stakes are lower—should something really gross get caught in an old sock, you don't have to toss out a good microfiber cloth.)

Paper towels

Cleaning toothbrush

Natural-bristle broom

Plush microfiber cloths

Iron-handled scrub brush

Heavy-duty push broom

Dustpan

Yacht mop or flat-head mop

Wringer bucket

Wave 1

TIDY AND ORGANIZE (5 to 30 minutes, depending on the space)

Wear work gloves and possibly a face mask to protect you from breathing in debris and mold (or else, you'll become Sir Sneeze-a-Lot). If your space is really, really dusty, consider wearing protective eyewear, too. Here's what to do:

1. Start at 12 o'clock and begin to move everything out of the space. A cellar is simple: move everything out of the room. If you're cleaning your garage, move everything onto the driveway. If you're cleaning your basement and you can't move everything out, do half the space at a time: move everything over to one side, clean that entirely, and replace what belongs there (waves 1 through 3). Then, when you go to do the next side, lay down a drop cloth on the clean area to avoid getting the clean floor dirty again.

2. Inherent to this work will be a bit of decluttering; I find it naturally happens whenever I visit this space. Have three distinct piles: keep, toss, and donate. Sort items into these piles. Stay on track, my friend. It is very easy to get sucked into opening old photo albums or looking at boxes of love letters and concert tickets. But now's not the time to reminisce, you are here to CLEAN. So keep moving.

3. While you're doing this, remember to take note of any areas that will require extra attention during wave 2. When you get back to your starting point, the space should already look tidier.

Wave 2

Disclaimer: This is some of the grittiest cleaning a home requires, so keep that protective gear on. You never know if you'll encounter mold or mildew, risk a splinter, or touch a dead creature, and also, you'll be kicking up a lot of dust and debris.

HIGH DUSTING (5 to 10 minutes)

Here's what to do:

1. Use the shop vacuum with the brush attachment or your high duster. Starting at 12 o'clock, walk around the room with your tool angled to capture any cobwebs where the wall meets the ceiling, making sure to to get windowsills, light fixtures, and any venting.

2. If needed, once you've completed dusting the perimeter of the room, hold up the vacuum or high duster and walk in an S-pattern back and forth across the room, to be sure you capture anything hiding in the ceiling beams and vents.

SUCK IT UP

A word about the shop vacuum. I strongly recommend this for unfinished spaces. It will suck up dead bugs, dirt, cobwebs, larger chunks of mystery stuff, superfine dust, and can also handle moisture (look for one that specifies being wet/dry). Don't use your regular vacuum; you *will ruin it* cleaning these areas. If you don't have a shop vacuum, try borrowing one from a friend or neighbor. Once you're convinced and you want to buy one, you'll find that they are quite inexpensive yet indispensible when you're standing in your basement facing a giant spider and you can't—and don't want to—figure out if it's dead or alive.

WINDOWS (2 to 3 minutes per window)

I know cleaning basement windows likely isn't on the top of your to-do list. But still, it's important to clean them occasionally, since the dirt that collects in the sills and tracks of the windows can harbor mold, and you don't want it to spread. We'll scrub out the dirt first, then clean the glass, then treat the sills and frame to inhibit mold growth. I recommend wearing disposable gloves and using paper towels for this task so that you can throw everything away when you're done, to eliminate the potential of transferring mold to other places.

1. Lightly dampen two paper towels with water and fold into quarters. You want them wet enough to pick up mold and mildew, but not so soggy that they will weaken and shred.

2. Run the paper towels along the window frames and sills to remove surface dirt and debris. Lightly scrub where needed.

3. Dampen a cleaning toothbrush with water and agitate the areas in the window tracks and corners.

4. Pat the sills and frame dry using a paper towel.

5. Spray the glass with glass cleaner and wipe clean using an S-pattern.

6. Quickly and thoroughly dry the sills and frames—you want the area completely dry before moving on.

7. Spray a thin and even application of a mold inhibitor and allow it to dry completely.

8. Spray a paper towel thoroughly with mold inhibitor and rewipe the sills and frames, then allow it to dry.

9. Dispose of the used paper towels and disposable gloves promptly.

You can use this method for any area, window or not, if you sense it has a slight mold or mildew issue. But for anything larger than a very contained area such as windows, you need to bring in a professional to deal with mold.

WALLS (20 to 30 minutes per room)

If you can write *clean me* on the dust on the walls with your finger, it's time to give them a cleaning. This method works on drywalled as well as unfinished walls. The idea is to capture sticky dust and cobwebs that are otherwise unattended to.

1. Start at 12 o'clock and use the shop vacuum with a hard-floor or bristle-brush attachment; if you don't have one, use a clean broom, angled at about 45 degrees against the wall.

2. Working from top to bottom in long, brisk strokes, vacuum or sweep the wall. Work section by section in a clockwise motion around the room.

3. Clean any vents as you go.

4. You may need to do a few passes until all the dust is gone, and you can do this by simply touching the wall and seeing what comes up on your finger. It doesn't need to be perfect, but it needs to be significantly cleaner. If you are using the broom, let all the dust fall to the ground; you'll deal with it in wave 3.

DUSTING STORED ITEMS (20 minutes to 1 hour)

The items you have placed in your keep pile will likely be quite dusty. I've recommended bringing some plush microfiber cloths along for this clean, because you're going to encounter a lot of dust and you want something that can painlessly absorb it. While you will mostly be using your cloth, keep your shop vacuum handy in case you encounter really thick layers of dirt or splintery patches. Splinters tend to get caught in microfiber, so avoid them where possible.

1. If necessary, vacuum the items in your keep pile using the shop vacuum and dust-brush attachment.

2. Spray a plush microfiber cloth with all-purpose cleaner and wipe each item or bin on all sides, using an S-pattern.

CLEANING DUCTS

I have seen many experts recommend that you have an annual cleaning of your heating and cooling ducts to maintain indoor air quality and improve the efficiency of the whole system. Interestingly enough, the EPA sounds a little more cautious about this, since there is not yet evidence that annual cleaning improves things health-wise or heating system–wise, and in fact, an improper cleaning can lead to trouble with the system or release pollution into the house. In other words, they recommend that the ducts get cleaned on an as-needed basis, rather than doing it regularly. I like these guys!

So how do you know when the ducts do need cleaning? If you are unsure, you can have a professional inspect the system. Dust in the return registers is not necessarily a sign that there is an excessive buildup in the system, but large amounts of dust is a concern, and large amounts of mold or mildew are a grave concern (ask the inspector to show you any mold found). You may find stuff that looks like mold, but only an expert can determine if it actually is—many microbiology labs will process a sample on a piece of tape for about $50. If there are conditions that are leading to the system becoming moldy, these will have to be corrected, in addition to replacing the parts that are moldy, in order to truly correct the problem.

CLEANING TRASH AND RECYCLING BINS (10 minutes active time plus 10 minutes inactive time per bin)

1. Bring bins outdoors (if they are not already there).

2. Empty any trash if necessary.

3. Spray down bins with all-purpose cleaner.

4. Toss baking soda around the damp surfaces and allow it to sit for 10 minutes.

5. Use an iron-handled scrub brush or a long-handled scrub brush to scrub well. Rinse with a hose and air dry.

Wave 3

I just want you to know how amazing you are. This is hard work and the fact that you're here is just fantastic. Think about how you'll reward yourself after while you do wave 3!

VACUUM OR SWEEP (5 to 20 minutes per space)

I strongly recommend using a shop vacuum for this, and if you don't have one, a heavy-duty push broom will do.

1. Plug in your vacuum as close to the exit point of the space as possible.

2. Use the brush-attachment tool and vacuum the area where the floor meets the wall and any corners, including those around the top or bottom of a staircase. If you come across any vents, vacuum these as well. If you're using a broom, do your best to get into these corners and sweep all the debris inward.

3. Switch to the hard-floor tool, if using.

4. Head to the opposite corner of where you've plugged in the vacuum and begin to vacuum sections of the space using the W-pattern. Each completed section should bring you closer to the outlet, until you vacuum yourself out of that space. If you are sweeping, work from left to right in sections and make all your broom strokes in the same direction, sweeping debris into a centralized pile. Using a dustpan or large piece of cardboard, sweep it all up and dispose.

MOP UNFINISHED CONCRETE FLOORS (5 to 10 minutes)

No worries about mop streaks here! Small victories. We use a cotton yacht mop for these jobs because they clean well on this type of surface. Use a bucket with a heavy-duty wringer, too.

1. Fill a bucket with hot water and 1 tablespoon of dish soap.

2. Soak the mop head for a few minutes to loosen the fibers and allow the product to soak in.

3. Wring the mop very well, clockwise, counterclockwise, and then clockwise again.

4. Start at the opposite corner to the entry point of the room (you will mop yourself out of the room).

5. Mop the floor with the S-pattern, section by section.

6. If using a twist mop, rinse and wring it every minute or so to avoid mopping floors with dirty water.

7. Put on rubber gloves (the water will be hot and dirty) and dump the dirty mop water. Refill the bucket with hot water, then rinse and clean the mop head. Wring well.

8. Repeat steps 2 through 6 to remove any sudsy, dirty water from the floor.

9. Allow the floor to dry.

10. Replace items where they belong, reorganizing the space as you'd like.

Now go shower, pour yourself a tall glass of lemonade (no one but you will know if it's spiked or not), and watch Netflix for a good, long while. You deserve it.

Finished Spaces—Laundry Room, Pantry, Mudroom

These rooms are at least a little prettier than the unfinished dungeons we just covered. There's your silver lining. Because these spaces show dirt more obviously than an unfinished space, it's a good idea to schedule cleaning these a little more frequently, although they still don't need it all that often.

FINISHED SPACES: EXPRESS CLEAN
(ESTIMATED TIME: 5 TO 10 MINUTES PER SPACE)

Air it out. If you have windows or a door to the outside in this space, open them, weather permitting, to let in fresh air.

Pick up! Get out that bin and toss in anything that doesn't belong.

Straighten up! Line up and tidy bottles and packages of product, and place any dirty clothing into a dirty clothing pile, and clean clothing into a clean clothing pile (baskets are best). Take the clean basket to the door, so that you have to deal with it on your way out.

Wipe it down. Starting back at 12 o'clock, take a general-purpose microfiber cloth dampened with all-purpose cleaner and quickly wipe up any stains, spills, or marks. Just go for whatever is at eye level or glaringly obvious. Your laundry appliances may have a layer of dust or spilled detergent; this is a great time to wipe that up.

Clean the sink. Quickly wipe out the laundry basin or sink with hot, soapy water. If it's quite dirty, do this with a sponge and mixture of dish soap and baking soda, then rinse well. If your plastic or acrylic sink is stained, I'll level with you: unless you want to spend a lot of your time and still get really poor results, just look at the stains as a form of patina and move on. These stains are nearly impossible to remove, and it's not worth your time to try.

Finish up with floors. Move on to the floor. For this, either use a vacuum with a hard-floor attachment or a nylon broom (natural-fiber brooms are for outdoor and unfinished spaces only). Start at one corner and sweep vigorously, forming a pile of debris and taking it along with you toward the door or exit point. If you're in the laundry room, vacuum the dryer lint trap slot with the crevice tool, too.

Mop it up. Quickly mop the floors with a flat-head mop and a spray bottle filled with the appropriate floor cleaner (see pages 18 and 19). Mop in sections, mopping your way from the farthest point of the room toward the exit point, ensuring that you mop yourself out the door.

Ditch the bin. Finally, grab that bin and deal with its contents. Take trash and dishes and glasses to the kitchen, books to the bookcase, and old papers and magazines to the recycling bin. Allow floors to dry, and you're done!

FINISHED SPACES: TOP-TO-BOTTOM CLEAN

These spaces get used for utility purposes and can become quite dirty and dusty over time—I'm looking at you, laundry and mudrooms. Consider doing a thorough clean quite regularly: monthly or every other month. Other spaces, like pantries, won't get that dirty, but a good cleaning a couple of times a year still makes sense. I'll assume this space doesn't have windows; if it does, refer back to one of the other sections where we discuss window cleaning.

PRODUCTS	TOOLS
All-purpose cleaner (see page 16)	Bin
Baking soda	Trash bag
White vinegar	High-dusting tool (see page 31)
Essential oil, such as tea tree or lavender	3 general-purpose microfiber cloths
Gasket cleaner (see page 25)	Plain cotton cloth
Hydrogen peroxide	Nonscratching sponge
Mild dish soap	Cleaning toothbrush
Rubbing alcohol	Paper towels
WD-40	Scraper
Disinfectant (optional)	

Wave 1

TIDYING AND ORGANIZING

Have a bin and a trash bag with you in the center of the room. Head to 12 o'clock, walk around the space and collect any items that don't belong; straighten up anything that will be staying. Line up bottles and packages neatly, and sort clean or dirty laundry. Remove shoes and boots and place in another space (outdoors, preferably) to free up the floor for further cleaning. In the pantry, everything should be placed back where it belongs. As always, pay special attention to any areas that will require extra attention during the second or third wave. The room should look tidy when you're done.

Wave 2

HIGH DUSTING (5 to 10 minutes)

These spaces can get dusty and house some pretty wicked cobwebs, so high dusting is key here.

Please note: Lights should be turned off during high dusting to avoid popping any lightbulbs.

1. Head to 12 o'clock and walk around the room with your high-dusting tool, gently moving it around the moldings and getting into ceiling corners; dust around any light fixtures.

2. Repeat this for any air vents high up on the wall or in the ceiling.

WALL FIXTURES (shelving, hangings, etc.; 2 minutes per item)

If you are fancy enough to have décor hanging in these spaces, I applaud you. I hung some artwork in my laundry room and seriously, I feel like I'm on the set of an aspirational TV show. This art barely requires any cleaning work, aside from the occasional dusting we've discussed in other chapters. What I want to focus on more here is the shelving, hooks, utility tools, and items that you may have hanging in these spaces that house supplies, food, or clothing.

1. Starting with the highest fixture, remove items from the shelves, hooks, or fixtures and place them on the floor or another space that has yet to be cleaned.

2. Spray a general-purpose microfiber cloth with all-purpose cleaner and wipe the fixture. Should there be an area that is stained, allow the product to sit on the stain for a few moments, then wipe away, or scrub the stain with a paste of baking soda and all-purpose cleaner. Wipe away with a damp cloth.

3. Wipe each item where needed with the damp cloth (think about those mucky laundry detergent bottles!) and replace neatly when the surface is dry. Remember, this is a good time to get rid of something you don't need anymore.

4. Move on to lower fixtures and repeat until done.

LAUNDRY APPLIANCES

Cleaning the exterior of your washing machine and dryer is a great idea—they can get so grotty, so fast. Cleaning the interior is equally as important, as it helps your machine work better, clean your clothes more effectively, and of course, not set your house on fire (lint traps!).

The Washing Machine (5 minutes active time plus 30 to 60 minutes inactive time)

1. Add 2 cups plain white vinegar and 10 drops essential oil, like tea tree or lavender, which will help with mildew and mineral deposits. Run a long hot-water cycle.

2. When that's done, using a general-purpose microfiber cloth dampened with vinegar, wipe down the agitator and drum. If there are any stains, try rubbing them with a paste of baking soda and water, using a nonscratching sponge.

3. For front-loading washers, clean the rubber seal: dip a general-purpose microfiber cloth into the gasket cleaner and give the gasket a rubdown, to inhibit any mildew.

4. Tackle the exterior parts using all-purpose cleaner on a general-

purpose microfiber cloth. Use a cleaning toothbrush to scrub any grimy areas or to clean the dispensing tray. Wipe clean.

5. Now that you've worked so hard, you'll want to leave the washing machine door ajar in between washes, to air it out and prevent any mildew or musty smells from developing.

The Dryer (30 to 45 minutes)

1. Unplug the dryer and empty the lint trap.

2. Take the discharge hose out of the back (that silver elephant trunk thing) and give it a good shake to dislodge debris.

3. (Consult the manufacturer's instructions before proceeding.) Unscrew the back panel of the dryer and remove it; vacuum up any visible lint using the brush attachment or crevice tool.

4. Vacuum the lint trap itself. If you are able to take this apart as well, vacuum any dust within.

5. Vacuum anything left behind in the drum. You might find a whole farm's worth of dust bunnies.

6. Wipe everything down with a cotton cloth dampened with all-purpose cleaner and reassemble.

HOW TO REMOVE PAINT FROM AN ACRYLIC SINK

Spilled paint here never looks pretty—it always looks like someone just puked in the sink. To remove it, here's what you can do: If the paint is latex, apply rubbing alcohol to the paint; if the paint is oil-based, spray WD-40 onto the paint. Allow either to stand for about 15 minutes or so. Now, get a scraper and begin to chisel away at the paint. It should come up easily. You may need to reapply treatment and repeat several times. When done, add a squirt of dish soap to a damp sponge and squeeze to spread the soap out. Scrub the sink down very well to remove any stains and leftover product. Rinse well and dry.

Laundry Basin (5 to 10 minutes)

This is the "everything but the kitchen sink" sink. It's used to fill buckets, clean dogs, handle painting projects, and aid in hand-washed laundry.

1. Spray down the sink with all-purpose cleaner and sprinkle baking soda over the top of the entire sink surface. This will help remove topical stains but won't get rid of everything if the sink is heavily stained (see previous page).

2. After 5 minutes or so, scrub the sink with a damp nonscratching sponge. If you notice any limescale on the faucet, treat this with white vinegar by soaking a cotton cloth in vinegar and draping it over the fixtures. Allow this to stand for an hour to overnight, depending on severity, and then scrub clean.

3. Rinse well and dry with a paper towel (microfiber may snag on rough surfaces in acrylic or plastic sinks).

CLOSETS (10 to 20 minutes)

If you have a mudroom with coat and shoe storage, you'll remember how to do this from the entryway closet. It's quite simple and helps keep a space looking streamlined and organized.

Please note: Treat the closet as three distinct zones: top shelf, hanging rack, and floor. That way, all areas can be efficiently cleaned.

1. Remove all items from the top shelf.

2. With a microfiber cloth dampened with all-purpose cleaner, wipe the shelf surface clean.

3. Tidy and organize the items as you replace them neatly on the shelves.

4. Hang up and straighten anything hanging in the closet. Move all spare hangers over to one end of the closet. Ditch anything that you no longer want or need—take this opportunity to declutter!

HOW TO CLEAN AN IRON (as needed; 10 minutes active time plus 5 minutes inactive time)

Have you ever wondered how an iron gets dirty, even though the only thing it ever touches is clean clothes? Good news—it's not some crusty habit of yours that's the culprit—it's just mineral deposits, and they're pretty straightforward to clean off. To prevent them from even forming, use only distilled water, and be sure to dump out the reservoir every time you finish ironing; it's the stagnant water that contributes to these deposits.

1. Make sure the iron is completely cool.
2. Make a paste of baking soda and water and apply it to any visible stains. Let it sit for 5 minutes, then wipe clean with a damp cloth.
3. Use a cotton swab dipped in distilled water to dab the steam vents clean.
4. Empty out any water sitting in the reservoir and add a small amount of distilled water. Turn the iron on to the highest setting and steam-iron a clean cloth. This will continue to flush out any internal mineral deposits.
5. Turn off the iron and let it cool, being sure to empty the reservoir again.

WALLS (10 seconds per mark)

The walls in these spaces can get stained and mucked up over time, especially in mudrooms, where fingerprints from the outdoors are prevalent and scuffs from shoes being kicked off are the norm. Pay attention to them!

1. Have a water-dampened nonscratching sponge in one hand and sprinkle ¼ teaspoon of baking soda onto a corner of the sponge. Have a microfiber cloth lightly sprayed with all-purpose cleaner in the other hand.

2. Examine each section of wall as you work, and if you come across a stain or scuff, first try wiping it with the damp microfiber cloth.

3. If the stain doesn't come off, use the sponge with the baking soda and gently clean the stain. (Matte-finish paint may rub off or be permanently "stained" by the sponge, so please test this in a hidden area first.)

4. Wipe the area well with the microfiber cloth to remove residue from the baking soda.

POINTS OF CONTACT (2 minutes)

Grubby hands abound in these spaces; we're touching dirty things and trying to clean them (or cook with them, in the case of the pantry). Cleaning points of contact is crucial.

Please note: Light switch plates connect to an electrical source, meaning they cannot be sprayed directly. Please spray a cloth to wipe clean a light switch plate.

1. Spray the point of contact with an all-purpose cleaner and wipe off.

2. Treat with disinfectant according to the bottle's instructions, if using.

BASEBOARDS (5 minutes)

Clean these as you see fit. I find these spaces do get dusty and dirty, so I'd encourage fairly regular cleaning of them, but I wouldn't say it is a huge priority, either. In other words, if you see they're dirty, clean them.

1. With a slightly damp cloth or dry cloth, wipe a section of baseboard from left to right. Alternatively, vacuum them or use your high-dusting tool.

2. Remove any dirt or marks by sprinkling baking soda onto a damp cloth; massage into the area and wipe clean.

Wave 3

Easy, right? This wave is quick, since these spaces tend to be quite small. If you don't feel like bringing out your vacuum and mop, you may find it easier to do it Cinderella-style instead. The benefit is that it all gets done in one shot: you use the cloth to wipe up dirt and debris as well as wash the floor by starting at the far end of the room and working in an S-pattern until you work your way out the door. But if you don't feel like being the non–belle of the ball, you can vacuum and mop in the traditional mode.

MATS (5 minutes active time plus 30 minutes inactive time)

In laundry rooms and mudrooms, mats help keep dirt at bay. Clean these up and keep them debris-free! If the mats are machine washable, pop them into the wash every couple of months or so, too.

1. Take your mats to an area where it's safe to do this (I usually bring it outdoors, around to the side of my house). Shake mats well and lay them flat.

2. Sprinkle baking soda onto the mat and gently rub it in using a patting motion. Leave this for 30 minutes.

3. Shake the mat out and vacuum, then roll it up and bring it inside.

4. Unroll the mat once the floor has been cleaned (after the next task!).

5. Wipe salty boot trays with a cloth dipped in a solution of white vinegar and water.

FLOORS
Vacuuming (7 to 10 minutes)

1. Move all items that can obstruct vacuuming out of the room temporarily to a location adjacent to the room you are in.

2. Plug in your vacuum as close to the exit point of the room as possible and attach the crevice tool.

3. Vacuum any corners or hard-to-reach spaces with this, including between appliances. Do this methodically by working your way around the room.

4. Now, put on the hard-floor attachment and vacuum using a W-pattern, working your way from one area to the next. You don't need to worry about beautiful cut lines here!

5. Vacuum the floor of the closet and tracks, if you've got a closet in the space.

Mopping (3 to 5 minutes)

Fill a bucket halfway with hot water and add the appropriate cleaner for your floor.

1. Dip your mop into the solution and wring well.

2. Use the S-patttern and mop thoroughly, working your way out the door.

3. Remember to rinse and wring your mop every minute or so, to avoid mopping floors with dirty water.

4. Leave the room, let the floors dry, and then replace shoes in closets, furniture, and rugs.

That's it! And now you can cross cleaning these spaces off your list for a nice, long time. And after these (sometimes scary) miscellaneous spaces in particular, I prescribe a nice, flavorful cocktail or a dense, towering slice of cheesecake.

CHAPTER 12

laundry

Oh my dear mother. At the dawn of time, she handled all our laundry, folding it neatly and arranging our stacks of clean clothes in the basement for me and my sister to *theoretically* collect and put away. But instead, we would just leave all the laundry right there, and go to the basement to get dressed (which felt perfectly reasonable at the time). One day, I had a friend over, and she and I were lounging around in the basement. At one point, my mother came downstairs to check on us and found my friend sitting *on top* of one of the clean laundry piles. I think the visual of all my mom's hard work being smushed into wrinkled oblivion by two careless kids put her over the edge, because that was the end of my golden laundry era. After that, she made us do our own—it was every daughter for herself.

Still, I wasn't given much of a tutorial. It was something like, "Wash the darks and the lights separately, and turn the dial *here*." That was it. I didn't understand the machine, what the other settings were or did, and I certainly didn't know how to remove stains. So far as I knew, everything went into that machine and hopefully came out clean (and the right color). Folding was another mystery. When you're a teenager, it doesn't matter if your clothes are perfectly clean and wrinkle-free. But as I grew older and needed to look presentable, I had to learn how to do laundry like a grown-up.

Clothes need a lot of maintenance, and the more you care about your clothes and your personal appearance, the more important it is to get their care right. If you want to look polished, professional, and stain-free, then you need to really master the rules of doing laundry. And like with so many other things, having a system will be a big improvement over not. Your laundry piles won't get tall and stinky, your favorite items will always be in great shape when you want to wear them, and all your clothing and linens will last longer when you treat them well. Clean clothing makes you look better, and when you look better, you feel better, and when you feel better, you're unstoppable!

HOW FULL SHOULD YOUR WASHING MACHINE BE?

A washing machine is designed to wash clothing and spin it to remove moisture. For a traditional top-loading machine, you want there to be enough room for the agitator to freely spin; if it's too filled up, it can't move, and your clothing won't get clean. Three-quarters full, loosely packed, works best. For high-efficiency machines, too *little* clothing will mean that there is *not enough* agitation, either. Make sure it is at least a third full (choose "light load"). Half full is a regular load, and two-thirds to three-quarters full is a large load. Anything more than that may (adversely) affect the machine's ability to wash your clothing.

Products

The laundry product aisle is, in a nutshell, insane. There are hundreds of variations of seemingly the same product and other products that make you scratch your head and stare blankly. Fear not! I'm going to help you decide exactly what you need and what you can leave behind. The more you know . . . you know?

Not all detergents are created equal. Let's break it down:

POWDER, LIQUID, OR PORTION PACK?

Though many of us grew up using powder detergent, it's falling out of favor these days, since it can get clumpy in the wash and not dissolve properly. I love liquid—it dissolves quickly, can double as a stain pre-treatment, and is convenient to use. Portion packs are super easy to use, but they need to be kept far away from small kids, who seem to think they look like a treat. Plus, with portion packs, you can't always adjust for the exact amount of detergent you require. In short, I prefer liquid, but if you must use the packs, I get it.

DYES AND SCENTS?

Sure, the smell of fresh laundry is one that taps deep into our happy-memory place. But if you find that you or someone in your family is particularly sensitive to chemicals, scent- and dye-free detergent is a no-brainer. (I just prefer it. I went scent-free years ago and I haven't looked back. Now I smell like my nice, classy French perfume instead.)

HIGH-EFFICIENCY FORMULA?

Choose powdered or liquid detergents made *specifically* for HE machines if you have one. (Not sure if you have one? Just look for the blue "HE" logo on your machine.) For a non-HE machine, look for a detergent without that labeling—you need something that works better in a machine that uses more water and agitation. Trust me, this stuff matters.

DO YOU PREFER A HOT OR COLD WASH?

Cold water may not dissolve detergent as well as hot water can, so consider a product designed to be used in cold water if you tend to do a lot of cold loads. Similarly, don't use a product designed for cold water in your hot-water loads. (More on hot versus cold washes later in this chapter.)

I like to experiment with different formulations, and lately, I've been going for scent-free, dye-free. Current favorites include Tide Free & Gentle; Purex Dirt Lift Action Free & Clear liquid detergent; Oxi-

Clean HD liquid laundry detergent; Seventh Generation Free & Clear; and Persil ProClean Power-Liquid Sensitive Skin laundry detergent.

DISHWASHING LIQUIDS

The cleaning workhorse of the kitchen and, frankly, the whole home, dish liquid is designed to—wait for it—lift dirt and grease off the filthiest pots and pans, and it works similarly on fabrics. Just don't get too overzealous with it; the sudsing can be problematic in your washing machine. Dab onto each stain sparingly and add a maximum of only three dish-liquid-treated garments per load.

DELICATES LIQUID

Certain delicate fabrics can't handle regular detergents, but you still want something that can remove odors, dirt, and stains. In a pinch, I've even used baby shampoo (or hotel shampoo, when I'm in a traveling pinch). I like the Laundress Delicate Wash.

OXYGEN BLEACH OR CHLORINE BLEACH?

Many of us grew up in homes where chlorine bleach was used on just about everything. And every now and then, you'd get an ugly orange splotch on a dark garment or holes would suddenly appear in otherwise brand-new clothing. As it turns out, chlorine bleach is a high-maintenance diva. Sure, it works, but only if used on the right fabric, with the right dilution, added at the right time during the wash cycle, etc. Ironically, it can even *yellow* some white items. It's certainly not good to get it on your skin or in your mucous membranes. It can create toxic fumes if mixed with other cleaning agents, such as ammonia. As I see it, you need a master's degree in bleach to use it properly, and frankly, I just don't have time. I need an easier solution that works well for brightening, whitening, and stain removal. There are plenty of bleach alternatives that are safer and easier to use, and that's why I am a big fan of oxygen bleach. You can even use it as a pretreatment for stains; just whip up a batch according to the package instructions and soak the garment before laundering.

FABRIC SOFTENER AND DRYER SHEETS

I prefer white vinegar (just the 5 percent white vinegar will do) to commercial fabric softener or dryer sheets for reducing static and softening fibers. To use vinegar as a fabric softener, you'll essentially sub it in where fabric softener went before. Fill your fabric softener compartment with white vinegar to the maximum fill line (more won't harm even a smaller load), or if your machine requires you to manually add it mid-cycle, add a cup to your wash when you would normally add your fabric softener. When paired with dryer balls (see tools, below), white vinegar produces the same result without any strong scent or waxy residue and I love that I can easily sub a pantry item for something I'd otherwise have to purchase (and in the case of dryer sheets, throw away).

TOOLS

Laundry tri-sorter, or three baskets for lights, colors, and darks

Basket for towels (if possible, otherwise collect weekly)

Basket or bucket for used (but dry) cleaning rags

Mesh bags for delicate items

Iron and ironing board

Handheld steamer (optional—but awesome!)

Air-drying rack

Flat drying rack (optional, but helpful for certain garments)

Lint brush

Sweater shavers

Dryer balls

Sweater stone, sweater comb, and/or sweater shaver: By simply dragging these over the fabric, you can help remove those little balls or pills that form on your clothing. Use the stone for thicker knits and the comb for thinner and delicate ones. The shavers can be a little harsh, so proceed with caution.

Dryer balls: To help remove static and fluff up clothing, plus speed drying time, I toss two to four dryer balls in a given load of laundry, depending on the size of the load. I prefer the plastic variety, since wool balls are not good for drying synthetic fabrics.

Understanding Your Washing Machine

High-efficiency machines are designed to use less water and to use smarter ways to remove soils from your clothing. If you find you're not getting the kind of results you are used to with your high-efficiency machine, consider doing a presoak of your clothing before it goes into the wash cycle—just do it in the sink or basin with a little oxygen bleach, then press out the liquid and place it in the washer for a regular load.

The **wash phase** of a cycle is where all the laundry magic happens. While many believe hot water is king for whitening whites and removing stains, recent tests have shown that newly formulated detergents and supplementary laundry products work just as well in cold water as they do in hot. Cold water is also more energy-efficient. I've switched to almost always washing with cold water, and I feel fresh as a daisy. But you be the judge! If you're washing undershirts, underwear, and socks, go ahead and use the hottest water you can, if you prefer. Hot water gets out tannin stains (like wine, coffee, and tea) and can sanitize clothing (depending on how high the temperature is) but can also shrink clothing, fade colors, and set protein and grease stains. Use it wisely!

The **spin phase** is quite powerful. It spins garments around to remove as much water as possible. The intensity of the spin varies from very fast for regular cycles to slow for permanent press and practically nonexistent for delicates. It isn't always the nicest to clothing, so the more delicate a fabric, the less intense of a spin you want.

The **regular**, **normal**, or **cotton** setting is designed to remove stains and soil from cotton clothing, linens, towels, sportswear, kitchen towels, and undergarments, as well as to sanitize when you choose hot water. It typically combines hot water with a fast-agitation phase as well as a fast-spin phase. This cycle is the harshest on your fabrics, which is why synthetic fabric, and more delicate fabrics like wool and silk, can't be laundered on this setting.

Don't let the name of the **permanent press** setting confuse you. This setting was designed to minimize wrinkles and is best for jeans, synthetics, and any other fabrics more delicate than your heavy-duty cotton. In general, this cycle is not quite as good at getting things clean, but it helps reduce color fading, wrinkling, and fabric wear and tear.

The **delicate** or **gentle** setting is a safe bet for fabrics that you aren't quite ready to hand wash or take to the dry cleaner but that are too delicate to place in a regular or permanent press cycle. Fabrics that get this gentle treatment—so long as the care label says the garment is machine washable!—include silk, wool, cashmere, rayon, acrylic, and acetate. Consider not only the fabric itself but also the *construction* of the garment when deciding if you should use this cycle or not. If you have a garment that you are particularly concerned about, place it inside out in a mesh laundry bag, to protect it from agitation.

HOW TO RESCUE A SHRUNKEN ITEM

Some shrunken items are ruined for good, like the time my gorgeous blazer from Anthropologie came out of the wash looking fit for a classy toddler. But some items can be saved: Fill a sink with lukewarm water and add a capful of gentle shampoo (this will relax the fibers). Agitate gently with your hand, then let the item sit for 30 minutes. Gently squeeze out the water (no rinsing!). Lay the item on a clean towel and roll it up to squeeze out some moisture, then roll it out on another clean towel and stretch it gently by hand. Leave it to dry. If there is any hope of getting it back to size, this trick will work.

Hand Washing

When in doubt, if something is frilly, sexy, delicate, or expensive, you may want to think about hand washing it. Your care label may require it, in fact. If that's the case, here's what you want to do:

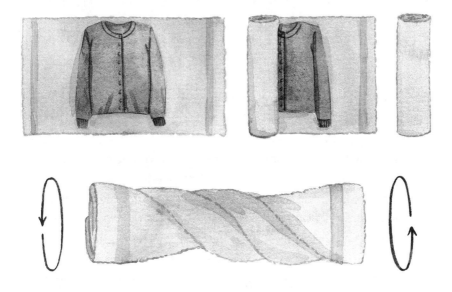

1. Fill a clean basin (if you have a double sink) or bucket halfway with cool water and add the appropriate dose of gentle detergent. Mix well.

2. Start with the lightest item and work your way to the darkest; you'll start to see some color (and dirt) come out in the wash.

3. Immerse each item into the bucket and agitate with your hands. Avoid pulling, wringing, or rubbing fabric together; too much action can cause pilling. Instead, take a small chunk of fabric and squeeze it a bunch of times, gently rubbing it with your hands and squeezing some more. Spend less time doing this with very delicate items, like pantyhose, and keep items that bleed easily in water for as little time as possible.

4. Squeeze each item well over an empty sink to get rid of soapy residue, then rinse well with cool water. Keep rinsing until the water runs clear and you don't feel any slippery soap on the garment.

5. Squeeze excess moisture out of the garment by pressing it up against the side of the sink or basin. Don't wring.

6. Lay out a dry towel and roll up the garment like a burrito to remove any excess moisture.

7. Lay flat or hang up to dry.

HACK! RESTORING A STINKY ITEM WITHOUT WASHING IT

There are several great options for keeping clothes smelling fresh between washes. The sun is a wonderful clothing deodorizer! Hang a garment outdoors in direct sunlight for an hour. If armpits are particularly smelly, sprinkle baking soda over the armpit area, allow it to sit for up to 30 minutes, and then shake it out well. To make your own fabric refresher, mix ½ cup white vinegar, ½ cup water, and ¼ cup fabric softener in a clean spray bottle, shake well, and spritz on clothing.

Understanding Your Dryer

If you had all the time, space, and good weather in the world—along with an arsenal of Cinderella's bird friends to help you with this lengthy chore—the ideal way to dry clothing is on a clothesline. The sun works wonders on clothing—it makes them smell fresh and lightens whites, too. In many parts of the world this is still the norm, and if you do line-dry, you can skip this section because you're already performing at the gold standard! But for everyone else who uses an electric dryer, keep reading.

If you aren't concerned about clothing shrinkage and know the fabric can handle heat, go ahead and put it in the dryer. You always want your articles of clothing to be entirely dry before putting them away; storing damp garments will allow for mildew growth and musty odors. Plus, fully drying helps ensure that no wrinkles will form. (One exception: if you are planning to iron, you'll have an easier time with it if items are still a little damp.) But even if the label says the dryer is okay, any time you are concerned about shrinkage, which is often permanent, hang the item to dry, just to be safe.

A load that's too small won't toss around and may take longer to dry, so if you're running a small one, place something dry in the dryer that's a similar material to everything else in the load to help speed the drying time; as a bonus, those added items will get a little dewrinkling (without chemical peels or Botox!). If the load is too bulky, items can't dry effectively, either, and will often end up quite wrinkled. The ideal load size is about half your dryer.

When your dryer buzzer goes off, it doesn't care if you're in the middle of an intense episode of your favorite show. It's telling you that if you don't act fast, your garments, which are nice and toasty, will stay wrinkle-free for about seventeen seconds. As soon as that heat stops blowing in and your load isn't tossing around, wrinkles will start to set. When you hear that buzzer, get up and get that load out, and fold or hang garments ASAP. Yes, it's annoying. But you know what? You and your clothes will look fabulous, and you won't have to haul out the iron.

TEMPERATURE AND CYCLE SELECTION

Regular tumble dry is a hot setting, which is great for heavy fabrics that won't shrink, or items that you don't care about shrinking, like linens, towels, flannels, cotton undergarments, and sturdy clothing.

Medium tumble dry or **permanent press** operates at a reduced heat level, which makes it great for anything you'd wash on the permanent press setting that can handle going in the dryer. It doesn't use enough heat to damage synthetics and won't be as likely to shrink something.

Low tumble dry or delicate is perfect for those fine items; it uses very little heat but still provides a good tumble for wrinkle-free and soft garments.

The fluff cycle provides blowing air only—no heat—so it can fluff up fabrics, such as terry or bathroom rugs, that have been hung to dry and are now as crispy as corn chips. A quick little fluff will restore their softness.

HACK! WRINKLE FIX

If you end up with a wrinkly item, there are three things you can try before you get out the iron. Place the item, along with a damp washcloth, in a mesh bag (to avoid rubbing it against more delicate fabrics), and turn on the appropriate dryer cycle for 10 minutes. Alternatively, consider getting a portable steamer. I keep mine in my bathroom, and when I want to dewrinkle something quickly in the morning, I just hang up the garment, steam, and go. But if you don't have a steamer, look to your hair arsenal: smooth a small area (like cuffs and collars) with a flat-iron (be sure to still mind the settings, choosing low heat for delicate items) or run over (slightly dampened) wrinkles with a blow dryer.

The Laundry Symbols Chart

Think of it as the periodic table of laundry. Unless you have a serious affection for chemistry, you probably hyperventilate when you try to understand one. But that's only because you don't have the chart at the ready to explain the translations of those little hieroglyphs. Well, good news! Unlike in tenth-grade chemistry, you don't need to memorize this biz. Take a page from my book (literally) and frame it for your laundry room, so you have it at the ready for reference, and it almost looks cute!

Please note: Always remember to empty the lint trap before you dry your clothing! Even after one load you can pull out a veritable

LAUNDRY SYMBOLS CHART

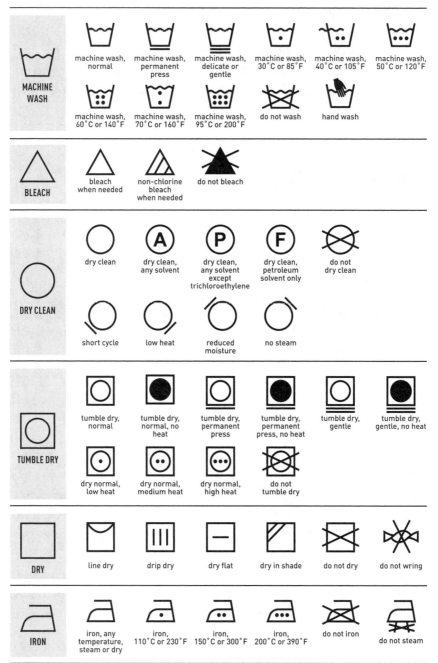

MACHINE WASH

machine wash, normal | machine wash, permanent press | machine wash, delicate or gentle | machine wash, 30°C or 85°F | machine wash, 40°C or 105°F | machine wash, 50°C or 120°F

machine wash, 60°C or 140°F | machine wash, 70°C or 160°F | machine wash, 95°C or 200°F | do not wash | hand wash

BLEACH

bleach when needed | non-chlorine bleach when needed | do not bleach

DRY CLEAN

dry clean | dry clean, any solvent | dry clean, any solvent except trichloroethylene | dry clean, petroleum solvent only | do not dry clean

short cycle | low heat | reduced moisture | no steam

TUMBLE DRY

tumble dry, normal | tumble dry, normal, no heat | tumble dry, permanent press | tumble dry, permanent press, no heat | tumble dry, gentle | tumble dry, gentle, no heat

dry normal, low heat | dry normal, medium heat | dry normal, high heat | do not tumble dry

DRY

line dry | drip dry | dry flat | dry in shade | do not dry | do not wring

IRON

iron, any temperature, steam or dry | iron, 110°C or 230°F | iron, 150°C or 300°F | iron, 200°C or 390°F | do not iron | do not steam stuffed animal–size piece of lint from that trap, and leaving it in there is a fire hazard. Have it become part of your routine when you're doing laundry so that you don't forget.

Preparing Clothing and Other Items for the Wash

One old-fashioned tenet of laundering that you absolutely must stick to is separating loads into like piles—as anyone who has ever accidentally left a red sock in with a load of whites can tell you. (PS—there is a fix for that! Just run the load through with a dye remover, such as Rit Color Remover.) I have found that the easiest way is to have a **tri-sorter**, a three-sectioned sorting bin, which acts as a hamper. Come laundry day, all the sorting has already happened. Designate one section for darks, one for whites, and one for colors.

In addition, you will want to keep **bins** or **baskets** in your laundry room for towels and washcloths. I even keep a separate one for used cleaning cloths (their microfiber powers can be undermined if they get washed with other items—plus they will cling like crazy to anything they're washed with). Be sure these items are dry before placing them in the bins, to avoid musty odors.

In addition, you'll want to check over the garments and get them in their best orientation for washing, to minimize fading and popping of seams, hooks, buttons, or zippers. Empty pockets (unless you love that soft confetti that sticks to everything after washing a used tissue). The jury's out on buttoning buttons—some say the washing process tugs on buttons and can loosen them, so I err on the side of laziness and leave everything unbuttoned. Clip up clips, hook up hooks, fasten Velcro, and loosely tie up any drawstrings, since you have better things to do with your time than try to fish out a drawstring that got sucked in during the wash.

✓ **PRO TIP: DESTINKIFY!** If your linens or any other items develop that sour musty smell, run them through on a second wash cycle using white vinegar in place of detergent.

STAIN REMOVAL RULES

There is so much to know about stains, I could write a whole book about it. But no one wants to read that book. So here are the basics that will get you really far.

Stain rule 1: The faster you treat them, the more likely you will be able to get them out. Gently scrape, blot, or physically remove as much of the stain material as possible before you treat the stain; this will reduce the amount of work you have to do and prevent the stain from spreading further.

Stain rule 2: Treat the type of stain with the appropriate product. **Oil-based stains** (most food and makeup stains) are best removed by first sprinkling with something to absorb the oil—think cornstarch or baby powder—then shaking off the excess. Next, pretreat with the original grease-remover: dish soap! Just dab it right in there and launder as usual (though don't put too many dish soap–treated items in the machine at once, or you will end up with an *I Love Lucy* situation with an overflow of bubbles). **Tannin-based stains** (coffee, tea, wine, or fruit) should get a 30-minute soak in cold water, then treatment with something like dish soap if still needed, before washing. **Protein-based stains** (basically all the unmentionable bodily fluids) should be blotted up first, then treated with oxygen bleach and laundered. Never wash or dry these items with heat, however, unless you are sure the stain is out, since heat sets protein (and oil) stains.

Stain rule 3: There are some effective last-ditch efforts:

- Scrub **toothpaste** into a dried bloodstain, then let it dry. Or **spit** on it! Spit, which contains enzymes, works wonders at breaking down fresh protein stains.

- Soak the garment in **oxygen bleach**. Fill a clean sink or basin with hot water and add the oxygen bleach powder, ensuring that it dissolves fully. If the garment (and stain) can take hot water, add it; otherwise wait for the mixture to cool first. Soak between 1 to 6 hours, then squeeze out excess liquid and launder as usual.

- For a freakish stain on your most prized possession, **take it to the cleaners**. Some things aren't worth risking. Just let the pros handle it.

✦ **HANDY HABIT: Dealing with Pet Hair.** Sometimes it feels like my cats' hair weaves itself right into the fibers of my clothing. The dryer removes a lot of pet hair, but to aid in that removal, simply snap your item of clothing in the air (think: "Whip it!") a few times before washing and again before hanging to dry or putting into the dryer. You can remove an extra bit of hair on air-dried items by tossing them into the fluff cycle for a few minutes after they are all dry.

✓ **PRO TIP: GET RID OF YELLOW PITS!** If you get unsightly pit stains on your white tops, there's a really easy fix. Create a paste of equal parts baking soda and water and apply the paste to the area. Allow it to sit overnight, and launder as usual the next morning. The paste totally annihilates those stains.

Ironing and Steaming

The need for ironing and steaming can be practically eliminated if you are fast to move your laundry out of the wash and into the dryer, and remove items from the dryer quickly. If you are hanging to dry, you can smooth out any areas that might wrinkle with your hands. But every now and again—when you're dealing with a fancy linen skirt or collared shirt, for example—you have to trot out the iron.

1. Arrange your garments based on care labels: one dot means cool; two, medium; and three, hot (it's easier to heat up an iron than it is to cool one down). Ensure your iron is clean—dirty irons leave marks (see page 225 for how to clean one)!

2. Fill your iron with water; I try to use distilled water, to avoid any chalky buildup.

3. Heat the iron to the coolest setting and select your garment, starting with the one requiring the lowest heat setting, and work your way up, adjusting the heat as you go.

4. If you don't have a steam iron, spray garments lightly with a mist of water (or plan ahead—I take them out of the dryer when still slightly damp).

5. Iron garments and hang them when finished.

Tips for the Person Who Doesn't Iron Too Often

• Wrap a sheet of aluminum foil under the ironing board cover; the foil will transfer the heat to the underside of the garment, which will reduce the amount of time it takes to get wrinkles out.

• Always keep the iron moving so that you don't burn the garment.

• If you are concerned about scorching a delicate item or getting that annoying iron shine, use a clean—I mean really clean—white dish towel or pillowcase as a buffer between the garment and the iron.

- If you accidentally iron a wrinkle into a garment (which I once did live on national television), just keep a spray bottle filled with water handy. Spray the wrinkle down and re-iron. Boom.

- Use a slow, steady W-pattern on garments, applying moderate pressure, and use the pointed tip of the iron to get into tighter corners like collars, cuffs, and pockets.

- Don't iron over any metal or plastic.

- For pleated skirts and dresses: My time (and yours) is more valuable than figuring out how to keep all those folds crisp. Take them to the cleaners.

HACK! FIX AN IRONING SNAFU

If you get that shiny gleam on your clothes from ironing, stroke it out with a red lint brush or dampen a clean white cloth and wipe it off.

STEAMING TIPS

It used to be that I would pass by my gorgeous, delicate garments in the morning because they were wrinkly. Rather than not rocking my pretty things, I decided to keep a steamer handy, and my fashion game has never been better. Steamers won't give you sharp creases and can't work dewrinkling magic on thick fabrics like an iron can, but they will certainly make a dent in wrinkly clothing, giving your garments a clean look.

To Steam a Garment

1. Hang up the garment in a clear, easy-to-access area.

2. Fill the steamer with water (read the instructions first; many are quite finicky) and allow it to heat up properly.

3. Run the steamer away from clothing and your body for a minute or two. The steamer will sputter and spray out hot water—just let it get it out of its system.

4. When the steamer is producing hot, consistent steam, stretch the garment gently taut with one hand (be very careful to avoid burns) while moving the steamer up and down with the other, focusing on wrinkly areas in particular.

5. If you notice an area by a seam or a pocket flap that's really wrinkly, hold the steamer over it for longer to help relax the fibers.

6. Give the garment a minute to dry.

TRUE STORY!

Honest admission here: I don't fold my underwear. I think there are a few things, like underwear and bathing suits, where it really, truly doesn't make a difference whether or not it's folded, both in storage and in maintaining the garment. Instead, I just create sections in my drawers using adjustable drawer dividers and dump items into each section.

Folding

To fold, you want a flat, clean surface to work on. I usually have the TV, music, or a podcast going when I am folding. It's pretty boring, so at least I can entertain my brain a bit.

The goal with folding most items (aside from socks and undergarments) is to create a rectangle. So, the first step for any item with awkward shapes (say, the sleeves on a shirt or an A-line skirt) is to fold them in, to turn the item into a rectangle. Then folding becomes much easier. When storing folded items, it is preferable to "file" them standing up in the drawer rather than stacking them one on top of the other. The stacking not only makes it harder to locate a garment, but the weight of the

other garments stacked on top sets creases. To file, fold your garment in half once more, after the basic fold is completed (folded edge up to shoulder line, for example), and file with the neat edge pointing up.

Don't subject your socks to the dreaded sock ball—that only stretches out their upper halves, leaving you with loose socks that slip down when you're walking down the street or pop off when you remove your boots.

Instead, pair your socks together and roll them up, like sock sushi, then stand them up in the drawer like you're packing a sushi-to-go order. If the pair is falling out of its coil, wrap an elastic band around it before placing it into the drawer.

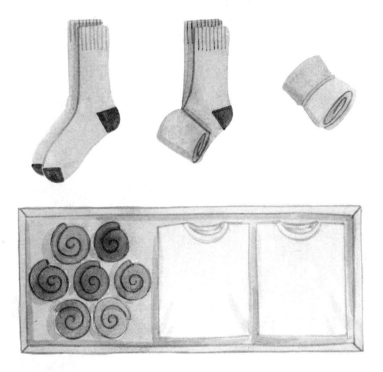

You know what the best thing is about learning the right way to do laundry? You arrive at a net of zero extra work, since presumably you are already doing laundry in some form—now you'll just know how to do it the best way. No, let's make that *less* work, since my methods reduce or eliminate the need for ironing. You're welcome!

SOME LAUNDRY NO-NOS

Don't mix towels or linens with the rest of your clothing. The fabric weights and textures are different, and the terry material from a towel will create friction on your softer garments and cause pilling.

Don't leave your washing machine door closed between uses. It's a damp, dark place, and closing it up will encourage mold and mildew growth, leading to a stinky, dirty machine.

Don't think your machine is self-cleaning! I explain on page 222 how to maintain your machine, and you should do it every so often. You can't get clean clothes from a dirty machine.

CHAPTER 13

routines and schedules

The Last (but Not Least) Step of the Maker Method

Who doesn't want to live in one of those pristine, magazine-story homes that look as if they've never had a speck of dust settle on a single surface? I sure do, but at the same time, I don't—at least, I wouldn't be able to, unless I had the means to employ a full-time housekeeper. There's the fantasy, and then there's what's realistic and manageable.

I have come to accept that I get a little tidier each day, but my home, despite my cleaning chops, is nowhere near magazine-home perfect at any given moment. I've dropped the need to live in a perfect space. Don't get me wrong, I love a clean house, but I also value my time and know what is really important to me (sanity, relationships, work, family, fun). When I have that unrealistic expectation of living in a perfectly clean home, I am unhappy; I feel inadequate, less-than, and I certainly don't feel motivated to clean. So, I choose to do what I can and what's most important to me (my MIAs). I master those tasks and know exactly how to do them so that they require as little brainpower, time, and resources as possible. Those that I can, I work into my existing daily routine. Those that I can't, I add to my schedule—literally putting them on my calendar, to ensure they get done.

That's the essence of step 3 of the Maker Method: to get great, lasting results, you have to *both* tweak your daily routines *and* make appointments—that you keep—for doing the bigger jobs. Now, let's be clear: this isn't going to be an overnight transformation, a crash-diet style prescription, since we all know that crash diets don't work. I want you to ease into this and be nice to yourself. The good news is, cleaning, unlike dieting, gives you immediate results that you can feel great about *right away*. As you master the tasks and realize that they take less time than you thought, you will be inspired to add another few things and work them into your routine. Clean begets clean. Trust me, cleaning is habit-forming. And remember: **I'm not necessarily telling you to do *more* work than you're doing now; I'm teaching you how to be way smarter about it. Efficiency for the win!**

ESTABLISHING YOUR ROUTINES AND SCHEDULE

I'm laying it all out here, but keep in mind that my suggestions are just that: suggestions. Your cleaning plan is completely customizable and ever evolving. At first, like a new athlete, you will be making only one or two small changes to your existing routine, and adding in only one or two larger jobs to your week. Think of this as laying the foundation—as you start to build that cleaning muscle, and get better and quicker at things, you'll add in more tasks. And of course, you are going to schedule in only what is most important to you and what you can maintain (although I do recommend challenging yourself!). Anything else, you will either just accept that it won't be cleaned, hire help, or schedule in time to do it on an infrequent basis. That way, at least you have it planned, and you can psych yourself up for it and reward yourself appropriately when the work is done.

In planning, you'll want to take these three things into account:

Consideration 1: Time You Have

I hear from hundreds of people every day about cleaning. Most dislike it, but every now and then, I come across the rare gem who really, truly likes it. And I can tell you, even people who *like* cleaning can't find the time to do it. A couple generations back, when it was common for women to stay at home, they had the time to cook and clean. These days, even stay-at-home parents are extremely busy; school is more competitive and more parent-involved, there's more driving, more preparing, more to manage. Life is just busier these days. And we're all doing our best.

So what's your number: 10 minutes per day, or 30? How big is your family? Who's helping you? What absolutely must get done? Right now, I spend about 20 to 30 minutes cleaning—most days—and so does my husband—so that equals about 40 minutes to an hour of attention that our home receives per day.

Consideration 2: Time It Takes

Consider the planning worksheet on pages 274–285, keeping in mind your MIAs. Tally up how many minutes each task should take. Is there a time discrepancy? Some small tasks, like a dirty backsplash, are easy enough to absorb in a daily routine—just add a backsplash wipe-down to your nightly postdinner wash-up routine. If a whole room is an MIA, on the other hand, you'll have to think about what priorities need to shift or where you need to adjust time available.

Consideration 3: *When* Do You Have That Time?

Now, think about what your average day of the week looks like. If you are a 9-to-5 type, your weekdays look one way and your weekends look another. If you work shift work, you may have a few days on and a few days off, or work nights one week and days the next. Either way, determine times of the day that make sense for you.

I like to do a lot in the morning. The more I can get out of the way, the better I feel about the rest of my day; it significantly reduces my stress and I feel extremely accomplished before I walk out the door. I wake up at least 90 minutes before I have to leave in the morning, which gives me enough time for some exercise, breakfast, getting ready, and some chores (usually dishes and laundry). When I get home from work, more kitchen cleaning happens, and some tidying up or a few key tasks or spaces get tackled as required. Weekend mornings are also great for me—I still get up early (I wasn't programmed with the chip that allows you to sleep in on weekends) and I am able to do a big job, say, give the kitchen or bathroom a Top-to-Bottom Clean.

Over the years, I've found what works for me. So, think about your schedule and your life, and when you're at your peak energy or motivation, plan for that to be the time to weave in some extra cleaning tasks.

WHAT ARE YOUR DAILY ROUTINES?

We all have daily routines, and I see them as opportunities to add in some extra cleaning by rethinking the manner in which we go about executing them. Think about what you do each day for the chunks of time listed below and approximately how long that activity takes you. (These chunks are based on your average Monday through Friday, 9-to-5-type lifestyle. If your life doesn't follow this setup, then examine any of those chunks of time where you find yourself at home.) Go ahead and pencil it in—unless you borrowed this book from the library. Then behave and get some scratch paper. Once you map it out, you'll be better able to see where you might be able to pick up some small new habits that yield big results.

- Morning routine
- Coming-home/before-dinner routine
- After-dinner routine
- Before-bed routine

On the next page is my morning routine, both *before* I changed my ways and *after* I started weaving in some chores (and even a bonus *after* to show you it won't clash with your exercise commitments, either!).

Wait! Do you get it now? The difference in what you have to do *is so subtle*, but the results are so incredibly different. In my "before" scenario, the kitchen was messy from making breakfast and lunch, and laundry piled up for days until I was left with *that* pair of underwear. The dishwasher was still full when I'd get home from work, which delayed my time making dinner and, of course, made walking into my kitchen utterly unenjoyable.

MY MORNING ROUTINE

———— ★ ————

BEFORE

- Wake up
- Use the bathroom (1 minute)
- Feed the cats (2 minutes)
- Boil hot water for lemon water (twiddle thumbs while waiting; 3 minutes)
- Drink lemon water while making breakfast (10 minutes; thanks, smoothies with 600 ingredients . . .)
- Drink smoothie and go on laptop/phone (30 minutes—embarrassing), leave smoothie cup out
- Shower, personal hygiene (13 minutes)
- Get dressed, hair, makeup (10 minutes)
- Make lunch (5 minutes)
- Clean up after breakfast and lunch prep—3 to 5 minutes (doesn't always happen)
- Leave the house

AFTER ON A NONEXERCISE DAY

- Wake up
- Use the bathroom (1 minute)
- Pull anything out of the bathroom that doesn't belong there or grab a load of laundry and walk it directly down to the basement; run a load through (5 minutes)
- Feed cats (2 minutes)
- Boil hot water for lemon water and unload dishwasher (3 minutes)
- Drink lemon water and make breakfast and clean up before eating (12 minutes)
- Drink smoothie and go on laptop/phone (30 minutes—still embarrassing)
- Rinse and dry smoothie cup or dish, place washed clothes into the dryer (7 minutes)
- Shower, personal hygiene (13 minutes)
- Get dressed, hair, makeup (10 minutes)
- Make lunch and clean up mess (7 minutes)
- Pull laundry out of the dryer (if I have time, and if it's a load where I care about wrinkles, 3 minutes)
- Leave the house

AFTER WORKOUT!

- Use the bathroom (1 minute)
- Brush teeth and wash face (3 minutes)
- Change into workout clothes (1 minute)
- Pull anything out of the bathroom that doesn't belong there or grab a load of laundry and walk it directly down to the basement, run a load through (5 minutes)
- Feed cats (2 minutes)
- Work out (30 or 60 minutes)
- Place washed clothes into the dryer or on the drying rack (7 minutes)
- Shower (10 minutes)
- Get dressed, hair, makeup (10 minutes)
- Boil hot water for lemon water and unload dishwasher while water boils (3 minutes)
- Drink lemon water and make breakfast (10 minutes)
- Make lunch and clean up mess (8 minutes)
- Leave the house with smoothie in to-go cup

Now by the time I get home, all I need to do is fold or put away that clean clothing on the bed and get started on dinner. Which means coming home feels amazing! My kitchen (a major MIA for me) is clean, and my laundry is done, without me really paying it too much mind. Incidentally, you don't see making the bed here, because Chad and I work opposing hours. He is still in it when I leave for work, so he's in charge of making the bed. Otherwise, that would be tossed into the mix, too.

Ready for another one?

COMING HOME FROM WORK

★

BEFORE

- Walk in from work, step out of my shoes, and toss my coat and stuff on the chair in the living room (1 minute)
- Place my lunch bag on the kitchen counter—there's no room for the containers in the dishwasher, and I just got home, so I'm not going to instantly kick in to unloading mode (20 seconds)
- Change and put dirty clothing in tri-sorter, but clean clothing I'd leave hanging over the tri-sorter (I'll do it later . . . ; 2 minutes)
- Do anything to take my mind off the mess or things I actually need to do, like playing a game on my phone (life-avoidance; 20 minutes)
- Try to start dinner, which really means unloading the dishwasher and cleaning the kitchen (usually from last night's dinner), putting my lunch containers into the dishwasher (20 minutes)
- Actually make dinner (20 minutes)
- Eat dinner (20 minutes)

AFTER

- Walk in from work and place my shoes and coat in the closet (1 minute)
- Place my purse, laptop bag upstairs (1 minute)
- Empty out my lunch bag into the empty dishwasher (2 minutes)
- Take clothing upstairs and fold/put away (5 minutes)
- Change and put dirty clothing in tri-sorter, hang up clean clothes (2 minutes)
- Life-avoidance (20 minutes)
- Make dinner (20 minutes)
- Eat dinner (20 minutes)

You've noticed by now how not only is the new routine so much more productive, but that it builds on all the mini chores I did this morning, so that I am actually doing *less* work and enjoying a much cleaner space. It's a self-reinforcing cycle! Maintaining is so much easier than hard-core cleaning.

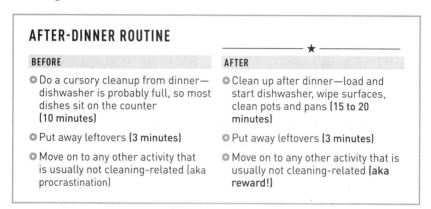

AFTER-DINNER ROUTINE ★

BEFORE

- Do a cursory cleanup from dinner—dishwasher is probably full, so most dishes sit on the counter (10 minutes)
- Put away leftovers (3 minutes)
- Move on to any other activity that is usually not cleaning-related (aka procrastination)

AFTER

- Clean up after dinner—load and start dishwasher, wipe surfaces, clean pots and pans (15 to 20 minutes)
- Put away leftovers (3 minutes)
- Move on to any other activity that is usually not cleaning-related (aka reward!)

This way, my kitchen is clean and ready for the next meal. This is such a satisfying way to end a day!

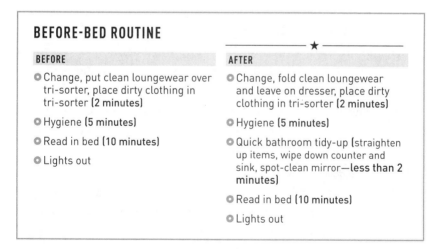

BEFORE-BED ROUTINE ★

BEFORE

- Change, put clean loungewear over tri-sorter, place dirty clothing in tri-sorter (2 minutes)
- Hygiene (5 minutes)
- Read in bed (10 minutes)
- Lights out

AFTER

- Change, fold clean loungewear and leave on dresser, place dirty clothing in tri-sorter (2 minutes)
- Hygiene (5 minutes)
- Quick bathroom tidy-up (straighten up items, wipe down counter and sink, spot-clean mirror—less than 2 minutes)
- Read in bed (10 minutes)
- Lights out

There's nothing really wrong with the "before" routine—we're all winding down at the end of the day. But notice that with the simplest of tweaks, I set myself up for more order when I open my eyes in the morning.

IDEAS ON HOW YOU CAN TWEAK YOUR EXISTING ROUTINES

Aside from tweaking yours the way I have mine, which I recommend adopting (and adapting) where you can, try integrating these ideas into your routines. You'll become so much more productive!

Hands Full

I learned this principle after many grueling years as a restaurant server. When you have six tables, you find ways to work smarter. Hands always had to be full whenever I was on my way from here to there. If they weren't, some manager would eagle-eye me and remind me to help clear a table or refill water pitchers. That lesson never left me. When I leave a room, I always take something with me and drop it off in the right place if I am headed in that direction. For example, when I leave my bedroom to head downstairs, I'll fill my hands with water glasses that need to go into the dishwasher. Sounds easy, but I promise you, this is a game changer.

Upstairs/Downstairs Bin

If there are items that need to go up- or downstairs, we leave them in neat piles at the top and bottom of the stairs. The rule is, whoever heads up or down next is in charge of taking that item where it needs to go. Families may wish to employ a bin or basket system, where everyone in the house gets assigned a basket, and their items get placed in the basket.

Automatic Replacement

Finished cleaning the kitchen? Immediately take dirty cloths and dish towels to the laundry bin and replace them with fresh ones. You'll never be left with gross, stinky kitchen linens again.

Get Ready, Get Rid

Have a donation bin going at all times. Pick a location for this bin and always take items you don't use—the very minute you question the usefulness of that item—to that bin. This will help manage the clutter.

Ruthless Reader

As soon as you finish reading newspapers, magazines, or catalogs, clip out anything you need to keep, store it, and then march them directly to the recycling bin. Leaving old magazines and newspapers around is asking for clutter.

Couch Tomato (or Whatever the Opposite of *Potato* Would Be)

If you're watching TV and still get commercials, stand up during those breaks and clean something nearby; tidy or straighten. Do an Express Clean over two commercial breaks.

Warm Up

When something is heating up—we're talking a clothes iron, your curling iron, or your dinner—get moving! A two-minute pickup can be more powerful than you know.

Shower Wipe-Down

Squeegee shower walls and tub when you're done showering, every time. This move prevents soap scum buildup and saves you from ever having to deep-clean your shower area. Trust me on this; it's an amazing addition to your routine and takes about 60 seconds.

Schedule It In

Your MIAs can be mostly accounted for in your routines, and I'd encourage you to include as many of them in your daily routines as you can—this is the best way to ensure that they stay as clean and tidy as you wish. But for areas where you can't incorporate them into your routine, you're going to have to schedule them in.

Taking into consideration the amount of time you have and the time of day that you're most likely to clean, make specific cleaning appointments and put them on your calendar—i.e., "bathroom, Saturday, 9 a.m." Just do it. I know you probably have an explosive calendar and feel overwhelmed when you have to think about planning *fun* events, but this scheduled cleaning appointment is very, very important.

As you start to schedule these appointments, I want you to use the following chart for reference (see pages 274–285). One column refers to how often, *in an ideal world*, these tasks would get done. (But keep in mind that each space is a little different, and I don't think overcleaning is a good idea. So don't take this first column as a generic prescription for cleaning that's going to have you spending your free time scrubbing.) The next is my personal column—so you can see how I shift the basic chart to reflect my personal priorities and MIAs. Finally, there will be a blank one, for you to start shaping your own schedule.

Columns

When you're looking at my column, keep in mind that I have an 1,800-square-foot home, and while we're pretty lax about it, Chad and I have a fairly high standard of cleanliness (hey, I am Melissa Maker). We've determined that for our level of clean, we need about 4 hours a week, or 30 or so minutes of dedicated cleaning time a day. Dedicated cleaning time means **scheduled specific cleaning tasks that change every day**, not those routine cleanups, such as washing dishes and tidying the kitchen after dinner, that take place every day. Some people might find that they can keep their house as clean as they like without additional cleaning during the week, but then knocking out a big three-hour clean every Saturday, or even every other Saturday. Whatever works for you. But these scheduled quality cleanings are key to keeping the house cleaner, longer. The better *quality* of the clean, the less *quantity* you need to invest in cleaning time; a cleaning done properly will indeed last longer. Your efforts will truly go the distance.

Even so, my personal column represents my personal ideal, but it doesn't mean that life unfolds that way every single week. The schedule is a starting point. It's not perfect, but it keeps me sane. If I want it cleaner, I will either carve out more time or hire help. If I want a special project done, I make extra time for it. I've learned that "giving up" 30 minutes per day helps me feel better about my space, giving me a home I am proud of. If my 30 minutes slip by one day without cleaning, I don't stress out and stop trying altogether (doesn't that sound like a diet to you?). There are always Express Cleans to save my bacon if someone is coming by, and I can simply pick up right where I left off with my schedule. The important part is to not let it build up; that's when it starts to feel unmanageable, and that's the feeling we want to avoid. So take some time and plan out your scheduled appointments, based on your column and your MIAs.

Working Together

It never ceases to amaze me how much work can get done when *two* people clean together. Take my word, it is extremely efficient and *way more* gets done in the same period of time (or less). I used to harbor a lot of resentment toward others whom I lived with when I was cleaning by myself. In my home growing up, cleaning didn't feel collaborative or balanced and that's why I really hated it. Now I've learned that cleaning together—as in, with Chad—makes everyone in the household feel better about it. Everyone makes a mess, so everyone pitches in. Some days I do more cleaning and Chad does more messing, and other days it's the opposite. But since we both clean (in fact, Chad is excellent at tidying and organizing and I excel at actually cleaning), I know the work balances out. My resentment about cleaning, which was quite burdensome for years, has lifted.

During the week, Chad and I tend to clean together—not side by side—but we each tackle a space or a task for a set period of time. We will usually have a discussion that sounds like this: "Okay, after dinner, let's take a few minutes to clean up. I am happy to clean the family room and empty the litter box—[here's where Chad says what he's going to do]—then we've got to hit the grocery store and return that thing to the mall. Can we be out of the house at seven thirty?" At that point, we start moving—the clock is ticking. I find setting the stage together helps us both remain focused and goal-oriented. Plus, no one is bossing the other around. It is always a collaborative conversation. You don't want to be the nagging wife or the dictatorial husband—you want to be a partner.

IT'S NOT 1950 ANYMORE.

Can we just take a moment to address what I consider the obvious? Historically, caring for the home has fallen on the woman's shoulders, but this is an outdated notion that causes more fights and more sore feelings among couples than I can tell you. Listen, everyone, if both members of a household work, or even if one works and one stays home and raises children—because that raising-children business still counts as a job—then it's time to divide the housework equitably, regardless of your sex. End of story.

SETTING GOALS AS A TEAM

When I speak to people about cleaning, they'll often share with me that they have challenges managing cleaning with their partner (spouse, roommate, sibling). If you have found that it is challenging to get family members to help out, here are some ideas on how you can approach the topic. Just remember, having a heated conversation where blame is involved makes the other party feel defensive. Make the other party feel safe by speaking from a place of "me" and "my needs," not "you" and what "you should" be doing that "you aren't" (see the diff?). This may start off as a bit of a crunchy conversation, but in my experience, both parties tend to walk away much happier when it's over. Have a kind, honest conversation by following these steps.

1. **Outline your common goals for your space.** What does "acceptably clean" mean to each of you? If your partner feels strongly that there should never be dishes in the sink, you need to find a way to honor that. And, if you feel that the bed needs to be made daily, your partner must honor that, too. If one partner is significantly neater or cleaner than the other, try to find a middle ground. It will require some negotiation, but it will be one of the healthiest things you do for your relationship.

2. **Outline each of your MIAs.** After you determine what level of clean is mutually acceptable, then you each need to establish what your MIAs are. By understanding your partner's MIAs, you can be more mindful as you move through that space, and your partner will respect your MIAs, too. This will also help inform your cleaning schedules and routines as you plan your time.

3. **Discuss timing.** How much time can each of you dedicate to cleaning in order to achieve your goals, and when will that take place, given your schedules? Talk through an average week; where is there some time you can work to get your tasks done? Do you want to work together or separately?

4. **Identify who likes to do what.** Lots of people find cleaning, well, a chore! And in their assumption that it is all drudgery, they might forget the possibility that one person's most dreaded task is another's little piece of heaven. If your partner really, truly doesn't want to clean, what else *can* he or she do to help run the house? I hate, and I mean hate, vacuuming. Chad doesn't mind it. So, he vacuums. But he hates cooking (and I happen to love it), so I cook. We have gone through what needs doing in the house, cleaning and otherwise, and we have divvied up

the chores that we can both do. The rest, we either decide aren't important to us and we kind of ignore until they become a glaring issue (yes, that's real life) or we hire out. Each of you will be more inclined to do your work, because you actually like it (or at the very least, feel neutral toward it).

5. **Talk through challenging routines or spaces.** If you know there's an area of the home that triggers someone, talk it through and discuss tweaks and adjustments to make it manageable. (Remember, despite the urge to trot out the expletives here, keep it classy. You catch more flies with honey.) These small conversations can really go the distance. For example, "Since I really value a clean front entryway, it feels frustrating when stuff is left at the front door. Can we just make it a thing that when anyone comes home, their coat has to be hung up right away, shoes lined up neatly, and bags placed in their appropriate spots? That would make a world of difference to me." Then, and here's where you need to take a deep breath and remind yourself that you're an amazing and equitable human being, you say, "What can I do for you?" Or, if there's a messy area, for example, where the kids play, talk about what's not working and how it needs to change. "The toy area is insane! Can we implement a cleanup song with the kids and have them tidy up before dinner each night? That would save us so much time!" These conversations may seem silly, but they are priceless. They save relationships.

6. **Rethink your routines.** If there is a routine that you or your partner can tweak to better accommodate maintaining your MIAs, talk through that and see what can change. For example, when Chad empties the kitchen garbage, I stand right there with him and place a fresh bag in the can. We do that now because for the longest time, he'd empty the trash and forget to replace the bag (moving on to other, more exciting things!), and I'd get pissed off when I would go to throw something into the trash and there would be no bag. So we tweaked it. Also, give your routines

time. It doesn't have to be perfect at first; it just has to start somewhere. Resolve to make it work. Imagine if your parents stopped potty training you the first time you peed in your pants. Make your routine your new norm and adjust accordingly.

7. **Set a schedule for larger jobs**. Anything that can't be managed through routines can be scheduled in. Whether it is cleaning a room, cleaning the whole house, or doing a larger or one-off job, take the time to schedule it and commit to doing it together. Use the format that makes the most sense for you—hang a monthly calendar up on the fridge, update a spreadsheet in the Cloud, use an app, have a shared calendar on your phone . . . whatever. There are lots of options!

GETTING KIDS TO CLEAN

In a sense, kids are just like anyone else in the household: they pitch in when making the messes, so they should pitch in to help clean up. But unlike a spouse or roommate, who can take care of a chore on his or her own, kids need help—at least at first. Plus, they'll respond well (as in keep up the behavior and create habits) when they feel positive about what they're doing. Here are some tips for making it a positive experience for everyone:

Be clear. If, say, the basement play area is completely trashed after a get-together, don't just say, "Clean that basement." Kids under ten years old will need more specific instruction. "Charlotte! You gather all the costumes and get them back in the costume box. Frank: walk around with this bag and put any trash scraps in it. Veronica: straighten the craft area, putting scissors and googly eyes back in their containers, making sure all the markers are capped and put away, and store your creations that you'd like to keep and toss the ones that you are done with."

Be realistic. Ask kids to do small tasks for manageable periods of time (a seven-year-old isn't likely to clean without assistance for 30 minutes, but 5 or 10 might be a good bet). Help them build confidence with tasks that are age-appropriate and make them feel really good about the work they're doing and how it is helping the family ("You're so helpful—thanks for bringing the dirty dishes to me, Jack!"). Build on their skills as they get older ("Nate, now that you are ten, I think you're ready to handle loading the dishwasher on your own. I'll show you what to do. You're going to be great at it and it would be a big help to me!").

Be good! Model good behavior. Don't be an armchair quarterback—get up and participate. Kids are geniuses when it comes to sniffing out hypocrites.

Build it into their routines. A kid as young as two years old can start clearing his or her dish when finished eating. Set up stations where they can have their own coming-home routine, with low hooks for coats and backpacks and a designated area for shoes. Make it a family habit to do a ten-minute pickup either while dinner is cooking or after cleaning up and before watching TV together. Emphasize the idea of putting something away as soon as they are done playing with it (it will take years for them to get good at it, but it is worth starting now!).

Listen to them. As with other family members, spend time trying to learn what your kids like to do and nurture that. Lots of kids love washing dishes, and you might even find that some get a kick out of things like sweeping or pushing the vacuum around (plus, it makes for amazing social media fodder #kidoftheyear). Sure, they may not perform up to your standards, but if you start teaching them these life skills, and that they can feel good about pitching in, it will set them up for a lifetime of good habits—and that's worth a few not-quite-perfectly-rinsed plates here and there, don't you think?

Hiring Cleaning Help

Maybe you've crunched the numbers, and even with all your new knowledge under your belt, you simply can't find the time to clean the way you'd like. If it is in your means to do so, then it is time to hire a cleaning service. It might be to do the regular Top-to-Bottom cleaning of your house, because you just can't fit it in; but even if you are cleaning regularly, you might want to outsource who handles your bigger jobs, or the tasks you just don't want to do (no judging). My cleaning service business has many clients whose homes are quite tidy and well kept. They do a great job at upkeep, but they don't want to do any of the heavy-duty work. That's where we come in.

Even if you don't have the budget for a regular cleaner, I still recommend finding a way to hire help occasionally to take care of the stuff you know you don't want to do, you keep avoiding, or that should get done but are low on your MIA list. It takes such a load off. In many cases, my company will be hired out to visit a home, say once per quarter, to complete a list that has been provided to us by the client. They are very grateful when the jobs that have been causing them headaches are handled by professionals.

If you can hand your cleaning person a list of the tasks you want done (and you have a specific list now because you know what needs to be done—yay, *Clean My Space*!), you had better believe he or she is going to be efficient and take care of exactly what you need. That's where the experts shine (literally!). It's not extravagant—it's freeing up, say, three hours of your time, and it's getting done exactly what you need done. This is such a relief to an individual, a couple, or a family who simply doesn't have the time. It is a sanity-saving, marriage-saving investment. The money is well spent.

TIPS FOR HIRING CLEANING HELP

When you are looking to hire cleaning help, ask for referrals from friends and family and do some online snooping: see what other people have to say. Remember, a company with a perfect rating should be just as suspect as a company with a zero rating. Although many people go with a private individual, rather than a service, keep in mind that there are risks involved with going that route, since you won't be dealing with a company with standard policies and insurance coverage. Here are some questions to ask depending on which route you decide to take:

○ When looking, find out if the company or individual is bonded (this means that you are protected by an insurance bond in the event of theft) and insured (this means you are protected in case something happens to your home that is caused by the cleaner, instead of the liability being on you as the homeowner).

○ Find out if the company or the individual is protected by worker's compensation. This means that if something happens to the cleaning person while on your premises, he or she has coverage to insure against injury, or is that a risk you need to take?

○ Find out what the breakage-and-damage policy is for the individual or company; will they repair or replace something they have broken or damaged?

○ Find out their rates and see how they compare to other service providers, but keep in mind that you get what you pay for. With cleaning, you really want someone who knows what they are doing and someone you can count on. Remember, it costs more to run a business that carries insurance, incurs overhead expenses, and provides ongoing training than it does to be self-employed, and those higher operating costs are built into that hourly rate.

○ Ask if the provider brings their own supplies and tools, or if you need to provide them (I prefer to provide my own in the event I hire help—it feels more sanitary and I can control what's being used).

○ Ask if they take customer requests for each visit, or if they follow a set cleaning routine.

○ Ask about payment methods and what happens if you are dissatisfied with their work—will they come back to fix it for you?

○ Remember to be *amazing* to your cleaning person. Cleaning is hard work, and your cleaner deserves a lot of respect and appreciation. Leave a kind note and cold drinks. Greet them warmly and make them feel like welcome guests in your home (this goes a long, long way). Tipping is always optional. A happy cleaning person is a good cleaning person (and someone who will want to stick around!).

○ Find someone who you are comfortable giving feedback and clear instruction to. If you feel bad about giving feedback to someone or can't communicate something clearly, that's going to pose an uncomfortable challenge for you. Find someone you get along with.

○ Become the king or queen of lovely feedback. There will come a time when you're dissatisfied with something your cleaner has done. Rather than just saying, "Melissa, you didn't clean under my bed last week even though I asked you to," which would make me feel pretty crap-a-doodle-doo about myself, I much prefer when clients frame their feedback like this: "Hi, Melissa, I really like the way you made my bed last visit, thanks so much for that. I did just want to mention that last time I had requested for under my bed to be cleaned as well and I noticed that it wasn't. Would you mind including that in today's clean as well as future visits? It's really important to me. Thank you!" When a client is courteous in this way, all I want to do is make them happier. In fact, I couldn't work harder to please them.

Really Big, Overwhelming, Specialty, or, Frankly, Really Scary Jobs

Oftentimes, people ask me how to clean a certain thing (fancy window treatments! Silk rugs! Designer handbags!) and I tell them the same thing: take it to the pros. There are certain jobs that are big tasks to take on or that require professional expertise or equipment, and then there are the ones that are downright intimidating. You don't have to do it all. Simply schedule times throughout the year to have these jobs done, hire a local, reliable professional, and move on with your life. Some service providers even do multiple tasks, like the steam-cleaning professional I use who can tackle carpets, upholstery, mattresses, and window coverings in one go. Other tasks, like getting the ducts cleaned, should happen once every few years, and since specialty equipment is needed for that, there's no way you could do it yourself. If something feels too overwhelming to take on because the PTT is highly specialized or the stakes are high, bring in the pros. Head online or ask around for referrals. If you can get your neighbors in on certain jobs, the service provider may be willing to lower the price, too.

MELISSA'S TRIED-AND-TRUE TIPS FOR KEEPING CLEAN

Avoid buying extras or bulk. You just need to find storage for it. Buy only what you need when you run out. A six-pack of paper towels is fine; a thirty-six-pack is not.

Put everything away when you come in each day. Everything. Immediately. Trust me, you won't get to it later.

Remember that furniture surfaces are decorative, nothing else. Your dining room table isn't also a temporary storage zone for papers and bags and boxes.

Make your bed each day and change the sheets once a week. You will feel like royalty when you go into your room.

Make it convenient for you. Have your products and tools ready and maintained. If supplies are remotely a hassle, that will be one more hurdle to getting the work done.

Schedule the time to do it. What gets scheduled gets done.

Make it as enjoyable as humanly possible. I like to turn on a twenty-minute podcast and do my thing; Chad blares a music playlist.

Have a system that works for you. Do you like a dry-erase board, a monthly calendar, reminders on your phone, a spreadsheet? Create a system that you're actually going to follow.

CLEANING SCHEDULES: IDEAL, MELISSA'S, YOURS

M=Monthly W=Weekly Y=Yearly 2M=Twice Monthly Q=Quarterly 2W=Twice Weekly 2Y=Twice Yearly D=Daily

Room	Task
FRONT ENTRYWAY	
WAVE ONE	
	Tidy and organize
WAVE TWO	
	High dusting
	Clean light fixtures (removing them, dusting them, replacing them)
	Front door
	Mirrors and windows
	Picture frames and art
	Horizontal surfaces
	Clean purse, work bag, or knapsack
	Points of contact
	Walls
	Closet
	Baseboards
	Welcome mats
WAVE THREE	
	Vacuum floor
	Sweep porch
	Mop floor
LIVING ROOM	
WAVE ONE	
	Tidy and organize
WAVE TWO	
	High dusting
	Mirrors and windows
	Windowsills
	Picture frames and wall art
	Fancy display items
	Horizontal surfaces
	Points of contact
	Walls
	Baseboards
WAVE THREE	
	Upholstered pieces
	Rugs
	Vacuum floor
	Mop floor

	Time	Page	Rating	Ideal frequency	MM	Yours
	5 to 15 minutes	60		W	W	
	90 seconds	61		M	Q	
	7 minutes/fixture	61		Y	As needed	
	2 minutes	61		M	Q	
	90 seconds/surface	62		2M	As needed	
	30 to 60 seconds/piece	63		2M	M	
	1 to 2 minutes/piece	63		W	W	
	10 minutes	64		As needed	Q	
	2 minutes	64		W	W	
	10 seconds/mark	64		W	As needed	
	10 minutes	65		Q	2Y	
	2 minutes	65		2M	M	
	5 minutes active, 30 minutes inactive	66		As needed	As needed	
	3 to 5 minutes	67		W	As needed	
	3 to 5 minutes	67		W	W	
	2 minutes	67		W	W	
	5 minutes	73		W	2W	
	90 seconds	73		M	Q	
	90 seconds/surface	75		2M	As needed	
	30 seconds/sill	75		2M	M	
	30 to 60 seconds/piece	75		2M	M	
	Varies	76		2Y–3Y	As needed	
	1 to 2 minutes/piece	78		W	2M	
	2 minutes	78		2M	2M	
	10 seconds/mark	78		2M	As needed	
	5 minutes	79		2M	M	
	2 to 5 minutes/piece	80		2M	M	
	10 minutes active, 30 minutes inactive	80		As needed	N/A	
	5 to 10 minutes	82		W	W	
	3 to 5 minutes	83		W	W	

Room	Task
DINING ROOM	
WAVE ONE	
	Tidy and organize
WAVE TWO	
	High dusting
	Chandelier
	Mirrors and windows
	Windowsills
	Picture frames and wall art
	Fancy display items
	Horizontal surfaces
	Points of contact
	Walls
	Baseboards
WAVE THREE	
	Upholstered pieces
	Rugs
	Vacuum floor
	Mop floor
KITCHEN	
WAVE ONE	
	Tidy and organize, pretreat
WAVE TWO	
	High dusting
	Upper cupboard fronts
	Exhaust hood
	Backsplash
	Countertops
	Lower cupboards and drawers
	Refrigerator (exterior)
	Stovetop and oven (exterior)
	Freezer (interior)
	Refrigerator (interior)
	Oven (interior)
	Oven racks

Time	Page	Rating	Ideal frequency	MM	Yours
5 minutes	73		W	2W	
90 seconds	73		M	M	
1 to 20 minutes (depending on method)	74		Y–2Y	2Y	
90 seconds/surface	75		2M	As needed	
30 seconds/sill	75		2M	As needed	
30 to 60 seconds/piece	75		2M	M	
Varies	76		2Y–3Y	As needed	
1 to 2 minutes/piece	78		W	2M	
2 minutes	78		2M	2M	
10 seconds/mark	78		2M	As needed	
5 minutes	79		2M	M	
2 to 5 minutes/piece	80		2M	2M	
10 minutes active, 30 minutes inactive	80		As needed	N/A	
5 to 10 minutes	82		W	W	
3 to 5 minutes	83		W	W	
5 to 10 minutes	89		W	W	
1 to 2 minutes	90		M	As needed	
5 to 7 minutes	90		2M	As needed	
5 to 10 minutes active, 10 minutes inactive	91		W (exterior), Q (interior)	2M (exterior), 2Y (interior)	
5 minutes	91		W	W	
10 minutes	92		D	D	
5 to 7 minutes; 10 minutes	93; 97		2Y	2Y–Y	
4 minutes	95		W	W	
5 to 10 minutes	95		W	W	
20 minutes	104		Q	2Y	
5 to 10 minutes	106		Y	Y	
10 minutes active, 3 to 4 hours inactive (self-cleaning); 20 to 45 minutes active, 10 minutes inactive (non-self-cleaning)	108		Q–2Y	2Y	
10 to 20 minutes active, up to 10 hours inactive	110		Y or as needed	Y or as needed	

Room	Task
KITCHEN (continued)	
WAVE TWO (continued)	
	Dishwasher (exterior)
	Walls
	Kitchen table
	Picture frames and artwork
	Mirrors and windows
	Windowsills
	Points of contact
	Baseboards
WAVE THREE	
	Faucet and sink
	Vacuum floor
	Mop floor
	Trash and trash can
	Dishwasher (interior)
	Microwave
	Toaster
DEN	
WAVE ONE	
	Tidy and organize
WAVE TWO	
	High dusting
	Mirrors and windows
	Spot-cleaning walls
	Picture frames and artwork
	Horizontal surfaces
	Points of contact
	Polishing wood
	TV
	Remote control and game controllers
	Electronics
	DVDs and video games (disc cases and shelving)
	Game consoles, stereo, cable boxes, DVD/Blu-ray players
	Speakers and sound bars
	Windowsills
	Baseboards
WAVE THREE	
	Upholstery
	Fireplace

Time	Page	Rating	Ideal frequency	MM	Yours
3 minutes	98		W	W	
10 seconds/mark	99		2M	As needed	
3 to 5 minutes	99		As needed	As needed	
30 to 60 seconds/item	100		2M	M	
90 seconds/surface	100		W	W	
30 seconds/sill	100		2M	As needed	
2 minutes	100		W	W	
5 minutes	101		2M	M	
3 to 5 minutes	103		As needed	As needed	
5 to 10 minutes	103		W	W	
3 to 5 minutes	103		W	W	
5 minutes active, 10 minutes inactive	103		M	Q–2Y	
15 to 20 minutes active, up to overnight inactive	110		2Y	2Y	
5 minutes	111		2M	M	
5 to 10 minutes	112		Q	N/A	
5 to 15 minutes	118		W	W	
90 seconds	119		M	As needed	
90 seconds/surface	120		2M	As needed	
10 seconds/mark	120		2M	M	
90 seconds/surface	121		2M	M	
1 to 2 minutes/piece	122		W	2M	
2 minutes	123		W	W	
3 to 5 minutes/piece			As needed	As needed	
2 to 3 minutes	123		2M	2M	
30 to 60 seconds/each	125		2M	M	
60 seconds/item			2M	As needed	
30 seconds to 20 minutes	126		Q	Q	
60 seconds/item	127		M	As needed	
60 seconds/item	127		M	As needed	
30 seconds/sill	129		2M	M	
5 minutes	129		M	M	
2 to 5 minutes/piece	129		W	W	
20 minutes active, 5 minutes inactive	132		2Y	N/A	

Room	Task
DEN (continued)	
WAVE THREE (continued)	
	Plants
	Vacuum floor
	Mop floor
BATHROOM	
	Pretreat
	Exhaust fan and high dusting
	Shower and tub
	Shower curtain, shower curtain liner, bathroom rug/mat, nonslip bath mat
	Clean and polish chrome fixtures
	Toilet
	Towel bar and toilet paper holder
	Walls
	Mirrors, medicine cabinet, and windows
	Windowsills and blinds
	Vanity top
	Cupboards and drawers (interior)
	Soap dish and toothbrush holder
	Points of contact
	Sink
	Baseboards
	Floor
BEDROOM	
WAVE ONE	
	Make bed
	Change linens
	Tidy and organize
WAVE TWO	
	High dusting
	Mirrors and windows
	Picture frames and artwork
	Walls
	Horizontal surfaces
	Points of contact
	Windowsills and blinds
	Baseboards

Time	Page	Rating	Ideal frequency	MM	Yours
1 minute/plant	132		M	As needed	
5 to 10 minutes	134		W	W	
2 to 5 minutes	135		W	N/A	
5 to 10 minutes	140		W	2M	
3 to 5 minutes	141		As needed	As needed	
10 to 15 minutes active, 5 to 10 minutes inactive	142		2M	2M	
30 minutes inactive, 2 minutes active	145		Q	Q	
1 minute/fixture	145		W	W	
3 to 7 minutes active, 5 minutes inactive	147		W	W	
30 seconds	147		W	W	
10 seconds/mark	148		Q	Q	
5 to 7 minutes	148		W (mirrors/ medicine cabinet), M windows	W (mirrors/ medicine cabinet), Q windows	
30 seconds/item	149		2M	2M	
5 to 8 minutes	149		W	W	
5 to 10 minutes/cupboard/drawer			2Y–Y	Y	
1 to 2 minutes/item active, 5 minutes inactive	150		M	M	
2 minutes	151		W	W	
2 to 3 minutes	151		W	W	
2 minutes	152		M	M	
3 to 5 minutes	152		W	2M	
2 to 10 minutes	159		D	D	
5 to 10 minutes	159		W	W	
5 to 10 minutes	162		W	W	
90 seconds	163		M	As needed	
90 seconds/surface	164		M	M	
30 to 60 seconds/piece	164		2M	M	
10 seconds/mark	165		M	As needed	
1 to 2 minutes/piece	165		2M	2M	
2 minutes	166		2M	2M	
30 seconds/sill	166		2M	2M	
5 minutes	166		M	M	

Room	Task
BEDROOM (continued)	
WAVE THREE	
	Vacuum floor
	Mop floor
HOME OFFICE	
WAVE ONE	
	Tidy and organize
WAVE TWO	
	High dusting
	Mirrors and windows
	Windows and window coverings
	Picture frames and artwork
	Walls
	Horizontal surfaces
	Office chair
	Books and bookshelves
	Keyboard
	Mouse
	Monitor
	Speakers
	Printer
	Computer tower
	Telephone
	Tablet
	Laptop
	Points of contact
	Baseboards
WAVE THREE	
	Vacuum floor
	Mop floor
HALLWAYS, STAIRCASES, AND OTHER PASSAGEWAYS	
WAVE ONE	
	Tidy and organize
WAVE TWO	
	Chandelier
	High dusting
	Mirrors and windows

Time	Page	Rating	Ideal frequency	MM	Yours
7 to 10 minutes	167		W	W	
3 to 5 minutes	167		W	N/A	
5 to 10 minutes	173		2M	M	
90 seconds	174		M	As needed	
90 seconds/surface	175		M	As needed	
30 seconds/item	175		2M	2M	
30 to 60 seconds/piece	176		2M	M	
10 seconds/mark	177		2M	M	
1 to 5 minutes/piece	177		2M	2M	
2 to 10 minutes	179		2Y	As needed	
2 to 10 minutes/shelf	179		2M (shelves), Q (removing books)	As needed	
3 minutes	180		Q	N/A	
1 minute	181		Q	N/A	
2 minutes	182		M	N/A	
1 minute/speaker	182		Q	N/A	
1 minute	183		2Y	N/A	
2 minutes	183		M	N/A	
1 to 2 minutes	184		2M	N/A	
30 to 60 seconds	185		W	W	
2 to 5 minutes	186		M	M–Q	
2 minutes	187		2M	2M	
5 minutes	187		M	M	
7 to 10 minutes	188		W	W	
2 to 3 minutes	189		W	N/A	
3 to 5 minutes	193		W	2M	
10 to 20 minutes	194		Y	Y	
2 to 5 minutes	194		M	M–Q	
90 seconds/surface	195		2M	N/A	

Room	Task

WAVE TWO (continued)

	Windowsills and blinds
	Picture frames and artwork
	Walls
	Staircase
	Horizontal surfaces
	Points of contact
	Baseboards

WAVE THREE

| | Vacuuming (not including stairs) |
| | Mopping floors (not including stairs) |

STORAGE SPACES

WAVE ONE

| | Tidy and organize |

WAVE TWO

	High dusting
	Windows
	Walls (unfinished)
	Horizontal surfaces (finished spaces)
	Dusting stored items
	Clean trash and recycling bins
	Wall fixtures (shelves, etc.)
	Washing machine
	Dryer
	Laundry basin
	Closets
	Walls (finished)
	Points of contact
	Baseboards

WAVE THREE

	Vacuum or sweep floors (unfinished spaces)
	Mop floors (unfinished spaces)
	Floor mats
	Vacuum floors (finished spaces)
	Mop floors (finished spaces)

Time	Page	Rating	Ideal frequency	MM	Yours
30 seconds/sill	195		2M	N/A	
30 to 60 seconds/piece	196		M	M	
10 seconds/mark	196		W	2M	
5 to 15 minutes	197		W	W	
1 to 2 minutes	201		2M	N/A	
2 minutes	202		W	W	
5 to 10 minutes	202		2M	M	
7 to 10 minutes	204		W	W	
3 to 5 minutes	205		W	W	
5 to 30 minutes	211; 220		2Y (unfinished), Q (finished)	Y (unfinished), Q (finished)	
5 to 10 minutes	212; 221		2Y	2Y	
2 to 3 minutes/window	212		M (finished), 2Y (unfinished)	N/A	
20 to 30 minutes/room	213		Y or as needed	As needed	
2 to 5 minutes/item			2M	2M	
20 to 60 minutes	214		Y or as needed	As needed	
10 minutes active, 10 minutes inactive/bin	215		Q	Q–2Y	
2 minutes/surface	221		2M	M	
5 minutes active, 30 to 60 minutes inactive	222		Q	Q–2Y	
30 to 45 minutes	223		Q	Y	
5 to 10 minutes	224		Q	M	
10 to 20 minutes	224		Q	Q	
10 seconds/mark	226		M	Q	
2 minutes	226		2M	M	
5 minutes	227		M	M	
5 to 20 minutes	216		Q–2Y	As needed	
5 to 10 minutes	216		Q–2Y	As needed	
5 minutes active, 30 minutes inactive	227		Q	Q–2Y	
7 to 10 minutes	228		2M	M	
3 to 5 minutes	228		2M	M	

The End

Well, here we are. We've been through a lot together; I've taught you everything I know about cleaning, and you've had the gumption to get through this book (and that deserves a high five!). Hopefully my ideas are seeping into your subconsciousness. You may have even had a dream about cleaning with the S-pattern or being chased by the high-dusting ghost. I still can't believe I've spent the past ten years learning about cleaning, but I am so glad I did, because if it makes *your* life even a little bit better or easier, I've done my job.

I remember when I started to make these changes myself, I was not only learning for my company but I was also trying to clean up my own life. At first, I was clumsy with my moves and did the work begrudgingly. Even today, I don't necessarily have a smile on my face every time I'm changing a sheet or swiping away with my high duster. But now, at least I know what I'm doing and I can get the job done lightning-fast.

There are plenty of people who find cleaning meditative, therapeutic, and enjoyable, and if that's you, kudos! But let me be clear: I still hate to clean, and you know what? I'm at peace with that. Over the years, I've learned that I don't have to love everything that I *need* to do in life. Instead, I focus on the outcome—how much I love a clean space—and having it is reward enough for the work. That alone has helped me shift my attitude and see that it's a profoundly important life skill to possess. If you enjoy cleaning, I sincerely hope this book has helped you build out your skills and take even more pleasure in the work you do. For those like me who don't like cleaning, I *know* this book has the power to change you. Whomever you are and whatever your stance on cleaning, I hope you have learned *how to clean better, faster—and love your home every day*. Being a person who cares for my surroundings has changed my life and changed who I am. It has had long-lasting effects of which I am still discovering the positive reverberations, every day.

I'm so proud of you for learning about my Maker Method: your MIAs, the PTTs, and figuring out how to schedule everything you really want cleaning-wise into your day. A clean space makes for a happier, healthier, and more productive home that is simply wonderful to be in, and that is my wish for you. You've got this.

Please share your journey with me on social media, or reach out with any questions on my website, CleanMySpace.com. I can't wait to hear about how *Clean My Space* has helped you!

MAKE SURE TO FOLLOW CLEAN MY SPACE ONLINE:

Website: **www.cleanmyspace.com**. You can also subscribe to our free newsletter, The Dirty Dish, on our website.

Instagram, Pinterest, Twitter, and Snapchat, you can find us **@CleanMySpace** and me **@MelissaMaker**.

My YouTube videos are available at **YouTube.com/CleanMySpace** and we post new videos every week. Subscribe to catch the latest!

On Facebook, we're at **www.facebook.com/CleanMySpace**. I'd love to see you online and hear your story.

To purchase Maker's Cleaning Cloths, my line of microfiber cloths, which are *simply incredible* (seriously, I tested more than a hundred before picking these ones), visit **www.makersclean.com**.

Acknowledgments

In embarking on this project, I've learned that a book doesn't get written by one person in a vacuum (yes, cleaning joke). I had no idea where to start, how it would all come together, and how my companies would keep afloat. A successful person never gets anywhere without copious amounts of support from many other helpful and talented people. This book has come together because those people have believed in me, supported me, and helped bring my vision to fruition, and for that, I'd like to extend my deepest gratitude.

My team at Clean My Space—my cleaning service based in Toronto—Sarah Ricketts, Andrea Dorton, and all our Cleaning Specialists, has been dynamite. Your hard work has allowed me to take time away to focus on this project for the past year. Both Chad and I thank you all for supporting me throughout and working so hard.

My team at Clean Digital Productions, the company that runs our Clean My Space media operations, has also gone the distance. Reuven Ashtar has been my trusted business manager, lawyer, and agent who not only handles negotiations and contracts but also offers up straightforward advice, humor, encouragement, and has continually pushed me to do better. The ideas, creativity, and patience of Lucas Bombardier, our producer, editor, and camera B, have been invaluable. Lindsey Rosen, my right-hand power woman, has handled everything I haven't been able to; she's a real gem. All these folks at our two companies have helped us bring our vision forth. We can't wait to see where we go next!

Our audience has been a key player in this even though I've kept the book a secret from the time I started talking about it with publishers in October 2015. I've learned so much from our audience and have thrived from their support; I'm always in awe of the stories they share with me about how my information has changed their lives. I cherish the connections we've created. Our audience has fueled me to keep talking about an admittedly tedious subject and is endlessly supportive of me and Chad. Thank you, all!

I didn't know how to write a book when I actually started writing a book. Thank heavens for Lesley Porcelli, my coauthor. Talk about someone who went above and beyond the call of duty! She took my chapters and worked them into what you read today. She gave me tons of advice, helped with research, and was a sounding board for my thoughts and concerns. We worked through each page together, and Lesley was super dedicated to making this book something special. She was the book's first guinea pig, too, trying out recipes, techniques, and DIY tools in her own home (and she's a busy mom of three!). I could not have asked for a more delightful and talented person to collaborate with on this. We had a blast working together and I'll always remember our writing trip with fond memories.

The publishing world is a new and different place for me. Fortunately, I believe I got the opportunity to work with the very best in the business. My agent, Judy Linden, has been outstanding. She's one of the hardest working people I know—I could not have asked for a better advocate. Her dedication, advice, and help have been the backbone of this project. Lucia Watson (and team Avery USA) and Andrea Magyar (and team Penguin Canada), my editors, have both believed in my book, supporting me and helping me craft this cleaning masterpiece. They've been encouraging, thoughtful in their suggestions, and have done everything to make this book special and unique. Working with these teams and editors has been a dream come true. I am very grateful to Meghann Stephenson, the illustrator of the book, who has brought all my crazy little cleaning concepts to life with her beautiful artwork.

Deepest thanks to Alex Goldberg, research scientist; Jonathan Yoder, epidemiologist at the Center for Disease Control; and Katharine Chang, pediatrician, for taking time out to help us understand and hash out the absolute best and most up-to-date advice for maintaining home hygiene.

Family and friends, most who initially thought I was nuts for getting into cleaning, have also been wonderful to me as I've built up my career and written this book. Mom and Dad (Sandi Maker and Sol Maker), thanks for *everything*. Isn't it great that I was such a messy terror growing up? As you can clearly see, it was a brilliant, strategic career move. Samantha, my wonderful sister, has always been by my side and has believed in me from the word *go*. Thanks as well to my wonderful in-laws, the Reynolds family: Cindy, Dwight, Gary, Sandra, Scott, Lisa, Andrew, Alexandra, Alisabeth, Noah, and Wilson. Aunts, uncles, and cousins have all been supportive and present for me, so hats off to all of you. A special thanks to my uncle Larry Maker, who has been a guiding light for me since I started Clean My Space. Alli Gaffen, Dalia Mail, Johanna Markowitz, Yaniv Bitton, Bryan Williams, Jenny Kalen, Oksana Vialykh, Ana Veliz, Rob and Laurie MacFarlane, Gemma Stafford, and Alejandra Costello (and all your partners) are my nearest and dearest friends, and on my toughest days, I could go to them for anything. Thank you, friends.

Finally, my deepest gratitude to Chad Reynolds, my husband and business partner. He met me in 2006 when I was a twenty-three-year-old bank employee looking to follow my dreams. He encouraged me, practically on our first date, to go out there and pursue entrepreneurship. Five years later, he encouraged me to start making YouTube videos. Thank you for everything you have done for me, everything you have sacrificed for me. You've backed your wife's career for the past ten years, and that's no easy task. Your support, guidance, creativity, energy, humor, smarts, dedication, and love have been invaluable. You've challenged me and dared me to dream big, and you have been right there with me through the highest highs and the lowest lows. I love you with all my heart and I can't wait to see where things go from here!

Wow, what a long list. I feel blessed to have such a big crew of people to thank. Thanks for reading, and thanks for buying this book. Now without further ado, let's get cleaning!

FURTHER READING

If you want to read more on this topic (bless your heart!), here are the books that I found invaluable during my formative years.

Cleaning Plain & Simple by Donna Smallin, 2005, Storey Publishing.

The Complete Book of Essential Oils and Aromatherapy by Valerie Ann Worwood, 25th anniversary edition, 2016, New World Library.

Home Comforts by Cheryl Mendelson, 1999, Scribner.

Martha Stewart's Homekeeping Handbook by Martha Stewart, 2006, Clarkson Potter.

Sidetracked Home Executives by Pam Young and Peggy Jones, Revised and Updated Edition, 2001, Grand Central Publishing.

Speed Cleaning by Jeff Campbell and the Clean Team, Third Edition, 1991, Dell Publishing.

INDEX